Corner House Publishers

SOCIAL SCIENCE REPRINTS

General Editor MAURICE FILLER

THE BORDER WARS

OF

NEW ENGLAND

SIR WILLIAM PHIPS ATTACKING QUEBEC.

(From a French print.)

THE BORDER WARS

OF

NEW ENGLAND

COMMONLY CALLED KING WILLIAM'S AND

QUEEN ANNE'S WARS

BY

SAMUEL ADAMS DRAKE

"Honor's a good brooch to wear in a man's hat, at all times."—B. Jonson

WITH MANY ILLUSTRATIONS AND MAPS

CORNER HOUSE PUBLISHERS

WILLIAMSTOWN, MASSACHUSETTS 01267

1973

To

LUCIUS TUTTLE, Esq.

CONTENTS

ILLUSTRATIONS

INTRODUCTION

A MONOGRAPH on the subject of the Indian wars
during the reigns of King William III. and Queen Anne
was a favorite project
with my father, Samuel
G. Drake, for which he
gathered a mass of ma-
terials in manuscript, but
did not live to see real-
ized. With the aid of
these, and other contem-
porary accounts, the
present volume has been
written.

Although told more or
less fully in all the general histories, the story
is nowhere connectedly
told, but is broken off
whenever other features

KING WILLIAM III.

of the general subject demand a hearing. This method
not only breaks the thread, but also the force of the
story, which is much more satisfactorily followed in a
compact form.

A twenty years' war, practically continuous, would
certainly constitute a critical period in the history of
any people, but to one only just beginning to take firm

root in the soil, and to stretch out a few feeble brancnes into the wilderness, it was really a question of life or death. It was the strategy of the enraged enemy to lop off these branches and thus prevent the growth of, if not finally kill, the tree itself.

At the breaking out of these wars, the New England frontier practically extended from the Hudson to the Penobscot, or from Albany to Pemaquid ; and while the rivers flowing southward to the sea, through the English settlements, were always so many avenues of danger to be watched, this whole extent of country was open to an enemy who needed nothing but the sun, moon, or stars to guide him. To guard this long frontier was impossible. To block up the mouths of the rivers with forts, isolated from all support, was equally idle, as was proved by the utter failure of every such attempt. Herein lay the weakness of the English. They were compelled to receive the enemy at their own doors, and that disadvantage they labored under from first to last.

As the English inhabited open villages, only one practicable plan of defence suggested itself. This was to make certain houses, better adapted or more favorably situated for the purpose than others, so many rallying points for all the rest, thus turning mere dwellings into what were called garrisons. Exquisitely homely as these ancient structures seem to-day, nothing could more forcibly press home the startling fact that in them the sole dependence of a settlement often lay, or in what a decisive sense every man's house was his castle. Realizing the uncertain tenure of these historic buildings, threatened as they are on every hand, I have reproduced as many of them as possible in these pages, believing too that, like the famous standard of Joan of Arc, as they had been through the ordeal, so with good reason they should share in the honor.

The earliest Indian names, as preserved by old writers, like Champlain, Lescarbot, and others, may with propriety be dispensed with, as having been given without adequate knowledge in the first place, and dropped as soon as a more thorough knowledge of the subject was obtained. For the sake of convenience, the English fell into the custom of calling the various tribes by the names of the rivers they lived upon, as the Kennebec, Penobscot, and St. John Indians, etc., but the French, with more accuracy, designated the three principal Abenaki Nations as Canibas, Malicites, and Micmacs, each speaking a different dialect. According to this classification, the Canibas occupied the Kennebec and its tributaries, the Malicites all between the Penobscot and St. John, the Micmacs, generally speaking, all now comprised in the provinces of Nova Scotia and New Brunswick. Besides these, the once numerous Sokokis, of the river Saco, dwindled to a handful, had mostly joined other tribes, and the Pennacooks, of the Merrimac, were no longer either very numerous or united, though still sufficiently formidable to be troublesome neighbors. Their villages were to be found in the neighborhood of the Amoskeag Falls, now Manchester, and at various points above, while the peaceful section, or Praying Indians, as they were called, lived at Pawtucket Falls, now Lowell, on a tract of land reserved to their use by the efforts of the Apostle Eliot in 1653. Although these people were friendly to the whites, there was much the same sort of intimacy between them and their pagan relations as between the seceding Mohawks and their friends, a fact sure to cast more or less sus-

picion upon their fidelity in time of war.   In the Connecticut Valley the Indians had been, for the most part,

QUEEN MARY.

dispersed during Phil-
ip's War, the fragments
going to other and
safer localities.   The
upper valley of this riv-
er seems to have been
reserved as a hunting
ground, or as a debata-
ble ground, roamed
over by different and
hostile tribes from time
to time.

Back of all these, in
the heart of the White
Mountains, lay what
was, perhaps, the old-
est village of the Soko-
kis, near what is now Fryeburg, Me.   This village was
Pigwacket, or Pequawket, long a thorn in the side of
the English from its almost inaccessible position, which
made it practically secure from attack, while the waters
flowing out of the mountains here led directly to the
Maine coast on one side, or to the New Hampshire coast
on the other.

For war purposes the rivers were connected by cross-
paths, easily traversed by the runners who carried the
war token from village to village.

And what of the Indian himself ?   What shall be said
of him ?   Undoubtedly there is much to admire, more to
arouse our pity.   We cannot but feel that he was the innocent victim of a cruel destiny.   We know that he was un-

justly dealt with. We admit that he fought for his rights as he knew them, and in treating of the question, from a moral stand-point, we are invariably driven to take the defensive. All we know is that the white man was the willing instrument, perhaps the appointed instrument, of the red man's extinction. If the decrees of an inexorable destiny are to be deplored, the world has been going wrong ever since the Creation. History is full of just such examples.

But at the moment when we are ready to admire the red man's noble traits, his ferocious cruelty, that rage of blood which delights in rending and tearing its helpless victims, disenchants us. We note how he measured success in war by the amount of havoc and misery he was able to inflict, and turn away from him in horror and disgust. With the tormented English borderers, self-preservation was the higher law. The final appeal must therefore be to a Higher Court than ours.

KING WILLIAM'S WAR

I

HOSTILITIES BEGIN

1688–1689

THE renewal of hostilities with the Abenakis, after ten years of peace, was distinctly the result of English aggressions. At the bottom lay the one irritating cause of all the Indian wars from that day to this, never to be removed except by the final subjugation of one or the other race. By the rapid growth and steady extension of English settlements, peace was working the downfall of the natives even more certainly **First cause of war.**

than war, for just as the wild grasses are eradicated by the cultivated sorts, so slowly but surely, step by step, the red man was being thrust back into the wilderness. Under such conditions little provocation was needed to fan the smouldering embers into a flame; and the

COTTON MATHER.

whole series of outbreaks, in their primary cause, may therefore be regarded as one.

The Ten Years' War, or Lamentable Decade, as Cotton

Mather tearfully terms it, is commonly known as King William's War, although it began some time before William ascended the throne.   But the momentous events, arising from the revolution in England, merged what was at first merely a local struggle into the larger proportions of a national conflict, as France and England soon went to war about the succession to the throne; and, willing or unwilling, the colonies found themselves drawn into it.

For New England no time could have been worse chosen for an outbreak.   It came just after the people were arbitrarily deprived of self-government, and put under the rule of a royal governor, whom they soon heartily detested.   This was Sir Edmund Andros, a favorite of James II. when Duke of York, and his governor of New **Governor Andros unpopular.** York after its recovery from the Dutch. With the mass of the people whom he was now sent to govern Andros had nothing whatever in common.   He was a thick-and-thin royalist, and they considered James II. a despot.   In his eyes they were little better than rebels and traitors; in theirs, he was the ready tool of a tyrant.   The people were therefore disconcerted, angry, and stubborn—by no means the best frame of mind for facing a great public danger.

Andros was, however, ready enough to assert the rights of his master, and the disputed Acadian boundary gave him an opportunity not to be neglected.   In the spring of 1688 he sailed to various points of the Maine coast, as far as St. Castin's trading-post, at Penobscot, still **Descent on St. Castin.** known by his name.   Sir Edmund purposed holding the place permanently, but the ruinous state of the old French fort there induced him to change his mind.   Before leaving, however, he plun-

dered St. Castin's house, respecting only the altar
and vessels of the Catholic mission. The baseness of
the act, so like to that of some roving buccaneer,
aroused the indignation of St. Castin's tribesmen, the
Penobscots, over whom he had unlimited control, and
they were now ready to dig up the hatchet whenever
he should give the signal.

Another, and even less justifiable, exploit soon followed. This was the seizure of sixteen Indians at
Saco, by Benjamin Blackman, a justice of the peace, in
retaliation for the killing of some cattle at North
Yarmouth. It is said that Blackman purposed selling
these Indians into slavery. Be that as it may, the act
set all the tribes buzzing with excitement. Reprisals
quickly followed. Immediately the Kennebec Indians
made a descent upon New Dartmouth (Newcastle),
taking Henry Smith, Edward Taylor, and **Indians seized**
their families, prisoners, and carrying **at Saco.**
them off to Teconnet. Egeremet, the chief sagamore,
angrily told Smith that these things were done in return
for the outrages committed at Penobscot and Saco ;
significantly adding that St. Castin had promised the
Indians all the powder and ball they might want to fight
the English with.[1]

At the same time a Jesuit missionary arrived from
Canada, bringing a present of powder and guns, and
furthermore announcing that two hundred Frenchmen
would shortly follow him.[2]

With the passions of the Indians inflamed against
the English to a pitch of fury, it is not strange that
some of the prisoners suffered death at the hands of their
captors. And thus matters stood in the autumn of 1688.

[1] SMITH's Relation to the Commissioners of the United Colonies, September 14, 1689.
[2] *Ibid.*

Fearing that he would soon have an Indian war on his hands, Sir Edmund first tried diplomacy. He im-

SIR EDMUND ANDROS.

mediately ordered all the Indian prisoners set at liberty, and called upon the savages to do the same by the English captives, and also to give up the murderers of any English without delay. These demands being treated with silent contempt, Sir Edmund found himself obliged to use force or confess defeat, with the result that his inefficiency proved as deplorable in war as in diplomacy.

Seven hundred men were hastily levied, and with Andros at their head, marched down through the eastern country, in the beginning of November. They found not one solitary Indian to fight, suffered incredible **Andros's futile** hardships, and loudly complained of being **march.** thus led about the country through frost and snow on a fool's errand. All the good that Andros really did, in this worse than foolish expedition, was to leave garrisons in the various frontier posts of Maine. [1]

---

[1] HE established a new post as a check to the Kennebec tribes, thus referred to in a letter from Wait Winthrop to his brother: "They have built something up Kennebec River which is called Fort Ann, where Captain Savage is with his Company." December 25, 1688. In December the governor was frozen up in the Kennebec.

Spring came, and with it news of the revolution in England. The arrest and imprisonment of Sir Edmund, at Boston, quickly followed. Being now without any lawful government, Massachusetts reassumed her old form, until such time as further orders could be received from England, and as the public exigency now demanded. Confusion in the administra- **Andros deposed,** tion of military, as well as civil, affairs **April, 1689.** necessarily accompanied these abrupt and bewildering changes. The garrisons posted along the Maine border took sides in the dispute. Many of the soldiers deserted, some were drawn off, and the rest with difficulty kept at their posts of duty.

Some effort was made by the new government to prevent further hostilities with the Indians, but the storm had been long brewing and was ready to burst at last; and when it did, all the old animosities were dragged forth to add to its fury tenfold.

II

THE SACK OF DOVER

June 27, 1689

DOVER is one of the oldest settlements in New Hampshire. By the year 1689 it had grown to be one of the most flourishing. There were, in fact, two settlements, a second having grown up at the first falls of the Cocheco River, just as, in the course of time, lumber was found to be the true source of wealth of the province. At these falls Richard Waldron had built a saw and grist mill. The forests stood at his door. The river very obligingly turned his mill-wheel.

Cocheco Falls.

It is needless to add that Richard Waldron was the great man of his village. More than this, he had held not a few important civil and military offices under the province, and was at this very moment a major of militia, then an office nearly equivalent to that of a county lieutenant in England, and in war-times one of high responsibility. Waldron was now about seventy-five years old, hale, hearty, and vigorous, and, unless report does him wrong, as hard to move as the dam of his own mill.

Richard Waldron.

Five block-houses guarded the settlement, for Dover touched the very edge of the wilderness. Waldron's, Otis's, and Heard's were on the north side of the river, and Peter Coffin's and his son's on the south side. All were surrounded by walls built of timber, with gates securely bolted and barred at night, at which time those families whose homes were not thus **Garrison houses.** protected came into the nearest garrison to sleep. In the morning, if all was safe, they went back to their own houses again.

This was Dover. This was border life. Yet even its dangers had their charm. It was the making of a robust race of men and women, whose nursery tales were the tragedies of Indian warfare or captivity, and who, as they grew up, became skilled in the use of arms, keen in tracking the bear or the moose, and almost as capable of withstanding hunger or hardship as the wild Indians themselves.

Though they did not know it, the people of Dover were actually walking between life and death. They had forgotten; but an Indian never forgets or forgives an injury until it is avenged. For years the memory of Waldron's treachery had rankled deep. It is no pleasant tale we have to tell, yet it is all true.

During the expiring struggles of Philip's War, some thirteen years before, Waldron had made a peace with the Pennacook, Ossipee, and Pigwacket tribes, by which the calamities of that war were wholly kept from him and his neighbors. It was a shrewd move thus to keep these restive Indians quiet. In the treaty the Indians promised, among other things, not to harbor any enemies of the English, meaning Philip's men. The Indians shook hands with Waldron upon it, and were allowed to come and go as freely as they liked.

This promise, however, was not kept. On the contrary, it is certain that many of Philip's followers fled to the Pennacooks for protection. Indian hospitality could not refuse these fugitives an asylum, hunted as they were by the unrelenting vengeance of their conquerors. To give them up was indeed a hard condition, which it is not surprising to find disregarded.   In other respects the tribes mentioned seemed to have lived up to their treaty obligations.

But other tribes, living on the Androscoggin and Kennebec Rivers, who had been parties to the same treaty, were easily led to take up the hatchet again, and were soon busy at their old work of killing and plundering the defenceless settlers.   Help being called for to put down this fresh outbreak, two companies were presently marched from Boston to their relief.

When these soldiers came to Dover they found some hundreds of friendly Indians gathered there, as it would seem, to trade with, or have a talk with, their father Waldron's   and friend, Major Waldron.   And though treachery.   they came armed, no good ground appears for supposing that they harbored any hostile intent whatever.

It was then and there that Major Waldron dealt them the most terrible blow they had ever received—a blow struck, as it were, behind the back.

The two captains, Sill and Hawthorne, having orders to seize all Indians who had been out with Philip, wherever found, upon being told that many of these very Indians were among those now present, would have fallen upon them at once without more words.   But Waldron was more wary.   A plan had arranged itself in his mind, by which the whole body of Indians could be taken without striking a blow.

He proposed to the Indians to celebrate the meeting by having a sham fight, after the English fashion, to which they readily consented. Meantime, he called up Captain Frost's company from Kittery, and got his own men under arms. These, with the two marching companies, gave him all the force he needed to carry out his deep-laid plan.

The next day the two bodies, English and Indians, were drawn up for the sham battle, into which the unsuspecting redskins entered with much spirit. Meantime, while going through with certain simple manœuvres, the English were quietly surrounding them. Still mistrusting nothing, the Indians opened the fight by firing the first volley. When their guns were discharged, the soldiers rushed in upon them, and seized and disarmed them without the loss of a man on either side. In this manner upward of four hundred Indians were taken like so many silly herring in a net.

They were then separated. Those known to be friendly were allowed to go in peace, but all those suspected of having aided Philip, numbering some two hundred in all, were sent under guard to Boston as prisoners, where seven or eight were hanged and the rest sold out of the country as slaves. It is true that those hanged were known to have been concerned in some of the bloodiest massacres of the war. Those sold helped to defray the expense of their capture. And all the people said amen!

So now, long years after, some of the same Indians who had been thus entrapped by Waldron laid their plans to be revenged. When it was found that the Dover people had fallen into careless habits, kept no watches, and would even let the Indians sleep in their houses, these plans were ripe for execution. It is true that some hints of intended mischief had been thrown

2

out in a vague sort of way, but the careless settlers hardly listened to them.

When Waldron himself was spoken to about it, he jocosely told the uneasy ones to go and plant their pumpkins, and that he would tell them when the Indians would break out.

As the time fixed for the assault drew near, the two chiefs, Kankamagus and Mesandowit, brought their followers to within striking distance of the village.[1] Indian cunning was then set to work. On Thursday evening, June 27, 1689, two squaws went to each of the five garrisons and asked leave to sleep there that night. It being wet weather, they were readily admitted to all except the younger Coffin's, though the people at Waldron's offered some objection, until the bluff but kind-hearted old major himself quieted them by saying, "Let the poor creatures lodge by the fire." They were even shown how to unbar the doors, and let themselves out, without troubling the people of the house. Coffin, more prudent, or less hospitable than the rest, bluntly refused them admittance.

Mesandowit himself went boldly to Waldron's, where he was kindly received, all the more readily because he announced that a good many Indians were coming there to trade the next day. While the two were sitting at supper, like old friends, the chief jestingly asked, "Brother Waldron, what would you do if the strange Indians should come?"

"A hundred men stand ready when I lift my finger, thus," was Waldron's lofty reply.

Not dreaming of the storm so ready to burst upon them,

---

[1] It is known that some of the assailants came all the way from the St. John River, showing wide-spread preparation.

the inhabitants went to bed at the usual early hour. So
far as known, not even one solitary sentinel stood guard
over the doomed village. When all was still, the faithless squaws noiselessly arose, quietly unbarred the doors
of the four garrisons, and gave the signal agreed upon—
a low whistle. Instantly the warriors, who had been
lying in wait outside, rushed in. Roused from sleep by
the noise, Waldron barely had time to jump out of bed,
pull on his breeches, and snatch up his sword, before the
infuriated wretches, who were in search of him, came
crowding into the room, tomahawk in hand. But the
fiery old man was not to be taken without a struggle.
Half-dressed, with his gray head bare, Waldron yet laid
about him so lustily as not only to clear his own room
of assailants, but also to drive them before him into the
next. There was still a chance for his life, and he hastened to improve it. His musket and pistols had been
left lying in his own room. Waldron therefore started
to secure them. Seizing the moment when his back was
turned, a savage sprang forward and brained the brave
old man with a blow of the hatchet from behind.

Grievously wounded, but still breathing, Waldron was
now dragged into the great room, a chair put upon a
long table, where he had often sat as judge, and his
half-lifeless body roughly lifted into it,   Waldron tort-
while his captors made ready to gratify   ured to death.
their long-nursed vengeance with savage ingenuity and
more than savage barbarity.

"Who shall judge Indians now?" they asked the dying man, with grim irony.

Not to cut short Waldron's sufferings, his tormentors
commanded other captives to get them some victuals.
When they had swallowed their hideous meal, with the

worthy major still sitting there, stunned and bleeding to death, in his chair, these miscreants first stripped him of his shirt, and then took turns at slashing him with their knives across the breast, each one crying out as he did so, "See! I cross out my account!" They then severed his fingers, one by one, at the joints, asking in mockery if his fist would weigh a pound now. [1]

By this time Waldron was so far gone that strength failed him. Seeing him about to fall, one of the Indians held up the point of the major's own sword, so that as the dying man pitched head-foremost upon the table, the weapon passed quite through his lifeless body.

After killing or taking all who were in the house, the savages first plundered it and then set it on fire.

Meantime, other parties, led by the chief Kankamagus, were similarly engaged at the other garrisons. Heard's was saved by the barking of the house-dog, just as the Indians were stealthily gliding in at the gate. One of the inmates, with rare courage and presence of mind, ran to the spot, thrust the intruders out, shut to the gate, and held it so by throwing himself flat on his back, and bracing his feet against the gate, until the rest of the people came to his assistance.

Heard's garrison saved.

The elder Coffin's house was taken and ransacked, but the lives of the inmates were spared. Finding a bag of money here, the Indians made Coffin scatter it by handfuls over the floor, while they amused themselves by scrambling for it, like so many mischievous boys. This was their way of making an impartial division of the money.

---

[1] IT was said that Waldron was in the habit of putting his fist into the scale as a make-weight against their furs.

Young Coffin stoutly refused to surrender, until the Indians brought out his old father, and threatened to kill him before his son's eyes. He then gave himself up. Both families were then put in a deserted house together, but not being closely watched, all made their escape while the Indians were engaged in plundering the captured houses.

This was a sad day for Dover. Twenty-three persons had lost their lives, and twenty-nine more were being carried off, captives. Five or six houses, with the mills, were burned to the ground, all being done so quickly that the elated assailants were able to decamp without meeting with the least opposition, loaded with booty and exulting in the manner in which they had " crossed out their account " with Major Waldron.

It is but just to add that the conduct of the savages during the sacking of Dover was not without some redeeming features. While certain persons seem to have been marked for unrelenting vengeance, others were spared, and still others not even molested. But the main circumstance is this : A new departure took place in regard to the treatment of prisoners. Instead of wearing out a miserable existence among the Indians, as in times past, they were now mostly taken to Canada and sold to the French, whose treatment was at least humane, although it was only a change of masters, not of condition, for the prisoners were held to belong to those who had bought them until ransomed by their friends. True, such conduct is wholly without warrant among civilized nations. But there was no appeal. The savages treated all prisoners as slaves, and disposed of them as such. And it must be admitted that the course taken by the English in selling their Indian captives into slavery fully justified this species of retaliation, by which the English were, by far, the greatest losers.   Be that as it may, just as soon as a living captive had a money value greater than a scalp, it became to the interest of the Indians to save, rather than slay, those who fell into their hands.   To this extent the policy is to be hailed as a distinct melioration in the conduct of these barbarous wars.

Sad to relate, the terrible calamity which befell the people of Dover might have been averted by the timely delivery of a letter.   The design was disclosed to Major Henchman, at Chelmsford, who immediately informed the Massachusetts authorities of it.   A letter containing this intelligence, and written by their order, was despatched to Major Waldron on the day before the massacre; but owing to some delay to the courier at Newbury the warning reached Dover some hours too late. Waldron in particular was notified that he was a special object of vengeance.   The feelings with which this letter was opened and read by his son may be imagined.[1]

---

1 THE letter is in Belknap's *New Hampshire*, I., Appendix.   The friendly warning is said to have come from Wanalancet, sagamore of Pennacook.

III

THE CAPTIVITY OF SARAH GERRISH

AMONG the captives taken at the sacking of Dover was Major Waldron's little granddaughter, Sarah Gerrish, a beautiful and interesting child, only seven years old, who slept at her grandfather's garrison on that fatal night.

Waked out of a sound sleep by the strange noises in the house, Sarah sprang from her warm bed and ran, in a fright, into another room, where one of her little playmates was sleeping. Child-like, the little simpleton crept into bed with her still more helpless neighbor, for mutual protection, pulling the bedclothes up over her head, as if imagining that in this way she might escape detection. With a beating heart she lay there listening to the muffled noises made by the savages in searching through the house.

Her hiding-place was, however, soon discovered, and she was rudely commanded to get up and dress herself, which she very obediently did, though the savages hurried her out of doors before she had time to finish putting on her stockings. With one foot bare she was presently marched off with the rest of the captives into the wilderness, after seeing her grandfather's house plundered and burned before her eyes.

According to their usual custom, when once clear of the village the different bands went their several ways,

after dividing the prisoners and booty. Sarah appears
to have gone with a party of Eastern Indians, doubtless
belonging to some Maine tribe, to whose village she was
first taken, and in which she remained till winter.

Sarah's first master, one Sebundowit, a dull sort of
fellow, was harsh, but not cruel. He, however, soon
sold her to another Indian, who was both harsh and
cruel, who carried her away to Canada to be sold.

No tongue can tell the hardships which this child of
tender years had to undergo during that long and terrible winter's march. Strong men have sunk down under
less than she endured, the petted darling of a once happy
home, now made desolate. But a Protecting Arm seems
to have sustained the little captive maiden when her feet
were ready to fail her, and her heart to break, under the
hardships of which she was the innocent object.

At one time her wretch of a master told her to go and
stand with her back against a particular tree, while he
began loading his gun before her eyes, with tantalizing
indifference. When the truth flashed upon the child's
mind, and she shrieked out in mortal terror at the thought
that her last hour was come, the hardened wretch, whose
ferocious instincts seemed now and then to get the better
of him, either relented or was satisfied with having attained his object in frightening her so cruelly.

At another time, as they were ascending a river, her
brute of a master ordered Sarah to run along the shore
with some Indian girls, while he paddled on in his canoe.
In this manner they had reached a spot where the bank
was both high and steep, when one of Sarah's impish
companions spitefully pushed the little white girl off
the bank and into the river, leaving her to sink or swim
as best she might. Fortunately the bushes here hung

out over the water, so that when Sarah rose to the surface she was able to lay hold of them and draw herself out of the water by their aid. Otherwise she must certainly have been drowned then and there. As it was, she rejoined her wolfish companions, wet to the skin, and frightened almost to death at her narrow escape. Yet when asked how she became so wet she dared not tell, for fear of meeting with still worse treatment from the Indian boys and girls, who were always very abusive to her.

Once again, having fallen into a deep sleep at the end of a long and hard day's travel, Sarah did not wake when the party was ready to move off in the morning, so she was left asleep, half covered up with fresh-fallen snow, like another babe in the woods, without a morsel of food to eat or any guide by which to know what direction her heartless companions had taken. Upon waking to find herself left alone in that frightful wilderness, the poor little captive may well have given herself up for lost, for, strange to say, she seems to have been even more afraid of the bears and wolves of the forests than of her inhuman captors. Terror sharpened her wits. Snow had fallen before the party set out, by which their tracks could be followed. Guided by these footprints in the snow, Sarah ran crying after them, until, after a long and weary chase, her tormentors let her come up with them again.

Yet one more ordeal was contrived, with devilish ingenuity, to play upon poor little Sarah's fears. One evening the savages heaped together a great pile of dry brushwood, to which they set fire, and when it was in a light blaze Sarah's master called her to him, and told her that she must now be burned alive in the fire. For the moment the child was struck dumb. Then she burst into tears. Turning to the inhuman monster who claimed her, she flung her arms around his neck and besought him so piteously to spare her life that the hardened cut-throat so far relented as to agree not to burn her alive if she would promise to be a good girl.

After escaping death by fire and water, Sarah reached Canada at last, where her sad story, no less than her bright face and winning ways, could not fail of exciting compassion. Indeed, it must have been a heart of stone not to have melted toward the friendless one. Her greedy master first took her to the Lord Intendant's, where much notice was taken of her by persons of quality. In the course of a week Sarah was bought by the Intendant's lady, who placed the child in a convent, where she was once more safe in the hands of Christians. Here she remained until the fleet of Sir William Phips came before Quebec, the next year, when through his means Sarah was exchanged, and returned to her friends again, after a captivity lasting sixteen months, into which years of suffering had been crowded.[1]

[1] BELKNAP tells the story briefly in a note, *History of New Hampshire*, I., 253. Phips had taken some French prisoners while on his way to besiege Quebec.

IV

PEMAQUID TAKEN; WITH THE RELATION OF JOHN GYLES

August, 1689

It was now St. Castin's turn to be revenged. True, an attempt had been made by the new rulers to pacify him with fair words, but all to no purpose. A more implacable foe never devastated the border; and though he dealt much with the English, by way of trade, being in no way averse to English gold, no hand was ever more ready to strike them than his. He had the twin passions of a true Bernais—love of war and love of money. His is a strange, eventful history. Reared a gentleman, and by profession a soldier, upon the disbanding of his regiment he had taken up the vagabond life of an Indian trader with as much facility as if he had never known any other; had taken a chief's daughter to wife; and had thus, to all intents, cast his fortunes for weal or woe among the filthy denizens of the forest. And the erratic Baron La Hontan, soldier, traveller, and author of the most amusing memoirs in the world, roundly asserts that St. Castin was so much respected by his savage clansmen that they looked up to him as their tutelar deity. If report was true, he had amassed a fortune of two or three hundred thousand crowns in "good, dry gold" among them. No wonder, then, that he stood ready to draw his sword in their behalf.

St. Castin of Penobscot.

Accordingly, there was much bustle of preparation at St. Castin's fort for the descent he meditated. This had for its object no less a place than the fort and settlement at Pemaquid, farthest outpost of the English dominions, in this direction, as Penobscot was of French power in **Pemaquid and Penobscot.** the other. The distance between them was considerable, yet St. Castin's hatred would not have cooled, even if the distance had been ten times greater.

When all was ready the war-party put off in their canoes. St. Castin and Father Thury, of the Indian mission, with the Abenaki chief Moxus, were the leaders. The scheme was a bold one, it must be confessed; **Moxus and Father Thury.** so bold, indeed, that there is little doubt of the invaders being well informed of the true state of the fort and garrison. Spies were sent ahead to New Harbor, an out-village of Pemaquid, to learn how the inhabitants disposed themselves in the daytime, and how best to strike them unawares.

The blow fell on one August afternoon in 1689. St. Castin's war-party gained the rocky shore undiscovered. They soon laid hands upon a white man, who disclosed the defenceless condition of the place. It was in harvest time, when the unsuspecting settlers were busy, either in the fields or about the shores. The main village, in which only the women and children were left, lay about a quarter of a mile from the fort. The farms, where most of the men were at work, were three miles higher up, at the Falls.

The assailants quickly arranged their plan of attack. One band threw itself between the fort and the village; the other between the village and farms. Then the work of slaughter began. As the men at the farms ran

for the fort, they found themselves cut off by the band
below.   In like manner, those in the village, who started
for the fort, were mostly intercepted before reaching it.

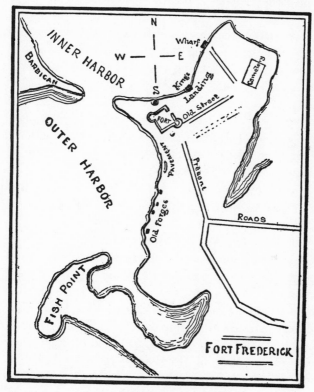

FORT AND APPROACHES, PEMAQUID, ME.

The few who did so owed their safety to fleetness of
foot.

The assailants next turned their attention to the fort.
A certain number threw themselves into some houses,
standing along the street leading to it, from which they

fired on every one who showed himself. The high rock, as conspicuous an object to-day as it was then, also served to shelter more of them, who were thus advanced so near the walls as to be able to drive the gunners from their posts.

Weems, the commander of the fort, held out until the next day, when having but fourteen out of thirty men left unhurt, besides being wounded himself, he gave up the place on condition that the garrison should be al-

The fort sur- lowed to depart unmolested. Fort and
renders. village were then given to the flames, after which the Indians took to their canoes, with their captives and booty, greatly elated at their conquest of this stronghold of the English.

The following relation, set forth by one of the captives, describes in a graphic manner the onset at the Falls:

" On the 2d of August, 1689, in the morning, my honored father, Thomas Gyles, Esq., went with some laborers, my two older brothers and myself to one of his farms, which lay upon the river, about three miles above Fort Charles, at Pemaquid Falls, and we labored there securely till noon. After we had dined, our people went to their labor, some in one field of English hay, some to another of English corn. My father, the youngest of my two brothers and myself tarried near the farm-house in which we had dined till about one of the clock, at which time we heard the report of several great guns at the fort. My father said he hoped it was a signal of good news, and that the great council had sent back the soldiers to cover the inhabitants (for on report of the revolution they had deserted).

" But to our great surprise, about thirty or forty Indians at that moment discharged a volley of shot at us from behind a rising ground near our barn. The yelling of the Indians, the whistling of their shot, and the voice of my father, whom I heard cry out, 'What now! what now!' so terrified me (though he seemed to be handling a gun) that I endeavored to make my escape. My brother ran one way, and I another, and on looking over my shoulder I saw a stout fellow, all painted, pursuing me, with a gun in one hand and a cutlass glittering in the other, which I expected in my brains every moment.

"I soon fell down, and the Indian seized me by the left hand. He offered me no abuse, but tied my arms, then lifted me up and pointed to the place where the people were at work about the hay, and led me that way. As we went, we crossed the spot where my father was, who looked very pale and bloody, and walked very slowly.

"When we came to the place, I saw two men shot down on the flats, and one or two more knocked on the head with hatchets, while crying out, 'O, Lord! O, Lord!' etc. There the Indians brought two more captives, one a man, and the other my brother James, who, with me, had tried to escape by running from the house when we were first attacked. This brother was about fourteen years of age. My oldest brother, Thomas, wonderfully escaped by land to the Barbican, a point of land opposite the fort, where several fishing vessels lay. He got on board of one of them and sailed away that night.

" After doing what mischief they could, the Indians sat down, and made us sit with them. After some time we arose, and the Indians pointed for us to go eastward. We marched about a quarter of a mile and then made a halt. Here they brought my father to us. They made proposals to him by old Moxus, who told him that those were strange Indians who shot him, and that he was sorry

Moxus is sorry. for it. My father replied that he was a dying man, and wanted no favor but to pray with his children. This being granted, he commended us to the protection and blessing of God Almighty; then gave us his best advice and took his leave of us for this life, hoping that we should meet in a better.

"He parted from us with a cheerful voice, but looked very pale, by reason of his great loss of blood, which now gushed out of his shoes. The Indians then led him aside. I heard the blows of the hatchet, but neither shriek nor groan.

"The Indians led us, on the east side of the river, toward the fort, and when we came within a mile and a half of the fort and town, we saw fire and smoke rising on all sides. Here we made a short stop, and then moved on to within three-quarters of a mile from the fort, into a thick swamp. There I saw my mother and my two little sisters, and many other captives taken from the town. My mother asked me about my father. I told her he was killed, but could say no more for grief. She burst into tears, and the Indians moved me a little farther off, and seized [1] me with cords to a tree.

"After the Indians had laid Pemaquid waste they moved up to New Harbor, about two miles farther east.

Embark at New Harbor. At this place there were, before the war, about twelve houses. These were deserted as soon as the rumor of war reached the place. When we turned our backs on the town my heart was ready to break. We tarried that night at New Harbor, and the next day went away in the Indians' canoes for Penobscot.

[1] A SEAFARING expression for tied him up.

"A few days after we arrived at Penobscot fort,[1] where I again saw my mother, my brother and sisters, and many other captives. I think we tarried here eight days. In that time the Jesuit of the place had a great mind to buy me. My Indian master made a visit to the Jesuit, and took me with him. I saw the Jesuit show my master pieces of gold, and understood afterward that he was tendering them for my ransom. He gave me a biscuit, which I put in my pocket, and not daring to eat it, I buried it under a log, fearing he had put something in it to make me love him. When my mother heard the talk of my being sold to a Jesuit, she said to me, 'Oh, my dear child, if it were God's will, I had rather follow you to your grave, or nevermore see you in this world, than that you should be sold to a Jesuit; for a Jesuit will ruin you body and soul.'

Antipathy to Jesuits.

"It pleased God to grant her request, for she never saw me more. Yet she and my two little sisters were, after several years' captivity, redeemed; but she died ere I returned. My brother, who was taken with me, was, after several years' captivity, most barbarously tortured to death by the Indians.

"My Indian master carried me up Penobscot River to Madawamkee,[2] which stands on a point of land between the main river and a branch which heads to the east of it. At home I had ever seen strangers treated with the utmost civility, and I expected like treatment here; but I soon found out my mistake; for I presently saw a number of squaws, who had got together in a circle, dancing and yelling. An old grim-looking hag took me by the hand, and leading me

Madawamkee.

---

[1] Now Castine, Me.　　　[2] MATTAWAMKEAG is probably meant.

3

into the ring, some seized me by the hair, and others by the hands and feet, like so many furies ; but my master presently laying down a pledge, they released me.[1]

" The next day we went up that eastern branch of Penobscot River many leagues ; carried overland to a large pond, and from one pond to another, till, in a few days more, we went down a river called Medocktec, which empties into St. John River.   But before we came to the mouth of this river, we passed over a

At Medocktec.

long carrying-place to Medocktec fort,[2] which stands on a bank of St. John River.   My master went before, and left me with an old Indian and two or three squaws.   The old man often said (which was all the English he could speak), 'By and by come to a great town and fort.'   I now comforted myself in thinking how finely I should be refreshed when I came to this great town.

" After some miles' travel we came in sight of a large cornfield, and soon after of the fort, to my great surprise.   Two or three squaws met us, took off my pack, and led me to a large hut or wigwam, where thirty or forty Indians were dancing and yelling round five or six poor captives, who had been taken some months before from Quochecho,[3] at the time Major Waldron was so barbarously butchered by them.

" After some weeks had passed, we left this village and went up the St. John River about ten miles, to a branch called Medockcenecasis, where there was one wigwam. At our arrival an old squaw saluted me with a yell, tak-

---

[1] THE owner of a captive might ransom him from torture in this way, if so inclined. Otherwise the custom was to first hand him over to the squaws, and afterward to the warriors.

[2] MEDOCTEC, a Malicite village on the St. John River.

[3] COCHECO, the Indian name of Dover, N. H.   The complicity of these Indians in that affair is thus proven.

ing me by the hair and one hand, but I was so rude as
to break her hold and free myself. She gave me a filthy
grin, and the Indians set up a laugh, and so it passed
over.   Here we lived upon fish, wild grapes, roots, &c.,
which was hard living to me.

"When the winter came on we went up the river till
the ice came down, running thick in the river, when, according to the Indian custom, we laid up our canoes till
spring. Then we travelled sometimes on the ice and
sometimes on the land, till we came to a river that
was open, but not fordable, where we made a raft and
passed over, bag and baggage. I met with no abuse
from them in this winter's hunting, though put to great
hardships in carrying burdens, and for want of food.
But they endured the same difficulty, and would often
encourage me by saying in broken English, 'By and by
great deal moose.'"[1]

[1] AFTER spending six years in captivity among the Indians of the St. John River,
young Gyles was sold to a French trader of that river, with whom he lived nearly three
years longer. He was not released until the peace of Ryswick, thus having been almost
nine years a captive. Gyles subsequently became a partisan officer of much merit, his
knowledge of the Indian tongue, gained during his captivity, standing him in good stead.
The *Memoir* from which the above extracts are taken, and put into coherent form, was
first printed at Boston in 1736. In a copy which belonged to Dr. Belknap, now in the
Boston Public Library, there is a note, in Dr. Belknap's hand, on the fly-leaf, ascribing
the authorship to Joseph Seccombe, chaplain to the garrison at St. Georges, afterward
minister of Kingston, N. H. It is a wretched piece of work, whoever wrote it.

V

CHURCH'S FIRST EXPEDITION

September, 1689

AFTER the fall of Pemaquid all the English settlements east of Casco, or Falmouth, were hurriedly abandoned, and this place now became the rallying point for the fugitives, who were still laboring under the evil effects of the panic, into which the enemy's successes had thrown them.

Aroused by the pressing nature of the emergency, the Massachusetts authorities, responding to the cries for help coming from all quarters at once, promptly called out six hundred men, who took up their line of march *Swaine's march,* from the rendezvous, at Berwick, on Au-*August 28th.* gust 28, 1689, to clear the border of enemies, strengthen the weak garrisons, and restore the failing courage of the inhabitants as they went. Major Jeremiah Swaine,[1] a good officer, was in command of this small army.

This was not done a moment too soon, as the daring enemy were now hovering about every settlement on the *Blue Point and* coast, from Berwick to Falmouth, killing, *Falmouth re-* scalping, and burning on every side, until *lieved.* Swaine's advance drove them back into the woods. At Blue Point,[2] in Scarborough, there was a smart skirmish, and when the troops reached Fal-

---

[1] SWAINE was of Reading, Mass.

[2] SINCE called Pine Point. Swaine urged holding the fort at Saco Falls on account of the saw and grist mill there. *Letter* of September 24, 1689.

mouth they found that place as good as invested by
the enemy, who made a sharp fight, in which ten soldiers
were killed, before being driven off the ground.

Having done the work assigned him in this direction,
and put new life into the desponding settlers, Swaine

COLONEL BENJAMIN CHURCH.

marched back to Berwick the way he came.   His march,
back and forth, disclosed the weakness of the whole
system of defence; for Swaine had no   **Durham**
sooner uncovered the towns in his rear,   **attacked.**
after taking with him every available man that could be
spared, than the Indians swooped down upon Durham,

N. H.,[1] killing eighteen men, murdering three or four children, and carrying off several persons into captivity.[2]

Swaine immediately despatched a strong scouting party toward Lake Winnipesaukee to hunt the assassins down, but, as usual, no Indians could be found, and the party returned empty-handed. These operations terminated Swaine's share in this campaign.

While putting forth these efforts to hold what was left of Maine, Massachusetts called the United Colonies[3] to her aid. A second expedition, acting in concert with Swaine's, but designed to carry the war into the devastated region, east of Falmouth, was raised chiefly in Plymouth Colony, and put under the command of Major Church, the tried veteran of Philip's War. A part of the two hundred and fifty men enlisted for this service were Church takes the field. Seconnet and Cape Cod Indians, some of whom had been out with Church before. They were true Indians. During their stay in Boston they had even sold their powder-horns and bullet-pouches to get money to squander for drink. Then the ammunition furnished was not of proper size to fit the bore of the guns. All this seems to have been unknown to Church, until the moment when he was going into action.[4]

[1] USUALLY called Oyster River in the accounts of these wars.

[2] THIS bloody affair took place at Huckins's garrison. Seeing all the men go out to work in the morning, the Indians ran between them and the house, killing all but one, who made his escape. They then attacked the house, in which there were only two boys, with some women and children. The boys kept them off for some time, and wounded several of them. At length the Indians set the house on fire, but even then these brave boys would not surrender until the Indians had promised to spare their lives. The wretches, however, immediately murdered three or four of the children, one of whom was impaled on a sharp stake before the eyes of its horrified mother. One of the boys escaped the next day.—Belknap, *New Hampshire*, I., 255, ed. 1792.

[3] A UNION formed by Massachusetts, Plymouth, New Haven, and Connecticut in 1643 for mutual defence.

[4] THE expedition was not half supplied with clothing, medicines, or provisions, and yet this was the season of autumnal storms.

Embarking at Boston, the expedition arrived at Falmouth on Friday, September 20, 1689. Immediately upon coming into the harbor Church found work ready cut out for him. He was hailed from a vessel and told that large numbers of Indians had been seen gathering on one of the neighboring islands, as if getting ready to make a descent. On board of a vessel lying at anchor, Church found a Mrs. Lee,[1] a redeemed captive, who said that she had counted fifty canoes, and knew that more were expected. To resist this formidable horde there were only two companies of soldiers in the fort and garrisons, besides the handful of inhabitants. Church had not come a moment too soon.

Gets to Falmouth, September 20th.

As soon as it was dark, Church landed his men, fully intending to go in search of these marauders at daybreak; but they saved him the trouble by coming up close to the neck, on which the village stood, some time during the night; so that the morning found them holding a position to cut off all retreat by land, whenever they advanced to attack the village.

In fact, when the sun was about an hour high, firing was heard in the direction of Anthony Brackett's farmhouse,[2] situated over against the neck, on the westerly side of a cove making in from the sea. Presently Brackett's son came running into the village with the news that the farm was swarming with strange Indians, who had taken his father prisoner. His own escape was owing to his fleetness of foot.

Though completely taken at a disadvantage, Church acted with promptitude and vigor. First, sending off

---

[1] A MARRIED daughter of Major Waldron, taken at Dover, N. H.

[2] SINCE the property of the Deering family.

one company belonging to the garrison, he followed it
with one of his own, expecting to send in the rest as
soon as they could be got ready.   It being low tide, the
two advance companies crossed the cove, and were im-
The enemy's at- mediately hotly engaged in and about
tack repulsed.   Brackett's field and orchard, thus putting the cove between them and their comrades. Instead
of coming promptly to their relief with his whole force,

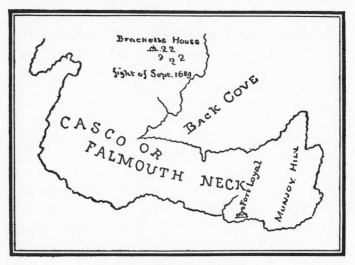

PLAN OF FALMOUTH NECK, PORTLAND.

Church now made the startling discovery that the bullets
were too large for the guns, causing a long delay, while
the bullets were being hammered into slugs, and putting
the small detachment, then fighting against great odds,
Church's critical in danger of being cut to pieces before
situation.   help could reach them.   When these laggards did come up, they found themselves cut off from
their hard-pressed comrades by the rising tide.   They,

however, opened a random fire across the cove. Church at length reached the spot. Seeing the danger his men were in, he succeeded in getting across the cove with his main body, higher up, and decided the combat by coming down on the enemy's flank. They then fled in confusion.

This fight, really forced upon Church before he was ready, or acquainted with the ground, was creditable only to the small number, who bore the brunt of it for several hours without flinching. It saved Casco, but did not help Church's reputation. His loss was twenty-one killed and wounded.[1] As the enemy followed their old custom of carrying off the dead and wounded, no estimate of their loss was **His losses.** possible. It was enough that they confessed defeat by making a precipitate retreat. That the battle was unexpectedly thrust upon Church is true; but that such an old campaigner as he should take the field so wretchedly equipped is certainly surprising.

By those who first faced the foe, the battle was gallantly, even desperately, fought. Among them, the inhabitants came in for a full share of the credit for the victory. There is a touch of humor in what Church says in his despatches[2] in regard to the fighting parson of Falmouth. " As for the minister of this place," the honest soldier declares, "I am well satisfied with him, he being present with us yesterday in the fight."

Having disposed of this body of enemies, who were probably ignorant of his arrival when they began their unsuccessful onset, Church now found himself at lib-

---

[1] A LIST of these will be found in S. G. Drake's *Additions* to Baylies's *New Plymouth*, p. 77.

[2] DATED at Falmouth, September 22, 1689.

erty to carry out his favorite idea of tracking the savages to their villages and striking them there. There were two of these on the Androscoggin, and as many more on the Kennebec, situated far enough inland not to be easily assailable, yet near enough to the sea to be dangerous neighbors. It was from these Indians that the English had most to fear, and it was they, no doubt, who had taken the lead in the recent assault.

Owing chiefly to the want of proper guides, nearly a month passed before Church was ready to set forth on this errand. Moving his force up to the head of Maquoit Bay by vessel, he struck across the great Indian portage uniting the waters of Casco Bay with those of the Andros-

Maquoit Portage. coggin, coming out on the banks of the Androscoggin at a point some forty miles below the Indian fort at which he was aiming. He found the low country everywhere flooded by the autumnal freshets. Abandoning his first design, he therefore turned down the river, marching on until his vessels took him up again in the Kennebec. He then set sail for Pemaquid, where his men did some scouting, but could find no Indians. All the fresh trails led eastward, thus indicating that the enemy's war-parties had drawn off from their inroads for the season. After taking on board some of the heavy guns belonging to the ruined fort, Church therefore sailed back to Casco, in a storm, and the campaign closed without a solitary exploit to its credit except the relief of Casco.[1]

---

[1] CHURCH'S *History* contains a lengthy, but rambling, account of his operations. Letters from him, written from Falmouth at the time, are much more coherent. See *Additions* to Baylies's *New Plymouth.*

VI

FRONTENAC'S WINTER RAIDS
March, 1690

AFTER this war had been going on for a year or more
with the Indians alone, a new enemy suddenly appeared
in the French, who, from this time forward, became
open enemies, instead of the secret ones they had been.
War had been formally declared between the two crowns,
England and France, and the colonies of **War with France.**
both must now bear their part in it.[1] It
is true that some sensible men had thought of a neutrality
for the colonies, as being a far more rational course
than cutting each other's throats without contributing
one iota to the final result between the great belligerents.   But this wise and eminently humane idea did
not meet with favor either at the French court or from
the man now at the head of affairs in Canada.   There
were fifty reasons why Louis should desire the conquest
of New England, to one why England **Canada not menaced.**
should wish to possess Canada, which at
that day she had no use for, and certainly did not covet.
Control of the fisheries, control of the Indian trade, but
more especially control over the one great gate-way to
Canada—the St. Lawrence—were the foremost of these
reasons.

[1] WAR was declared at Westminster, April, 1689; at Boston not until December.

On the other hand, New England asked only to be let alone. There was then no such thing as an American colonial policy, although war between the two great powers most interested in America was as certain to create one as that the sun rose and set. This conflict, which the French sought to bring about and New England wished to avoid, may be set down, therefore, as the beginning of the end.

No American policy.

The long series of hostilities, of which we are now at the beginning, should not be regarded, therefore, as so many hap-hazard blows struck in the dark, but as an issue to be fought out to the bitter end, or until one or the other adversary surrendered at discretion.

Count Frontenac, the man on whose shoulders Louis had twice put the burden of saving Canada, was beyond question without his equal as a commander in all the colonies. Though now seventy, he was to all appearance as vigorous in mind and body as ever. To a military training in the best schools of Europe he added the genius of audacity— the quick and brilliant conceptions which mark the great soldier. It was this rare quality which made him by far the most dangerous enemy that New England ever had. None knew better than he the advantage of carrying the war into the enemy's country, or of striking a disabling blow when your adversary least expects it ; and while the English thought that winter, with its rigors, had put a stop to warlike movements, Frontenac was raising war-parties to distress them to the utmost. In a few short years he could say, as his master said of the Pyrenees, "there is no longer a wilderness."

Count Frontenac.

By furnishing a few ambitious French officers to lead his war-parties, composed mainly of savages, Frontenac

made the most of his means, without exposing himself
to great loss, besides, in a manner, dignifying these descents with a character they were far from deserving, as
they were neither more nor less than de-   Make up of
liberately planned raids for robbery and   war-parties.
murder. We cannot, therefore, in conscience find a
place of honor for such deeds, although narrating their

SAMUEL SEWALL.

injurious effects. Frontenac thought much of crippling
his enemies, but cared little for the means; and it is to
his eternal disgrace that he inaugurated the policy of
indiscriminate massacre, which put him on a level with
the savages he employed.[1]

---

[1] IT is claimed that this was done in retaliation for outrages committed by the Iroquois in Canada. But the Iroquois also were savages, neither governed by the rules
of civilized war, nor led by English officers.

Frontenac had planned three expeditions, one against
Schenectady, and two against New England. It was in
the heart of winter, when nobody dreamed of an outbreak, that the three war-parties set out on their errand
of destruction. In February, news of the atrocious massacres at Schenectady sent a thrill of horror throughout the colonies, and served to put the exposed east-
Weak defensive ern settlements somewhat on their guard.
line. But this line was much too long and too
thin not to be easily broken through, as it consisted of
villages situated ten, twenty, and thirty miles apart, connected only by occasional patrols. The horsemen were
of course compelled to keep to the few highways, which
were easily avoided, while the footmen, who ranged

LIEUTENANT-GOVERNOR STOUGHTON.

the woods looking for
fresh tracks of an enemy,
often had to force their
way through swamps
and thickets where the
foot of man had never
trod before.

The venerable Samuel
Sewall relates that he
was present at a "treat"
or social gathering in
Boston when the news
of the shocking calam-
ity at Schenectady came
to cast its withering
blight over the spirits of
all the company. It was
a premonition of the coming storm which cast its dark
shadow before. It was a season of gloomy foreboding.

" Mr. Danforth looks very sorrowfully.   Mr. Stoughton thinks best to prosecute vigorously," are simple words, pregnant with meaning.

The second expedi-
tion, numbering only fifty-two men, one half Canadian bushrangers, and one half savages, were toiling on through snow and ice toward the New England coast. François Hertel was in command, with Hopehood, a Norridgewock chief, to direct the sav-
ages.[1]

CANADIAN SNOWSHOE RANGER.

On the 27th of March, 1690, the in-
vaders came out of the woods near Salmon Falls, a little village situated on the west bank of the stream dividing Maine from New Hampshire. Like Dover, of which it was then a part, Salmon Falls had grown up around **Salmon Falls.** the falls, which furnished excellent mill-
sites ; and lumber was here cut, sawed, and rafted down the river for shipment abroad.   At the time Hertel ap-
proached it a more dismal landscape could scarcely have met the eye, for in that bleak season winter still obstinately disputes the advance of spring.

[1] HERTEL had with him three of his sons and two nephews, namely, the Sieur Crevier, Seigneur of St. Francis and the Sieur Gatineau. His party set out from Trois Rivières.

Upon reconnoitring, Hertel's scouts found no watch kept. The advantage of coming on the place by surprise decided Hertel to attack, small as his force was. At daybreak, therefore, having previously divided it into three parties, the assault began on the three garrison-houses, placed to cover the rest of the village.

Though taken by surprise, the garrisons were stoutly defended, but in the end were forced to surrender one after another. After this success the enemy made short work of the undefended farmhouses and mills, first plun-

Hertel destroys it. dering, then burning them, with the barns and their contents, live stock included. Every species of property was swept away. Thirty of the bravest inhabitants were killed, and fifty-four made prisoners, chiefly women and children. No place could have been more thoroughly laid desolate.[1]

Upon an alarm that the English were coming to attack him, Hertel began his retreat. He was pursued by a hundred and forty men, hastily collected from the nearest towns, who came up with him at Wooster River, in

Combat at Wooster River. Berwick, where the stream was crossed by a narrow bridge. Hertel halted his men on the farther side, faced about, and succeeded in keeping his eager pursuers back until darkness put an end to the combat.

Both sides lost a few men, the English suffering the most, as they were the assailants. They gave up the pursuit here, and Hertel continued his retreat.

Hertel now struck across the country to the Kennebec. Upon reaching it he learned that Frontenac's second war-party, reinforced from the Kennebec villages, and

---

[1] *Massachusetts Archives.* Sewall's account was obtained from a "Frenchman, taken while making up his pack."

by St. Castin and his warriors from the Penobscot, had
passed down the river shortly before, on their way to
attack Casco.[1] Leaving his wounded at the Abenaki
village, Hertel set out to join the others, who, with this
addition to their force, mustered from four to five hundred men. Portneuf[2] was the commander, ably second-

WENTWORTH GARRISON, SALMON FALLS, N. H.

ed by Courtemanche, Hertel, St. Castin, Madockawando, Hopehood, the two Doneys, and others — a truly
formidable array of the most crafty and relentless marauders ever sent out on the war-path.

[1] The garrison was not without warning of this. Captain Willard, who was then in
command, wrote, April 9, 1690, to the authorities at Boston, giving an account of the
danger they were in, thirty Indian canoes having been seen in the bay, besides several
fires on the shore. This was six weeks before the assault took place, and shows that
one of the enemy's detachments was waiting for the others to join it. The enemy
also had made a descent at Wells, April 3, burning a saw-mill and several houses there.
"Council ordered 120 men sent out of Essex to their relief."—*Sewall Papers.*

[2] Third son of the Baron de Becancour.

Though only a poor village, Casco was one of the strategic points essential to be held if a foothold was to be retained in eastern Maine, the more so since the fall **Fort Loyal,** of Pemaquid had left Casco an outpost. **Casco.** For defence, there was Fort Loyal, a picketed enclosure, built on a low bluff at the seaside, and mounting a few light guns to command the approach as well by water as by land. A portion of the regular garrison were gone out on a scouting expedition, and Captain Sylvanus Davis, the commander at this moment, had just reported the works to be in a very bad condition.

Taking everything into account, the enemy could not have made their appearance at a worse time.

Outside the fort four garrison houses served as so many rallying points for the village, which lay in a natural depression, around the fort, with its rough clearings reaching back to the surrounding forests. Such as they were, fort and village covered but an insignificant space on the peninsula, now Portland, which, at most points, rose high above the water, and in some was even inaccessible.

At this time the number of inhabitants was somewhat increased by the fugitives who had been driven from the settlements farther east. Including this small **Portneuf at-** garrison, there were, in all, about a hun- **tacks it.** dred able-bodied men in the place when Portneuf came before it, on May 25, 1690. An ambuscade was quickly formed on the brow of Munjoy Hill, the lofty elevation terminating the peninsula at the northeast. All this passed without discovery.

Without doubt, Portneuf intended to throw his whole force upon the village before the unsuspecting inhabi-

tants were stirring in the morning, as Hertel had done
at Salmon Falls. The terror and confusion of a surprise would do the rest. But this purpose was frustrated
through the eagerness of some of his outlying Indian
scouts, who waylaid and shot Robert Greason, a settler,
as he was passing toward the village. They then raised
their scalp halloa. This put the English on the alert.
Thirty of them immediately started off on a scout in the
direction of the firing. Mounting the hillside, they
pressed on across the clearings, into a lane, fenced at
both sides, which led to a block-house,[1] standing at the
skirt of the woods. It was noticed that the cattle, turned
out to pasture, instead of quietly grazing were all staring
in the same direction, a sure sign that all was not as it
should be. Instead, however, of acting upon the warning thus plainly given them by these dumb sentinels,
the impetuous assailants dashed headlong into the ambuscade ; and, while penned up in the lane, they received
a murderous volley, almost at the muzzles of the enemy's guns, which brought thirteen to the ground and
put the rest in disorder. The enemy then sprang from
their coverts, behind the fences, and fell with swords
and hatchets upon the survivors, only four of whom succeeded in regaining the fort, and they were wounded.

Elated by this success, the invaders then rushed into
the village. The undefended houses were easily carried,
but the assailants met with such a rough reception at
the garrisons that they were obliged to draw off at nightfall, and Portneuf even began to doubt his ability to
take the fort.

The English, however, were convinced of their inability to withstand another onset. The loss of so many of

---

[1] THIS block-house was evidently left unguarded.

their best men thus early in the fight had seriously crippled them. Under cover of the darkness those in the garrisons therefore quietly withdrew to the fort. In the morning, finding the village deserted, the enemy first plundered and then burned it. Having carried the outworks, they then advanced to attack the fort. In reconnoitring it a deep gully was found running within fifty yards of the stockade, in which the besiegers, completely sheltered from the fire of the fort, could inflict considerable loss on the garrison. Its fire was, however, too hot to venture upon a direct assault. Portneuf, therefore, set his men to work digging a trench up to the palisade, with tools found in sacking the village. Meantime firing was kept up on both sides night and day. That from the fort, however, did not prevent the work of zigzagging toward the stockade from being pushed rapidly forward; and, though wholly unused to this species of warfare, both French and Indians labored so industriously with pick and shovel that on the third day the besiegers were close under the palisade. Portneuf then summoned Davis to surrender. Davis, expecting the return of his detachment, demanded a truce of six days. This being refused, fighting was resumed. The besiegers could now throw hand grenades over the stockade into the fort, while their fire, kept up under cover of the trenches, grew more and more destructive. As the end drew near they grew more bold. A barrel of tar, with other combustibles, was pushed up against the stockade in readiness for firing.

Seeing the moment of assault at hand, and fearing to risk its result, Davis hoisted the white flag. Up to this time he supposed he had to do only with savages. Knowing them to be utterly faithless, he demanded to know if there were any Frenchmen among them.   Being answered in the affirmative, he insisted on treating for the surrender of the fort with them only.   He stipulated that all within the fort, men, women, or children, well or wounded, should have good quarter, be   **The fort is** allowed to depart unharmed, and be fur-   **taken.** nished with a safeguard as far as the next English town. Davis would not be satisfied, he says, until, at his demand, the French officers swore "by the ever living God" to fulfil these conditions to the letter.

All were shamefully violated.   Instead of finding the promised protection the survivors were abandoned to the fury of the Indians, who wreaked their vengeance unchecked.[1]   Davis's indignant remonstrances were treated with derision.   He was told that he was a rebel and traitor to his king, as if that fact, were it true, absolved his captors from all pledges.   After plundering the fort the invaders set it on fire, and it was soon burned to the ground, leaving Casco untenanted, save by the unburied bodies of the slain.

French accounts make no mention of this act of treachery.   Charlevoix adds, however, that the place was scarcely evacuated when four English vessels hove in sight, bringing a reinforcement for the garrison.   Seeing no flag flying, those on board understood that they had come too late, and after waiting some time in vain for a signal from the shore they stood off to sea again.

The loss of this post threatened to lead to the total depopulation of Maine.   As it was, all the garrisons as far as Wells withdrew in a panic to that place, where they were hastily reinforced and ordered to make a

---

[1] No very clear estimate of the losses is attainable. Charlevoix puts the number of prisoners at seventy, without counting women or children.

stand.[1] This left the savages free to overrun the New
Hampshire border undisturbed. A war-party, under
Hopehood, fell upon Fox Point in Newington, slew
Fox Point, N. H.,   fourteen persons, carried off six, and
harried.   burned several houses. They were pursued by Captains Floyd and Greenleaf, were overtaken
and compelled to leave behind some of their captives
and booty. Early in July eight persons were killed
while mowing in a field near Lamprey River (Newmarket), and a lad taken. On the next day Hilton's garri-
Newmarket and   son at Exeter was assaulted, but was saved
Exeter.   by a timely reinforcement.[2] On the sixth,
two companies, who were out searching for the marauders, had for some hours a severe fight with them at
Wheelwright's Pond, in Lee, in which Captain Wiswall,
his lieutenant, sergeant, and twelve besides, were killed,
and several more wounded. Floyd, the other captain,
kept up the fight some time longer, but was finally
Captain Wiswall   driven off the ground. The victors then
killed.   went westward, leaving a bloody track as
they went, no less than forty people having fallen victims to their rage in one week. Such were the immediate results of Frontenac's two war-parties.

[1] CAPTAIN SYLVANUS DAVIS'S *Narrative* is in *Massachusetts Historical Society
Collections*, 3d Series, Vol. I. What relates to the siege is very brief. He says he
told Frontenac that his war-parties were no better than robbers and cut-throats.
Charlevoix, II., 52, has the fullest French account of the two descents. La Hontan
adds a little, and La Potherie a little. Mather, *Magnalia*, II., 603, has the fullest
English account.

[2] BELKNAP relates that one of the relieving party, Simon Stone, received nine
gun-shot wounds and two strokes of a hatchet. When his friends came to bury him,
signs of life were perceived, and by the use of restoratives the wounded man revived,
to the amazement of all. See Sewall, I., 325.

VII

PHIPS TAKES PORT ROYAL,[1] BUT FAILS AT QUEBEC
May—October, 1690

UP to this time the people of New England seem to have had no thought of invading Canada themselves, or felt much fear of being invaded from there. Thus far the war, on their part, had been a purely defensive one. But it was now clear to everyone that the real struggle was not so much between the English and Indians, as between the English and French, who kept the Indians constantly supplied with the means of carrying on hostilities, while enjoying entire immunity from its ravages themselves. The relation was as close as that between the hand and the weapon. Two flourishing provinces lay at the mercy of hostile incursions, which no power could foresee or prevent. The entire depopulation of both was imminent. All this continual harrying of defenceless villages, with its ever-recurring and revolting story of captivity and massacre, was fast turning the border back into a wilderness, which, indeed, was what the enraged savages aimed at. Every attempt to reach and destroy these vigilant foemen in their own fastnesses proved worse than futile. New England was losing ten lives for one; and in property more than fifty to one.

This being so, the plan of striking at the root of the evil was wisdom itself. True, the difficulties in the way

---

[1] So named by Champlain, 1604, on account of its spacious anchorage.

of successfully assailing Canada were wellnigh insurmountable. Nature herself seemed to have set up an impassable barrier between the belligerents; but no sooner was the necessity realized, than all obstacles

PHIPS RAISING THE SUNKEN TREASURE.

vanished before that spirit of stern determination with which the New Englanders were accustomed to grapple with the most arduous undertakings.

But hostile incursions from Canada were not the only evils to be redressed with the strong hand. Injuries scarcely less vexatious had long been accumulating in

another quarter, where no wildernesses forbade a settlement of the account. For years Acadia and its har-
bors had been a safe retreat for privateers   Acadia a nest
and corsairs, who robbed and ill-used the   of corsairs.
New England fishermen until those seas were become
no longer safe. Bad as it had been, the evil was now
made tenfold worse by a state of war. For depredations
of this sort Acadia, or Nova Scotia, is remarkably well
placed, and as New England subsisted mostly by her
fisheries the alternatives were either to see them destroyed or to put them beyond the reach of future spo-
liation.

Early in the spring of 1690, before Casco had been
assailed, an expedition sailed from Boston to attack
Port Royal, the chief seaport of Acadia, where a French
garrison was kept. Sir William Phips,[1] a man whose
simple force of character had raised him   Sir William
from poverty to affluence, and from an hum-   Phips.
ble ship-carpenter to Knighthood, was put in command.
His popularity, no doubt, contributed much toward setting the little squadron of eight vessels and seven or
eight hundred men afloat; but his appointment was a
wide departure from the traditions of the colony and
province, where social rank had always been considered
indispensable to high command.[2]

As this was the first venture of the kind in which
New England had ever engaged, the result   Port Royal
was awaited in painful suspense. Phips   taken.
was, however, completely successful. Port Royal sub-

---

[1] CONSULT Mather's and Bowen's biographies. Mather is too laudatory. Phips was
a protégé of the two Mathers.

[2] UP to this time Sir William does not seem to have been even a freeman of the
colony, by the following entry in Sewall's *Dairy*, viz.: "Saturday, March 22, 1690.—
Phips appointed to command the. forces. Court makes Sir William free and swears
him major-general."

mitted, and his reputation as a commander was made
at once.[1]

No doubt was now felt that, with a little greater effort,
Quebec and Montreal could be taken with all ease.
Phips himself seems to have been of this opinion. Nor
was it ill-founded. As a matter of fact, Quebec had
Plan to take been taken before, and it was not unreason-
Quebec. able to suppose that it might be taken
again. The concurrence of Connecticut and New York
being obtained, land forces were raised to attack Montreal by way of Lake Champlain,[2] while Phips, with a
fleet, should be thundering away at Quebec.

It was a good plan and well deserved success—the
self-same plan, in fact, by which the conquest of Canada was achieved seventy years later. By assailing two
points at once the chances of success were greatly improved.[3] But the army got no farther than the head of
Lake Champlain, leaving Phips to fight it out alone at
Quebec, where he was repulsed, as a matter of course;

[1] MENEVAL, commander of Port Royal, charged Phips with violating the capitulation, and even with robbing him of his own money. A violent scene took place at
a hearing before the Massachusetts Council, in the course of which Sewall, who was
present, says that "very fierce words" passed between Sir William and Mr. (John)
Nelson, who took Meneval's part.

[2] FITZ JOHN WINTHROP, who had served under Cromwell in England, was put in
command.

[3] AT a congress of delegates held at New York, early in May, it was agreed that
New York should raise four hundred men and the New England colonies three hundred and fifty-five, to which the Iroquois were expected to add the whole fighting
strength of their confederacy. Only a few Mohawks and Oneidas joined the expedition,
however, the more western tribes failing to appear. Of the white forces New York and
Connecticut alone furnished their contingents, Massachusetts and Plymouth having
their hands full in defending their frontiers. See *Journal of Major General Winthrop*,
N. Y. Col. Docs., IV., 193; *Sewall Papers*, I., 327, etc. News that the Montreal
troops were returning from Wood Creek, to which point they had marched, came to
Boston, August 28, during a Public Fast, eliminating, of course, all hope of ultimate
success. *Ibid.* Captain John Schuyler, with a detachment of New York volunteers and
Indians, made a bold dash to La Prairie, opposite Montreal, inflicting some loss upon
the enemy.

for as soon as Frontenac found that Montreal was in no
danger he hurried off to Quebec with every available man
and musket. Instead of a garrison weakly manned, Phips
really had to contend with the whole strength of the colony, led by a soldier every way his superior in military
knowledge and capacity. Quebec, too, had been made

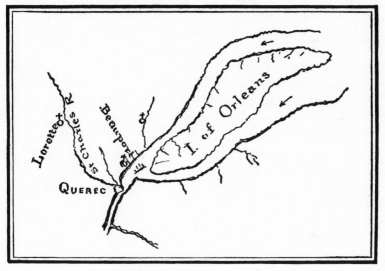

SKETCH MAP, APPROACHES TO QUEBEC.

very strong. But this fact did not become known until
it was too late to draw back.

Owing to various delays the fleet did not get in sight
of Quebec until the 5th of October, when, if anything
was to be done, it was necessary to act promptly, as the
season for active campaigning was draw-   **Phips's fleet
ing to a close. The fleet consisted of   and army.**
thirty-two sail, scraped together for this expedition, the
largest carrying forty-four guns, some a few only, and

the greater part none at all, being mere transports.[1]
Twenty-three hundred men were embarked.[2]

On the 6th, however, Phips summoned Frontenac to
surrender in terms which the old soldier hotly resented;
and, in view of the means at his disposal for enforcing
the demand, it must be admitted that Phips's language
was sufficiently offensive. But Frontenac was not to be
browbeaten into surrendering. He flew into a towering
passion, called the English rebels and traitors to their
lawful sovereign, and threatened the envoy, but finally
calmed down sufficiently to return Phips the dignified
and soldierly answer, "Tell him who sent you to do his
best, and I will do mine." To Phips the challenge could
scarcely have been encouraging. From his anchorage
in the basin below, the huge, rock-ribbed promontory of
Quebec towered defiant in the distance.
Its front, thrust boldy out into the St. Lawrence, was a precipice. Whichever way the eye wan-
dered no vantage ground offered itself in this direction.
Toward the country, however, the land fell off to a lower
level, showing the besiegers a line of lesser heights,
down which the road from the town led to a stretch of
meadow land bordering the river St. Charles, crossed
this at the usual fording place, practicable only at low
tide, and passed on to Beauport, where the shipping lay.

Quebec as it looked to Phips.

A morass, a ford, a steep ascent thus separated the
combatants in this quarter. Yet this, as Frontenac well
knew, was the one assailable side of Quebec,
and he had accordingly made up his mind
not to risk a general engagement beyond the St. Charles,
as Montcalm afterward did, but to let the English

Plan of defense.

---

[1] FOUR ships of war and twenty-eight others.—Sewall.
[2] WAIT WINTHROP to his son John.

themselves cross the river, and attack him in his defences, thus taking the fullest advantage of all the natural obstacles in the way of their advance or retreat.

QUEBEC, FROM AN OLD PRINT.

Such, in brief, was the position which Phips had come
so far to take, and Frontenac had labored night and day
to strengthen. Without making a careful reconnois-
sance in advance, misled by the out-of-date report that

it was not half fortified, and but weakly defended, Phips nevertheless, born fighter that he was, saw only his enemy within his reach at last.

The land forces, upon whom the brunt of the assault must fall, had now been cooped up for a month on shipboard, without any opportunity whatever of getting together for drill or discipline. All were raw militia. They were commanded by Major John Walley, a respectable civilian, who was yet to fight his first battle. The small-pox had broken out at sea ; and, from one cause or another, so many had fallen sick that of the 2,300 who had embarked at Boston, probably a third part were wholly unfit for active duty. The rest, however, showed no lack of spirit when called upon to fight.

The plan agreed upon embraced an assault upon the town, in the rear, while the fleet was cannonading it in front. But the troops were first to gain the desired position by crossing the St. Charles and storming the heights of St. Genevieve beyond ; then, when the greater part of the garrison should be drawn off to repulse this assault, Phips was to open his batteries upon the town. If the enemy showed weakness here, Phips himself was to attempt a landing at the Lower Town. Little fault can be found with this plan, but much with the way in which it was carried out.

Plan of attack.

Two days went by. The 6th passed, as we have seen, in fruitless negotiation. The 7th proved too stormy to attempt a landing. On the 8th, however, about 1,300 men were set on shore, abreast of the fleet, some four miles below the town, most of them wading through water knee deep from where the boats grounded on the flats. "Never were more men landed in less time," declares Walley.

The troops land.

The troops had scarcely begun their march toward
the town when they were fired upon from every copse
and thicket by the enemy's out-parties, who hung, like
swarms of angry bees, around the invaders, disputing
their advance from cover to cover, until routed by a
final charge, when they broke away and   Reach the
re-crossed the river to the town, and at   St. Charles.
dark the New Englanders encamped for the night on the
banks of the St. Charles. This opening affair had cost
them four killed and sixty wounded. Considering that
the ground had not been reconnoitred at all, it was by
no means discreditable to Walley's raw levies.

That evening a deserter came into camp, bringing the
unwelcome news of the garrison's being heavily reinforced from Montreal. This piece of news seems to
have taken all the fight out of Walley, who now found
twenty reasons for not advancing a step farther. And
he was still further disconcerted at seeing Phips weigh
anchor to attack the town, before the troops were in
position to co-operate with him.

Whether this manœuvre was intended to draw attention from Walley, and thus facilitate his crossing the St.
Charles, is uncertain. Walley says that the boats promised him for this purpose failed to appear; and furthermore, that a battery of eight guns, with a thousand men
in support of it, was waiting for him on the opposite
shore.

Be that as it may, toward evening, the four heaviest
ships moved up before the town, and were soon hotly
engaged with the enemy's batteries. Night   Phips cannon-
put an end to the conflict. It was resumed   ades.
in the morning, with the result, that, after being badly cut up in their hulls and rigging, without doing seri-

ous damage to the enemy, the ships were obliged to drop down, out of the fire, leaving the troops without support. During the cannonade, they had remained mere idle lookers-on, and, now, that it had failed, Walley shrank from making the assault alone. After holding his ground until the 10th, he appealed to Sir William to withdraw the **Phips is beaten off.** troops, and as Phips now realized that he was beaten, orders were given to bring them off without loss of time. This was effected on the night of the 11th.

Phips now thought only of getting away from Quebec as soon as possible. Before sailing, there was an exchange of prisoners,[1] by which Captain Davis and two daughters of Lieutenant Clark, taken at Casco, and little Sarah Gerrish, carried off from Dover, were released from captivity.

On the return voyage, the same ill fortune continued to pursue Phips and his defeated squadron. One vessel suffered shipwreck on the Island of Anticosti,[2] two or more were sunk, and several blown off to the West Indies.[3] One by one they came dropping into the port they had left with such full expectation of an easy victory. Now all was changed. No such terrible humiliation had ever before visited New England. Yet, alone and single-handed, she had struck the blow which was to be the key-note of future operations against Canada;

---

[1] On his way up the river Phips had taken several prisoners, among whom was the wife of the explorer, Joliet.

[2] " June 29, 1691 : Yesterday Rainsford arrived with 17 men that remained alive on Anticosti ; 4 dead of the small-pox since the long boat's coming."—*Sewall Papers.*

[3] " Friday, Nov. 8, 1690 : Between 9 and 10 at night, governor sends to me and enforms of the defeat at Canada. Shute comes into Boston that night or next morning ; hath thrown overboard more than sixty persons since his going hence, most Indians of Plymouth. Town much filled with the discourse and some cast blame on Major Walley."—*Sewall Papers*, I., 332.

and if, in this instance, it had not proved successful, if
the means and the leadership had savored somewhat of
inexperience, and yet more of over-confidence, the lesson, costly as it proved, was not thrown away. Present
failure only pointed the way to ultimate success.

The impoverished people were, however, at the end
of their resources.[1] For the present they could see
nothing but their overwhelming defeat. The returning
soldiers were loudly clamoring for their pay, and there
was no money to pay them with. In this extremity,
Massachusetts was forced to resort to the expedient of
issuing paper money to defray the expenses of the expedition, which, it had been confidently   First paper
hoped, would be met by the spoil of   money.
Quebec. And here was first opened the door to those
financial difficulties which ever after proved so vexatious
and so lasting in their effects.[2]

[1] PENHALLOW puts the cost of this expedition at £140,000 in money, besides the
lives of several hundred men.

[2] THE leading authorities on this expedition are Walley's *Journal*, in Hutchinson,
vol. 1, *Appendix*; *Diary of Sylvanus Davis* in *Mass. Hist. Coll.*, 3, 1, 101 ; Savage, *Account of the Late Action*, etc. (London, 1691) ; Winthrop, *Journal in N. Y. Col. Docs.*,
IV., 193 ; *Public Occurrences* (Boston, September 25, 1690). The French accounts
of Charlevoix, La Hontan and La Potherie, furnish details not given elsewhere. Char-
elvoix should be read for its detail of the land operations; La Hontan for the incident
of the summons.

5

VIII

CHURCH'S SECOND EXPEDITION

September, 1690-1691

WHILE Phips was on his way to Quebec, the Massachusetts authorities deemed the opportunity a fitting
one to chastise the hostile tribes who had desolated
the Maine border in the previous spring, now that the
French could afford them no aid. For this purpose
Major Church was again called into the service. It
required considerable persuasion to induce the old
ranger again to take the field, for he was still smarting
under the censures his previous expedition had called
forth; but he was at length prevailed upon to lay aside
his personal grievances and accept the command. Many
of his old soldiers, Indians included, immediately enlisted under him. In all, three hundred men were
raised, with whom Church was expected to give a good
account of himself.

It has already been explained why the rivers empty-
ing upon the Maine coast were so many points of
danger from hostile inroads. At safe distances up
these rivers, varying from sixty to a hundred miles, the
tribes who usually acted together against the English
had permanent villages, whence war-parties could easily
slip down unperceived to the coast, join their forces at
some point mutually agreed upon, and fall upon such
settlements as had been marked for destruction. Small

and insufficient garrisons posted at the mouths of these
rivers had utterly failed to put a stop to these inroads.
Scouting the border could not do it.   To destroy the
enemy's villages was the only alternative.   Root out
the nests and the vultures would fly away.

Church arrived in Casco Bay on September 11th.   He
was ordered to first strike the Indian villages on the
Androscoggin, which the high water had prevented his
reaching in the preceding year.   Landing, as before, at
Maquoit, he first marched up to Pejepscot Fort.[1]   Finding this abandoned, he kept on some forty   Church
miles higher up the river, to the enemy's   at Pejepscot.
principal village and fort.   When within gunshot of it,
his advance was discovered.   What few men were there
fled away in a panic, leaving the women and children to
their fate.   Church says that some three or four were
shot while attempting to swim the river.   Among the
dirt and filth of the wigwams five English captives
were found in a most pitiable plight.[2]   Six or seven of
the Indian prisoners were inhumanly butchered, Church
says, as an example to the rest.[3]   Two old women, too
decrepit to bear the fatigues of a march, were spared to
relate the story of the descent and slaughter to their
friends.   In his usual boastful vein Church told them
who he was, what great things he had done in Philip's
War, and what their tribe might expect if they continued to make war upon the English.   Then, softening
his tone somewhat, he bade the hags tell their warriors
that, if they wanted to see their wives again, they must

[1] BUILT and abandoned by the English.

[2] MRS. ROBERT HUCKINS, taken at Durham the preceding August; Mrs. Benjamin
Barnard, of Salmon Falls; Ann Heard, of Dover; one Willis's daughter, of Durham,
and also a boy of Durham.—Church's *Letter,* September 30, 1690.

[3] CHURCH'S *Entertaining History.*

bring in all their English captives to Berwick within fourteen days.

Nine women and children of the chiefs Kankamagus and Worombo were brought off as pledges for the good behavior of the tribe in future; for Church well knew that so long as they were in his power these chiefs would remain quiet.

From questions put to the only man taken there, whose life was spared at the earnest entreaty of Mrs. Huckins, Church learned that most of the warriors had gone over to the Saco River to collect provisions there for an expedition they had planned in concert with the Bay of Fundy Indians. Acting upon this information, he resolved to follow them without delay. After burning the fort, with its stores of corn, laid up for the winter, Church therefore marched back to his vessels, with his prisoners and booty.

He was here joined by young Anthony Brackett, who had been taken at Casco, but had made his escape upon hearing of Church's being up the river. Brackett's thorough knowledge of the localities proved of much use in Church's future operations.

Church now sailed round into Saco River, where some of the enemy were discovered making fish. His scouts killed two of them, and rescued Thomas Baker, an English captive, who told Church where these Indians had hid away their beaver at Pejepscot. Retracing Sails back to Saco. his course, that place was re-visited, and the plunder secured, but no Indians were seen. Some of Church's men now demanded that he should return home. Church demurred, but was overruled by his council, and after recrossing Casco Bay, the vessels cast anchor at Purpooduc Point, on Cape

Elizabeth, for the night. Three companies were allowed to encamp on shore. The Indians whom Church had been chasing about, but had never overtaken, had now got together in considerable force, and, un- Surprised at known to him, were watching his every Cape Elizabeth. movement. Finding a careless watch kept, they fell furiously upon the camp, at daybreak, and had nearly driven the English into the sea, before a sufficient number could be rallied to make head against them. Church hastened to their assistance. The assailants were then charged and routed in their turn. In this wretched affair the English had seven killed and twenty-four wounded.

Standing off from here to the westward, Church next made a landing at Cape Neddock, marched thence to Wells, and sent out scouts as far back to the eastward as Saco Falls [1] and Winter Harbor. [2] No enemy was found. Since striking their blow at Purpooduc, the Indians had scattered to the woods again. Having called in his scouts, Church returned to Portsmouth on September 26th, to brood over the cool reception that he knew awaited him at home.

As Church had foreseen, one good result followed close upon his capture of the Indian women at Androscoggin fort. In October several of the chief sachems came to Wells, where they held a talk with Captain Elisha Andros, under a flag of truce. With real or pretended sincerity—it is hard to say which—they declared that the French had made fools of them, A truce that they would fight against the English agreed to. no more; and that they were ready to make a treaty whenever the English were. A meeting was soon ar-

---

[1] Biddeford.   [2] Biddeford Pool.

ranged for, which took place at Sagadahoc, November 23d. By that time it is evident that the hostile Abenakis had heard of the repulse of Phips at Quebec, and, under French influences, were wavering or scheming to gain time, for they brought in only ten captives of the large number in their hands, and after prolonging the talk for six days, finally agreed only to a truce until the following May, at which time they promised to deliver the rest of their captives and conclude a lasting peace. We shall see how this promise was kept.[1]

No Indians appeared at the appointed time, though the English commissioners were on the spot, ready to proceed with the treaty. This keeping aloof from the rendezvous was of sinister omen, and forewarned another outbreak. Breathing time, however, had been gained, which was much to a people worn down and dispirited by the last year's reverses.

It proved, however, a mere lull in the storm. When questioned, the neighboring Indians pretended ignorance of the time fixed for the treaty. A further delay was granted. This also proved a blind. Convinced, at last, that the subtle enemy would soon be upon them again, the commissioners hastened homeward, promising to send reinforcements to Wells forthwith.

It was in June, 1691, that Captain James Converse was posted in Storer's garrison,[2] at Wells, with some thirty-five or forty soldiers, part of whom had but just joined him, when the chief, Moxus, assaulted it at the

---

[1] UPON this conference see Mather's *Magnalia*, 529-553; *Collections Massachusetts Historical Society's* 3d Series, I., 104, 105; Hutchinson, I., 358. Church was annoyed at being ignored in this affair.

[2] THE SITE is now identified only by the angle of an old wall, built of large, unhewn stones, brought here by water, for the purpose. It was on the main road through Wells, where the house of John S. Pope stands, as I write.

head of two hundred warriors, expecting an easy conquest. The assault was bravely repulsed, and Moxus drew off, swearing to be revenged. When **Wells assaulted.** Madockawando heard of it he laughed heartily. "So," said the amused chief, "my brother Moxus has missed it, has he? next year I'll go myself, and have the dog Converse out of his den."

SITE OF STORER GARRISON, WELLS, ME.

Foiled in their attempt on Wells, the enraged assailants next fell upon the little fishing hamlet at Cape Neddock, five miles farther down the coast, **Murders** and in York. Here they killed nine men, **at York.** who were loading a vessel, set the hamlet on fire, and then disappeared as suddenly as they came. The limit of this raid was, however, to mark the starting-point of one bloodier still, before many months had passed away.

Following close upon these events, four companies of English, commanded by Captain John March, were despatched in July to the enemy's old haunts at Pejepscot. They marched up from Maquoit, and they marched back again, empty handed.   No Indians had been met with; yet while the soldiers were re-embarking, they were violently attacked by the wily enemy, who expected to repeat the lesson they had given Captain Church, the September before, at Purpooduc.   Captain Sherburne[1] was killed before he could get off to his vessel.   This onslaught was excellently timed, when the vessels were left aground by the tide.   As soon as they were afloat again, they hauled off, for reasons unexplained in the accounts of the affair.

Except for roving scalping-parties, who killed seven persons at Berwick, two more at Exeter, and killed or captured twenty-one more at Rye, the remainder of **At Berwick**   the year was passed in comparative quiet. **and Rye.**   As usual, the English had suffered more loss than they inflicted.   But March's expedition was said to have checked a purposed descent upon the Isles of Shoals.   In November Port Royal was retaken by Governor Villebon without striking a blow, there being no garrison to defend it.   In gloom and darkness the old year went out and the new came in.

[1] SHERBURNE was of Portsmouth, N. H.

IX

YORK LAID WASTE, WELLS ATTACKED
February—June, 1692

ON the morning of the 5th of February, 1692,[1] the village of York lay locked in the arms of winter. Since daybreak it had been snowing heavily, so that few of the inhabitants were yet stirring. At this hour nothing could be heard but the muffled roar of the waves, beating against the ice-bound coast, or the moaning of the wind, as it swept through the naked forest. All else wore its usual quiet.

Suddenly a gunshot broke the stillness. At that sound the village awoke. The startled settlers ran to their doors and windows. Out in the darkness and gloom they saw a body of armed men fronting them on every side. Some tried to escape by their front-doors. A storm of bullets drove them back. They next made for the back-doors. Death met them at the threshold. They saw themselves surrounded, entrapped. On every side the rattle of musketry, mingled with the loud yells of the assailants, drowned the voices of nature—moaning sea and rising storm. The village was surrounded and retreat cut off; and a carnival of murder was to join its horrid uproar to that of the elements.

From the brow of Mount Agamenticus, the enemy had reconnoitred the village on the afternoon before. They

---

[1] MATHER'S date of January 25 is Old Style.

had bivouacked there that night in the snow. There was no warning of their coming. Under cover of the storm some three hundred savages had stolen upon the village, like famishing wolves upon a sheepfold. They found no watch set to give the alarm, as they silently filed out of the forest into the open fields beyond. Not even a dog barked. The fresh snow deadened their stealthy footfall. Until that signal shot was fired, nobody dreamed of an enemy near.

Then the slaughter began. The savages quickly burst open the doors with their axes, killing and scalping all whom they met. As soon as one house was carried, and its inmates butchered, it was first ransacked and then set on fire; the assailants then rushing off in pursuit of new victims. In a short time the village was blazing in twenty places.

At length it would seem as if the savages themselves grew weary of bloodshed, since some four-score persons escaped the tomahawk and scalping-knife. Among them were many aged women and little children, some of whom were set at liberty when the Indians marched off. Accounts differ as to the number slain, Mather **Number of** fixing it at fifty, others at from seventy- **killed.** five to a hundred. Many of the slain were cremated in their own dwellings. The blow was sudden, unlooked-for, deadly. It was not supposed that the place could ever rise from its ashes again.

Among the scattered houses, stretched a mile and a half along the river, four or five had been expressly constructed as a defence for the rest. These were, therefore, termed garrisons. Their thick walls of hewn timber were bullet-proof; a row of stout pickets kept an assailant at a distance; while the inmates were firing

deliberately from a secure cover, through the loopholes. Rude as they were, these primitive fortresses
proved of signal use in repelling such attacks as that
just narrated.

A few resolute, or desperate, men succeeded in breaking through their assailants, and so gaining the shelter
of some of the four garrisons. All were summoned to

JUNKINS GARRISON, YORK.

surrender, but in every case the summons met with a
stern defiance. Finding that nothing was to be had but
blows, the savages drew off without venturing to make
an assault. Except Alcock's, Harmon's, Norton's, and
Preble's garrisons, every house in the village was burned
to the ground.

The house of Shubael Dummer, the minister, stood
by the seaside, not far from Roaring Rock. He was
shot down at his own door, while in the act of mounting

his horse.   His wife and son were carried off into captivity, with the rest, and Mather pithily says that one of
Dummer   the "bloody tygres" strutted about among
slain.   the broken-hearted prisoners, wearing the
clothes of the murdered man.

These Indians belonged to the missions of Father
Thury at Penobscot, and Father Bigot at Norridgewock,
by whom the expedition had been set on foot.   Before
dividing their plunder, these so-called Christian converts chanted a Te Deum for their victory.   They also
chanted matin and vesper service, while on their homeward march, as their spiritual fathers had strictly
charged them not to omit the sacred offices of religion,
if they would have success reward their undertaking.[1]

A boy, four years old, who escaped the massacre,
afterwards grew up to lead an avenging band against
this same Kennebec tribe and mission, and extermi-
nated both.

As Wells joins York at the east, it was in a manner
isolated by the crushing blow dealt that place.   The
people of Wells, lonely outpost of a lonely frontier, now
talked of nothing but abandoning the place.   To in-
Wells an Out-   duce them to stay the garrisons were
post.   strengthened, stores collected, and the
country diligently patrolled for signs of the enemy.
Nothing happened, however, until June, when Madockawando made good his threat, in part, by coming at
the head of four hundred warriors, as he had said he
would.   Moxus and Egeremet were with him, the former burning to wipe away the disgrace of his defeat; the
latter as eager for English scalps as he had been ever

---

[1] UPON receipt of the news at Boston, Major Hutchinson was sent to the scene of
the massacre.

since the kidnapping of his friends at Black Point, five
years before.

Joined to this formidable body of savages was a
small band of Canadians, commanded by Portneuf, an
officer assigned to the expedition by his superiors,
active in setting it on foot, skilled in border warfare,
and now exercising as much authority as a horde of
undisciplined savages were disposed to   Portneuf in
yield to a white man. 'With Portneuf   command.
were the Baron St. Castin, a gentleman by birth, and a
savage from choice; also one La Brognerie, and one or
two other French officers.

To oppose this army Converse could muster only
fifteen soldiers of the garrison, to whom, if we should
add such of the inhabitants as had sought safety within its walls, the defenders could still count themselves
but a handful at best.   Fortunately, how-   Storer's garri-
ever, two sloops, laden with stores for the   son beset.
garrison, had arrived on the 9th, with fourteen soldiers
more, thus bringing Converse's force up to twenty-nine
fighting men.   To these should be added, of course,
those able-bodied inhabitants who had come into the
garrison, upon hearing of the enemy's approach.

This was not, however, to be a battle of numbers, but
one of courage, endurance, and skill.   Wells was but a
small, straggling village, drawn out for a mile along the
seashore it overlooked.   Storer's garrison stood on the
brow of a gentle rise of ground, commanding the little
salt water river, or creek, that makes the harbor.   At
low tide there is only a thread of water left between
banks of soft, sticky ooze.   The two sloops were an-
chored off in the channel, within pistol-shot of the
shore, ready to bear their part in the coming fray; and

as Converse had fully made up his mind never to yield while a man was left to fire a shot, or load a gun, the combat promised to be an obstinate one.

These preparations for defence were scarcely completed when notice was given of the enemy's presence by the cattle running in out of the woods, frightened and bleeding. The hunters of men were close at hand. That night was an anxious one for the garrison. As soon as it was light, contrary to their usual custom, the savages came swarming out of their hiding-places, screeching, brandishing their weapons aloft, and hurling shouts of defiance at the garrison as if they expected to frighten it into a surrender by a show of numbers and noise. After yelling themselves hoarse, **Enemy assault.** they let fly a random volley which hurt nobody, sheltered as the besieged were behind the stockade, while their steady return fire speedily drove the too confident assailants to their coverts again.

Failing here, the savages next turned their attention to the sloops, which promised to fall an easy prey, as they lay within short gun-shot of the shore. Lying near at hand on the bank was a pile of planks, and also a haystack. From behind these a galling fire was kept up on the vessels with musketry, and they were once and again set on fire with lighted arrows. The fire was as often put out, however, by the steadiness and coolness of the crews, who also managed, by a well-aimed shot now and then, to hold their assailants under cover. One, indeed, who rashly ventured an attempt to get on board, by shielding his body behind a slab of pine, was shot dead in his tracks.

This failure, however, seems to have suggested what followed. The besiegers having found a cart somewhere, proceeded to fit it with a shield of planks in front, made bullet-proof. As many savages as it would hold then got into it, and when the tide had left the vessels aground, a score or more of their comrades began pushing their ingenious machine out toward the helpless craft, under the direction of the Converse Holds Frenchman La Brognerie. It was thus Out. moved some distance when it stuck fast in the soft mud of the creek. La Brognerie put his shoulder to the wheel, to lift it, when a shot fired by Captain Storer from the garrison laid him dead on the spot. Another, who took La Brognerie's place at the wheel, fell a moment later, pierced by a bullet fired from the sloop. The machine remained immovable. As the tide rose it overset, so exposing those within it to a galling fire from the sloops, by which several more lost their lives while running to cover. When night put an end to the fighting, Storer's men had everywhere more than held their own.

Throughout the night, the savages kept up a dropping fire, designed to keep the besieged on the alert, and so wear them out. They lay so near, that the firing was interspersed with harmless banterings on both sides. " Who are your commanders ? " a voice in the darkness called out. The reply quickly came back, " We have a great many commanders." " You lie," retorted the first speaker, " You have none but Converse, and we'll have him, too, before morning."

In the morning the besiegers gathered together for a final and decisive assault, and at a given signal they made another blind rush for the stockade, firing their guns and yelling like so many demons let loose. Converse exhorted his men to stand firm. One man only, intimidated by the fearful outcries around him, stammered out some words about surrendering, upon which Converse threatened him with instant death if he dared breathe that word again. A rapid discharge of musketry was kept up from the loopholes, the empty guns being passed back to the stout-hearted women of the garrison, who loaded and handed them over to their male defenders again; some even firing away at the savages as undauntedly as the men. The assailants could not long stand before so hot a fire, on open ground, and gradually broke away to cover again.

Exasperated by repeated failures, the savages next made their most dangerous attempt upon the sloops, now lying lashed together for mutual protection out in the stream. A fire-raft was hurriedly put together, the combustibles lighted, the raft shoved off from the shore and left to drift down upon the vessels with the tide. The same fatality attended this effort as the others. A puff of wind drove the blazing mass against the bank, where it burned harmlessly out.

Force having failed, the discouraged besiegers resorted to stratagem. A flag was sent to demand a surrender. Ensign Hill went out to meet it. When the message was brought to Converse, he returned for an answer, "that he wanted nothing but men to come and fight him." The wrathful envoys retorted the threat to cut the English "as small as tobacco" before morning. Converse then broke off the conference with a brusque invitation to make haste, for he wanted work. The savage, who held the flag, then dashed it to the ground in a rage, and ran off one way, while Ensign Hill ran another, each one eager to get under cover as quickly as possible. It was well for Hill that he took the alarm when he did,

for a number of shots were fired at him from an ambush, treacherously contrived by the savages, in case
their demand was refused.   Thanks to fleetness of foot,
Hill got into the garrison unhurt..

This incident ended the siege.   After putting their
one captive, John Diamond, to death with excruciating
tortures, the discomfited crew of white and red savages
slunk silently away between dark and daylight, leaving
some of their unburied dead behind them.[1]

[1] CONTEMPORARY authorities for the attacks on York and Wells, are Mather's *Magnalia;* Charlevoix's, *New France;* Champigny, *Letter to the Minister,* October 5, 1692;
Villebon's *Journal;* Pike's *Journal.*   See also Hutchinson, *History of Massachusetts,*
II.; Williamson, *History of Maine,* I.; and Bourne, *Wells and Kennebunk,* for local
tradition.

6

X

REBUILDING OF PEMAQUID TO TREATY OF 1693

May, 1692—August, 1693

THUS far the war had been conducted under all the difficulties arising from an unsettled form of government. Self-preservation had, indeed, united all the people in a common effort against the common enemy. There was, however, an active undercurrent of social unrest, touching their political future, which now and again bubbled up to the surface, keeping the minds of all men in a state of dread and suspense highly injurious to interests of every sort. Since the accession of William to the throne of England the people had lived in hopes of having their old charters restored. All uncertainty was now set at rest by the arrival of Sir William Phips, with a new charter, in May, 1692.[1] The king, in his wisdom, had appointed Phips to be governor, not unwilling, it would seem, to set a limit to the demands of the old Puritan party, with whom it is clear that he had much less sympathy than was generally supposed. William was a deep politician. In Phips, for whose rugged honesty and personal bravery the king probably had a sincere liking, he saw an entering wedge likely to divide the

Sir W. Phip governor.

[1] MAY 14, 1692. "Sir William arrives on the Nonsuch frigate. Candles lighted before he gets into the town-house." *Sewall Papers*, I., 356. News of his being made governor reached Boston late in January.

strong republican sentiment of New England, and by
that sign to conquer. For certainly William had no
more sympathy with republicanism than his predeces-
sors. It was his trade to be king.

The new charter went into effect at once. By its provisions all the old traditions were swept away with a
stroke of the pen. It was in entire accord with the spirit
which had brought about this sweeping political change
that the new governor should himself be the obedient
creature of the royal favor.

Sir William found everything in the utmost confusion.
As if the calamities of war were not enough, a new and
secret enemy, intangible as the air itself, yet scattering
its deadly poison broadcast, so that all who breathed
the infection quickly yielded to its noxious effects, was
terrorizing the community beyond all belief. It was not
the ignorant alone, but also the wise, the learned, and
deeply pious who fell before this astonish-   The witchcraft
ing delusion. In February of this year   craze.
the fatal witchcraft delirium had broken out and was
now at its height. The most abject, unreasoning fears
were pressing heavily upon the hearts of the people.
Phips feared nothing in human shape, but was ill-
equipped for an encounter with demons. It is no wonder, then, that he should prefer the horrors of war to the
terrors of the invisible world. Leaving, therefore, the
judges and ministers of the Gospel to deal with the delusion, Sir William forthwith set himself to straighten-
ing out the military situation with his customary energy.
Moreover, the state of affairs on the eastern frontiers
was such as to demand immediate attention.

Realizing its importance, the king had directed the
rebuilding of the fort at Pemaquid at once, first to re-

cover lost ground, next to hold the Indians in check, and lastly to reassert the English claim to so much at least of the territory in dispute between the two crowns.[1] It was, as Hutchinson points out, a very ill-advised measure, Pemaquid being too remote to come within any well-digested plan of defence. He might have added that its very remoteness was one of the strongest reasons for attacking it, as it could not be reinforced except by sea.

Turning a deaf ear, however, to the grumbling which the proposal met with, chiefly on account of the enormous expense, Phips at once vigorously set about the work cut out for him. He immediately summoned the ever-faithful Church to his aid, levied several hundred men with dispatch, made Church his second in command, and set sail for Pemaquid early in August. On **Pemaquid rebuilt.** the way there the expedition put into Falmouth, interred the remains of the dead, who had lain there unburied since the sacking of the place by Portneuf, took off the great guns, and then proceeded to its final destination. Phips's operations were greatly facilitated by the undivided authority which had passed to him by the new charter, Plymouth, Massachusetts, Maine, and Nova Scotia being now under one government.

[1] THE fort was supposed to cover the Kennebec, Damariscotta, and some other small rivers draining the coast between the Kennebec and Penobscot. It was argued that the settlers would thus be encouraged to return to their deserted farms, and the Indians effectually kept out of those rivers for the future. But this would demand a garrison strong enough to act offensively, at need, outside the fort, instead of one so small as practically to be besieged inside of it ; and it was clearly beyond the ability of Massachusetts to maintain such a garrison as the professed objects required. But the real design being political, the fortress had a certain strategic importance in the eyes of the court at a time when fortifications were the rage in Europe. For further particulars about Pemaquid consult Johnston's *Bristol, Bremen and Pemaquid; Nooks and Corners of the New England Coast; The Pine-Tree Coast*, etc.

Upon his arrival at Pemaquid, Phips immediately set part of his force to work building the fort, while, with the rest, Church started off to harass the enemy in that quarter. Doubtless a secondary purpose was to keep them from finding out what was going on at Pemaquid. In the execution of his orders Church first looked into the Penobscot, and afterward went up the Kennebec as far as Teconnet, where the Indians set fire to their fort and fled to the woods at his approach.

Meanwhile work on the new fort was being pushed forward with the greatest vigor, and, on its completion, it was given the name of William Henry.[1] It was strongly built of stone, and armed with the heaviest guns then to be had—eighteen-pounders. Mather computes that above two thousand cart-loads of stone were used in laying up the walls. **Named William Henry.** Leaving sixty men, under Captain March, to garrison it, Phips ordered the remainder back to Boston, well satisfied with having, at last, put an iron curb upon the ambitious projects of his old enemy, Count Frontenac.

It was while the attention of every one was drawn to the eastern frontier that a series of unlooked for attacks broke out in the west again. At Lancaster, on July 18, 1692, a marauding party entered the house of Peter Joslin, while he was away at work, and butchered the whole family. When Joslin came home **Lancaster raided.** he found his wife, his three children, and a widow Whitcomb, who lived with him, lying in their blood, all having been tomahawked by the savages.[2] A similar onslaught was made on Billerica, August 1st. It

[1] For a description in detail see Mather's *Magnalia*, II., 536; or *Decennium Luctuosum*, p. 81.

[2] Harrington's *Century Sermon*.

is known that six persons here, belonging to two families, were killed at this time, the victims being Ann, the
Billerica suffers. wife of Zachary Shed, and their two children, Agnes and Hannah; Joanna, the wife of Benjamin Dutton, and two of her children by a former marriage, Mary and Benoni Dunkin. The records touching this event are quite meagre, but the list of victims shows that probably not more than two houses were assaulted at this time. Brookfield also was visited, at nearly the same time, on the same murderous errand.[1]

Brookfield, July 27. The first victims were Joseph Wolcot's wife and two daughters, who hid themselves in the bushes, but were discovered and slain, Wolcot himself escaping, with another child, to a distant garrison. The house of one Mason was entered while the family were at dinner, Mason and one or two of his children slain, and Mrs. Mason and her infant carried off. Thomas and Daniel Lawrence, two brothers, also were taken prisoners, Thomas being soon after killed for having deceived his captors with respect to the number of men in the town. Meantime a messenger had gone to Springfield for assistance. A company under Captain Colton set out in pursuit of the raiders. Mrs. Mason's infant was found knocked in the head and thrown into the bushes. Following the fresh tracks, the pursuers came upon the Indians' camp, which they had surrounded with a brush fence. The avengers of blood waited until daybreak and then fell upon the camp, killing fourteen or fifteen of the savages,[2] rescuing Daniel Lawrence and Mrs. Mason, putting the rest of the sav-

---

[1] THE details of this affair are narrated in Fiske's *Historical Discourse.*

[2] SEWALL has it five or six killed and two captives rescued, as the account first came to hand. *Papers* I., 381.

ages to flight, and capturing some of the plunder left behind in their haste.

During these troublesome times, John Nelson, a prominent merchant of Boston, had been taken prisoner while making a trading voyage to the St. John River, and carried to Quebec.[1]

It chanced that, in the course of these wars, Nelson had shown some kindness to certain French prisoners of rank, and now that the fortune of war had placed him in the same situation, his former conduct was remembered to his advantage. Frontenac   J. Nelson lodged him in the château, gave him a seat   taken. at his own table, and though keeping a strict eye on his prisoner, behaved like a generous enemy toward him.

Nelson spoke French fluently, had some knowledge of Indian dialects, was quick and observant, intelligent and penetrating. He had been in Quebec before; knew all the ins and outs of the place; had a heart to feel for the sufferings of others; and as the city was then crowded with our poor prisoners, dragged thither by the savages, Nelson humanely set himself to relieving their wants as far as lay in his power.

From such a man what was going on around him could not long remain hidden. In the first place, two ships of war arrived from France. Instead of unloading they began taking on board cannon and provisions. Then, a number of Indian chiefs were daily coming to Quebec, to receive presents and to have a talk with their French father, as Frontenac was styled by them. Among these was the Penobscot sachem, Madockawando, who was well known to Nelson.

By making good use of his eyes and ears Nelson soon

---

[1] NELSON was taken in October, 1691, with Colonel Tyng and John Alden, Jr.

learned beyond a doubt that a formidable expedition
was getting ready to capture Pemaquid, the new English
fortress commanding the coasts of Acadia; and afterward to ravage all the New England coast beyond.

In all probability his friends and kinsfolk were com-
pletely ignorant of the blow about to fall upon them.
In the course of some talk he held with Madockawando
Nelson drew enough from the wily savage to be con-
vinced that it was meant to be the heaviest stroke that
New England had ever known.

From this moment Nelson could think of nothing but
how to warn his friends of their danger.   His decision
was quickly taken to attempt it at all risks.   But how to
do this seasonably, and without drawing suspicion upon
himself, was a matter so beset with difficulties on every
side that almost any other man would have despaired of
success.

Though not restrained of his personal liberty, Nelson
was closely watched by an attendant.   He was not permitted to write letters.   Once, indeed, this vigilant attendant, in reality a spy upon him, had surprised Nelson
Thwarts   in the act of writing and had taken away
Frontenac.   his inkhorn.   However, where there's a will
there's a way; so, under the plea of illness, Nelson managed to write a letter in bed, at such odd moments as
could be snatched from this constant espionage.   When
he heard the attendant coming he would hide his unfin-
ished letter under the bedclothes.

His next care was to find a messenger or messengers.
This was done by bribing two soldiers to desert, who
succeeded in making their way first to Albany and then
to Boston, thus disclosing Frontenac's favorite project in
time to admit of strengthening the garrison at Pema-

JOHN NELSON.

quid; so that when the two ships-of-war did arrive
before it the commander judged the place too strong to
be attacked.

As this descent had been carefully planned in France,
Louis was very wroth when he heard how completely it
had failed, and Frontenac received a reprimand that
stung him to the quick. So when Frontenac was informed of Nelson's share in thwarting his well-laid plans,
as he presently was by the recapture of the two deserters,
his anger was aroused against the man who had dared
thus to beard him in his own stronghold. And the penalty exacted savored both of fear and revenge. These
feelings were no doubt aggravated by the King's reproof
for having treated Nelson with so much consideration.
He was now to experience treatment of a far different
nature.

Nelson was therefore shipped off to France as a state
prisoner of the most dangerous character. He was first
thrown into a dungeon of the Château Angoulême, where,
for two years, he was allowed to see no one except the
gaoler, who brought his food to the grating of his cell.
He might have died there, unpitied and unknown, if a
visitor, from motives of curiosity, had not one day
In the   stopped at his grating to ask if he could
Bastile.   do anything for him. Nelson entreated
that his friends in England might be informed of his
situation. This was done, with the result that a demand
soon came back for Nelson's release or exchange. Although the demand was ignored, it proved the means of
getting Nelson transferred to the Bastile, at Paris, in
which formidable fortress he was confined for two and
a half years more.

After many grievous disappointments, Nelson at last

got leave to go over to England, on his parole, upon giving a bond in a large sum for his return. This was generously

THE BASTILE, IN THE TIME OF LOUIS XIV.

furnished by a French gentleman. Nelson then crossed the channel to England. Upon hearing his story, the king laid his commands upon Nelson not to go back to

France. With a feeling which does him honor, Nelson disobeyed the order, recrossed the channel and gave himself up, thus redeeming his pledges. Peace being declared, Nelson was set at liberty. Broken in health, he returned to his family after an absence of ten years, during which he had dared and suffered as few men have for love of country.[1]

The vigorous measures inaugurated by Governor Phips brought a season of respite to the long-suffering inhabitants of the eastern frontiers. Except some minor depredations committed by small scalping parties at Oyster River,[2] and Quaboag,[3] the spring and summer of 1693 were passed in comparative quiet. Meanwhile, the indefatigable Major Converse, with four or five hundred men, was ranging up and down the eastern country, from Piscataqua to Pemaquid, and from the coast as far up the Kennebec as Teconnet,[4] keeping the Indians continually on the move, and thus preventing their assembling in any force for their customary raids.

With the active entrance of the French into the war, by sea as well as by land, the old timber stockades of former times had outlived their usefulness. Forts for sea-coast defence now began to be built with the view of resisting the heavy artillery of ships of war. Pemaquid announced this new departure from the primitive

[1] IT IS uncertain just how far Nelson's information was effective in this matter. His letter, dated at Quebec, August 26th and 27th, mentions Wells, the Isles of Shoals and Piscataqua, as the places to be ravaged. News of the rebuilding of Pemaquid might not have reached him so soon, though it was undoubtedly known to Frontenac. Nelson's letter arrived at Boston about September 25th, in ample time to strengthen Pemaquid before Iberville came before it, in October. Charlevoix is positive that Nelson's agency frustrated the design. Hutchinson (Vol. II., p. 68), while quoting Charlevoix says this is a mistake. Whether the authorities saw fit to act upon it or not, in nowise lessens the value of Nelson's warning.

[2] DURHAM, N. H.   [3] BROOKFIELD, MASS.   [4] WATERVILLE, ME.

methods which, at need, had so easily converted a common dwelling-house into a fortress. During this summer another strong work was built in Maine, near the site of Phillips's old garrison, at the falls of the Saco,[1] and at the head of ship navigation on this river, designed partly to cover the Saco settlements and partly as a trading-post, as a means of drawing the Indians of this region away from the French to the English interest, by furnishing them with better and cheaper goods than the French did.

Fort at Saco Falls.

Dismayed by the failure at Pemaquid, alarmed at seeing one avenue after another to the coast being steadily closed against them, of their own accord the hostile tribes now sued for peace. As the English were only too glad to meet them half way, a treaty was soon signed by some thirteen of the principal chiefs, by which they bound themselves not to commit any hostile acts for the future ; but to be true and faithful subjects to the King of England. Five Indian hostages were delivered as a pledge of good faith ; and to all appearances, the blessings of peace were now to blot out the ravages of war. This treaty was signed and sealed at Pemaquid, August 11, 1693, between Phips and the chief sagamores of the eastern tribes.

Peace with Indians.

[1] IT WAS an irregular pentagon, with a tower.—*Hutchinson.* It stood six miles from the sea, in what is now the Laconia Company's premises, in Biddeford.

XI

DURHAM DESTROYED
July 18, 1694

THUS, unexpectedly, the war seemed to have worn itself out. To both parties it promised a much needed season of respite. But beneath this calm, there lurked the gathering storm. In Canada, news of the treaty caused real consternation, as well it might. The French were alarmed for fear that the New England tribes **Treaty alarms** would finally go over to the English, if the **Canada.** peace should hold, thus defeating the policy, as crafty as it was cruel, of sacrificing the miserable Abenakis to the vain hope of regaining what was clearly lost to them forever. When the weapon had grown too dull tor further use, it would be cast away. But, meantime, this living barrier to Canada must not be broken down.

Instructed by their superiors, the French missionaries domesticated among the Kennebec and Penobscot tribes, now set themselves vigorously to work to break off the truce. The first step was to dispose of any lingering scruples on the score of conscience or honor; otherwise, even these rude barbarians, if left to themselves, might **Villieu's** have hesitated. They were told that to **efforts.** break faith with heretics was no sin. The ground being thus prepared, an officer, named Villieu,[1] went about from village to village, urging these tribes

---

[1] COMMANDANT at Penobscot.

to dig up the hatchet again. Large presents were given them; they were flattered, feasted, and cajoled to their heart's content; old wrongs were artfully dwelt upon, until the slumbering embers of rage and hate flamed up again with tenfold fury. A generous supply of brandy did the rest.

All this time the desolated border was enjoying a season of long-wished-for repose, of thrice happy relief from that state of care and watchfulness which had made life on the border not worth living. Once, indeed, the New Hampshire settlers were on the point of abandoning the province in despair. They were now told to go about their usual vocations without fear.

It is true that some mutterings of the coming storm had led to certain precautionary measures. Permanent garrisons were now established in Amesbury, Haverhill, Billerica (including Tewksbury), Chelmsford, Dunstable, Groton and Marlborough. To prevent the desertion of the frontier, the General Court, in March, 1694, enacted a law, providing that if any person having a freehold in the towns named should desert the same, during the war, his estate should be forfeited.

But in this state of false security the midsummer of 1694 found the inhabitants of New Hampshire. Their villages were mostly widely scattered farms, growing just a little more compact toward the central part, where the bare, barn-like meeting-house stood, like a shepherd tending his flock. For families so dispersed there could be no central rallying point. Every man must defend his own home as best he might. Nothing was more easy, then, than for a numerous enemy to cut off each dwelling from its neighbor.

Villieu's arts, backed by the efforts of the missionaries, had prevailed. Casting the treaty to the winds, Madockawando and Moxus, of Penobscot, declared for war. Portions of the Penobscots, Norridgewocks, and Maquoits, with a sprinkling of warriors from the tribes farther east, were out on the war-path again.

The three hundred warriors, thus scraped together by Villieu, had singled out the pretty little village of Oyster River, now Durham,[1] N. H., for fire and slaughter. No hint of their murderous intent had reached that peaceful settlement, although some few **Treaty broken.** Indians had been seen lurking in the neighborhood; but their presence had provoked no distrust, as they had disappeared without doing any mischief. These were really scouts sent on ahead to get exact information how best to assault the place.

Scattered along the high grounds were some twelve garrison-houses, enough to have sheltered all of the inhabitants, if warned in season. Most of them, however, not dreaming of danger so near, slept in their own houses, instead of going to the garrisons at night. And there being no suspicion, a loose watch was kept..

The settlement stretched out some miles along both banks of Oyster River, clustering thickest about the falls, where John Dean's saw-mill stood, with the meeting-house occupying a gentle eminence just beyond; and where also the roads, east and west, came together. The country round is pleasingly rolled about in low hills, then well wooded, rendering the approach of an enemy all the more easy.

Villieu reached the vicinity undiscovered on Tuesday evening, July 17, 1694. He halted near the falls till after dark, then divided his followers into two bands,

---

[1] FIRST forming a part of Dover.

one taking the south and the other the north side of the river, so as to make a clean sweep of the whole settlement. Bomazeen went with the Indians **Durham destroyed.** told off to the south side, while Captain Nathaniel put himself at the head of those on the north. The two bands then broke up into parties of eight or

WOODMAN GARRISON, DURHAM, N. H.

ten each, in order to fall on as many houses as possible at once, as soon as it should be light.

Had this plan succeeded, it is probable that a much greater loss of life would have been the result.

It chanced, however, that John Dean had planned to go on a journey that morning. He had risen early and was just leaving his house, near his mill, when he was seen, fired at, and killed on the spot. The alarm was thus given before some of the assailants had reached their

7

designated stations, giving some families time to seek
safety in flight, or to stand on their defence, as their
fears or their courage prompted them.

At the signal the Indians fell with fury upon the
settlement, and the butchery began.

Each house has its own sickening tale to tell. There
was little or no fighting. It was all downright butchery. At each the same course was pursued. The
savages surrounded it, beat down the doors, and rushed
in upon the startled inmates, awakened from slumber to
see a dozen painted assassins menacing them with instant
death. The men were mostly tomahawked on the spot,
the women, torn shrieking from their hiding-places,
dragged away to endure a captivity but little better than
death itself.

John Dean's death has been mentioned. His house
was quickly assaulted. Mrs. Dean, with her little
daughter, was seized and taken two miles up the river,
where they were left in charge of an old Indian, while
the captors went off to perform other exploits. The old
savage, who spoke a little broken English, complained
Mrs. Dean's   of having a bad headache, and asked Mrs.
escape.   Dean what he should do for it. Seeing
him have a bottle of rum, the poor woman told him to
drink that and it would cure him. The savage, nothing
loth, drank freely, and soon fell fast asleep. The
prisoners immediately fled to the woods, where they
lay hid until night, when, finding all quiet, they plucked
up the courage to return home. A heap of blackened
ruins was all that was left of it. The fugitives then
found a canoe, in which they paddled down the river to
Lieutenant Burnham's garrison, where they again found
themselves among friends.

Of course the garrisons were especially marked for destruction. Jones's was one of the first to be attacked. Awakened, just before day, by the barking of his dogs, he went out to see if the wolves were not prowling about his hog-pen. Finding nothing wrong there, he turned back to the house. Still uneasy, he climbed up into a flanker, and sat down on the wall to listen. He was hardly seated when the flash of a gun lighted up the gray twilight. Upon the impulse of the moment Jones threw himself backward, and drew his body up into a heap. The movement saved his life, as the bullet struck in the place he had just quitted. Finding the people here on their guard, the Indians drew off after firing a few shots out of spite.

Jones's adventure.

Adams's garrison made no resistance. Fourteen persons were killed here. Drew surrendered on the promise of having his life spared, but was immediately slain. His nine-year-old boy was then made to run the gauntlet of a double file of Indians who, at length, despatched him with their hatchets. Thomas Edgerly and his son, both wounded, made their escape by taking to their boat, and paddling off down the river. Beard's and Meader's also were abandoned, making in all five garrisons taken without firing a shot. The remaining, seven resisted every assault, although one or two had narrow escapes from capture. At Burnham's,[1] where the gate carelessly had been left open over night, the inmates barely secured it in time to save themselves from a surprise.

Thomas Bickford saved his garrison with rare courage and address. It stood near the river, surrounded by

[1] THE HOUSE in which Mrs. Dean took shelter.

the usual palisade. Hearing the alarm, he sent off his family in a boat, shut his gate, took down his gun, and stood on his defence, resolved to risk his life for his homestead. Soon the house was surrounded. He was **Bickford's defence.** urged to surrender; then threatened. But promises and threats alike failed to bring the wary Bickford out of his fortress. His only reply was to fire at his besiegers as fast as he could load his gun, showing himself first at one loophole, then at another, always in a different hat or cap, and shouting out his orders as if there were a number of men in the garrison with him. Deceived by these artifices, the Indians withdrew to some easier conquest, leaving the brave Bickford master of the property he had so ably defended.

As each house was carried it was set on fire, until some twenty, or half the settlement, were blazing at once, over the mutilated bodies of their inmates.

While the Indians were thus rioting in fire and slaughter, Father Thury, their chaplain and father-confessor, made his way into the Puritan meeting-house, where he amused himself by writing with chalk upon the pulpit what was probably meant as a warning to all heretics to beware how they provoked the just anger of heaven in future. Unfortunately, the purport of the message is not preserved.

Having completed their bloody work as far as possible, the scattered bands now came together again at the falls, whence they presently moved off in a body to assault Woodman's garrison,[1] which stood a little out

[1] THIS venerable structure, built by John Woodman about 1670, was still standing a little off the Madbury road when the above was written. Within thirty days after my visit to it, nothing was left but the tall chimney-stack, it having been burned to the ground on November 9, 1896. It was one of the best preserved specimens of its

of the village on a commanding eminence overlooking
the whole course of the morning's bloody work.
Finding Woodman prepared to give them　　**Woodman's**
a warm reception, and fearing that the　　　　**Garrison.**
country people would soon rally to attack them, the
assailants drew off, after hearing mass for their victory,

RUINS OF WOODMAN GARRISON.

with their prisoners and booty. Only one man of them
had been wounded, as they report.

They left Durham a shambles. Not far from a hun-

time to be found in New England. The situation is superb, overlooking the country
for miles around. On a beautiful wooded knoll to the south rest the remains of
seven generations of the Woodman family, from John Woodman, the earliest occupant
of these grounds, in 1659, to the latest in 1862.

dred inoffensive persons had been shot down or tomahawked, in cold blood.[1] About thirty were led away
into captivity. For six miles up and down both sides
of the river the place was in a manner laid waste.
Twenty dwellings were burned to the ground and many
cattle wantonly killed. The survivors were aghast at
the scene of desolation around them, and a great dread
fell upon the country far and near.

All, however, was not yet ended. The tale of blood
was to have its bloody sequel. While the enemy's
main body was making good its retreat, a picked band,
led by the chief Moxus, not satisfied with the carnage
just committed at Durham, struck off toward the Merrimac in search of more victims. A small party first
crossed the Piscataqua, where they fell upon some farm
laborers who were at work in the hay fields without a
guard, and killed Mrs. Ursula Cutts, widow of the late
chief magistrate of New Hampshire, with three others.

Avoiding the settlements lying farther to the west,
the crafty Moxus now made a large détour, crossed the
Merrimac unperceived, and after making such a march
as only savages out on the war-path are capable of, on
the 27th of July, at daybreak, made a determined
assault upon Groton, Mass., some thirty-two miles
from Boston. At Lieutenant Lakin's garrison the assailants were handsomely repulsed, but in the scattered parts of the village, where
the inhabitants were taken wholly unawares, twenty-two
persons were killed and thirteen carried off into captivity. Of one family of Longleys, the father, mother, and

Moxus strikes
Groton.

---

[1] THE accounts vary between 80 and 100. Sewall gives 90 odd ; Lieutenant-Governor
Usher, 93 ; Parkman follows Villieu, who says 130. By subtracting prisoners he obtains
104 as the number slain.—*Villieu to the Minister*, September 7, 1694.

five children were slain on the spot, and three children taken captives.[1]

This audacious blow, struck, as it were, within reach of the most populous parts of the province, brought the dread possibilities of the war home to every man's door. Having regard to its intimidating effects, it was, from the enemy's standpoint, much the most brilliant exploit so far of which they could boast.

It is supposed that this was the same band of marauders, who, at their returning, slew three persons at Spruce Creek (Eliot), one at York, and eight more at Kittery. These murders happened between August 20th and 24th. No loss worth mentioning had been inflicted in return.

Deep exasperation followed these wanton acts, yet it was the old story told over again. Truth to say, the English, or those who had the management of civil and military affairs, seem always to have been dull in estimating the value of Indian treaties or the Indian character, and presumed too much upon pledges of no more real worth than the scratch of a bear's paw. But the Indians had dealt their blow, and were now waiting to see the result of the storm they had so unexpectedly raised.

[1] THE town has since caused a monument to be erected to their memory on the site of their old home. One of the surviving daughters, Lydia, was baptized in the Roman Catholic faith, in Canada. John, a boy of twelve, was ransomed, but four years of savage life had so won upon him that he had to be brought away by force. Betty, another daughter, died in captivity.

XII

A YEAR OF DISASTERS
1694—1696

IT happened that some of the leaders in the horrid work at Durham had been recognized.[1] Among the number were the two Doneys,[2] of Saco, who had so lately put their hands to the broken treaty of Pemaquid. When the noise caused by that affair had a little subsided, Robin Doney, a most hardened wretch, and three more of his comrades, with brazen impudence, sauntered into the fort at Saco as if nothing had happened. They were immediately seized by the commanding officer's orders. In like manner, Bomazeen and two others were taken at Pemaquid and sent to Boston, where they were kept in close confinement. It is true that Bomazeen came into the fort under the protection of a flag; but his captors, in their eagerness to secure so redoubtable an enemy, were not more disposed to stick at a little deception than the Indians themselves, with whom such artifices were more often a merit than a crime. At any rate, the authorities now considered that they had obtained more substantial security than empty pledges, and the prisoners were accordingly held in close custody.

Indians seized.

November 24, 1694.

---

[1] STATEMENT of Doney's woman servant. who made her escape. *Mass. Archives.*

[2] SAID to have been the mongrel descendants of D'Aulnay, French governor of Acadia, whose name is so pronounced. Hutchinson, II., 81, *note.*

Meantime, in November, Sir William Phips had sailed for England in order to answer to certain charges preferred against him there of official misconduct.   In his absence the conduct of affairs devolved upon Lieutenant-Governor Stoughton, who belonged to the   Phips goes to old wing of the Puritan party, which the   England. force of events had lately pushed somewhat into the background.   While waiting for his case to be decided, Phips was seized with an illness, of which he died in February, leaving behind him the memory of a career as remarkable for its failures as for its successes, and of a personality in which the good and the bad were so mingled as to leave in doubt whether his brief rule was or was not of benefit to his country.

The year 1695 was one of comparative quiet.   One of those periodical epidemics, with which the Indians were now and then scourged, was again making frightful ravages among them.   This kept them from going out on the war-path, and, it was thought, would dispose them to listen to overtures for a lasting peace.   At any rate, the experiment was worth trying.   With this view, one of the hostages was released, and sent out as a mediator to the hostile tribes.[1]   In times past he had been one of the Apostle Eliot's converts, but had   Futile efforts relapsed into paganism again.   Through   for peace. his influence two captive children were brought to Storer's garrison at Wells, on May 1st, and several more

---

[1] SHEEPSCOT JOHN—so called. He carried a letter from Lieutenant-Governor Stoughton, couched in rather haughty terms, in which the various tribes concerned in the late atrocities at Oyster River and Groton were commanded to deliver up not only the prisoners taken, but also the chiefs who had taken part in the descents. To these demands Asacambuit, of Norridgewock, returned a most insolent reply, strongly suggestive of the hands of the Jesuit missionary, denouncing, in unmeasured terms, the violation of the flags sent into Pemaquid and Saco, and breathing nothing but revenge.

to Pemaquid on the 20th, with the promise that the rest should be given up within twenty days, at which time they would be ready to make a treaty. Commissioners therefore met the Indian delegates at the time appointed, at Pemaquid. As a first step the return of all English captives was insisted upon. Not seeing Bomazeen or his fellow-hostages there, whom they had fully expected to get back by an exchange, man for man, the Indians believed they were being cheated, and went off in a pet.

Notice was immediately despatched to put the frontiers on their guard; and again were the poverty-stricken settlers compelled to abandon their own homes, with such little comforts as they were able to command, for the narrow limits of the garrisons, which, indeed, promised safety, if little else. This sort of life, if life it can be called, had now endured for seven years, with only short intervals of repose from the daily and hourly menace of sudden death. Little wonder, then, if a stoical indifference to danger had grown up out of the habit of always facing it or that a great many lost their lives through sheer recklessness, or worse—as the long list of casualties, occurring between July and November, sufficiently shows.

Billerica, Saco, and Pemaquid. At Kittery, Me., Major Hammond was taken prisoner, and carried to Canada ; at Billerica [1] ten persons were killed, and five carried off into captivity ; at Saco Fort Sergeant Haley was slain ; at

---

[1] THIS occurred August 5th, in what is now Tewksbury. On that day a number of horsemen were seen approaching, but were not suspected of being Indians until they surrounded the house of John Rogers. Rogers received a mortal wound from an arrow while in bed and asleep. He woke with a start, withdrew the arrow, and expired. Rogers's son and daughter were taken captive. A woman who was scalped, and left for dead, recovered. Of John Leviston's family, six were killed and one taken. Dr. Roger Toothaker's wife was killed and his daughter carried off. It is said that the Indians had even tied up the mouths of the dogs for fear of being betrayed by their barking.

Pemaquid[1] four more were killed and six wounded, out
of twenty-four men at work outside the fort.   Nine persons were also captured at Newbury, and hurried off into
the woods.   Being overtaken at their first camp, the
marauders, according to their usual custom,   Newbury men
when hard pressed, tomahawked all the   taken.
prisoners on the spot.   Strange to say, none were killed
outright, though all subsequently died of their wounds,

INDIAN HEAD BREAKER.

except one youth, who luckily received the blow from
the hatchet on his shoulder, instead of his head, and so
escaped a lingering death.

Having had several men shot down, while at work
outside the fort, the garrison at Pemaquid were in a
revengeful mood.   Captain Pascho Chubb had relieved
Major March of the command.   His qualifications for
so important a post do not appear, yet a strange fatuity
seems to have put him there.   The sequel was a tragedy
in which Chubb showed himself utterly unfitted for the
trust committed to him.

In the month of February, 1696, on a Sunday, a party
of Indians came before the fort, with a flag, and demanded a parley.   Chubb and some others went out to
meet them.   Three noted chiefs, Egeremet, Abenquid,
and Moxus, were with the other party.   In only one respect is the account of what afterward happened at all
clear.   The object of demanding the parley was said to

[1] In September.   Hugh March was one of the slain.

be the exchange of prisoners. In view of the late attacks on the garrison, fear of treachery was no doubt upper-most in the minds of both parties. Mutual recrimination was probable. Yet what actually passed is shrouded in mystery. All positively known is, that the English suddenly fell upon the Ind-ians, that weapons were drawn, and that in the mêlée Egeremet and Abenquid, two as untamed spirits as ever lifted the war-hatchet, were killed on the spot. Two others of the party were slain, and one or more made prisoners.[1] Moxus freed himself from the grasp of his enemies and made good his escape. For thus putting himself on a level with savages, Chubb unaccountably escaped formal censure, perhaps, as Mather naïvely re-marks, because some well enough liked the thing that was done, although they did not like the manner of doing it. To his credit be it said, Mather was not enough of a Jesuit to stomach such unpardonable baseness.

Chiefs killed at Pemaquid.

It was but natural that the Indians should exact prompt and bloody reparation. With the spring, there-fore, a new chapter of massacres began, the Piscataqua settlements now being the particular objects of the en-emy's fury.

The densely wooded country around York, Me., out of which rises the blue dome of Mount Agamenticus, was threaded by a lonely horse-path uniting the villages of York and Wells. As Thomas Cole and his wife Abi-gail, with two others, were returning home from a visit to York, they were waylaid in these woods. Cole and his wife were shot dead. The others made good their

---

[1] CHARLEVOIX'S account that two English were slain in this encounter lacks con-firmation.

escape. On the 26th of June a large body of Indians crossed over from York Nubble to Rye Beach in their canoes, hid their canoes among the bushes, and made a violent assault upon the scat-   **York and Rye.** tered houses lying some two miles below Portsmouth. Fourteen persons were killed outright, one was scalped and left for dead, and four taken. After plundering the houses, the enemy set them on fire, and then hastily made off. They were so closely pursued by a party of militia from Portsmouth, that, having halted on the slope of a hill to eat their breakfast,[1] the captives and plunder were retaken, but owing to bad management the marauders got to their canoes again in safety. A month later the people of Dover were waylaid while returning from public worship, three killed, three wounded, and three carried away into captivity.

While the Piscataqua settlements were being thus ter- rorized, a blow was struck in another quarter which swept away every vestige of that easy-going confidence hitherto reposed in stone walls, as such, regardless of whether they were, or were not, properly manned or commanded. True, the poverty of the country com- pelled the strictest economy to be practised, yet adher- ence to a penny-wise, pound-foolish policy, born of a native reluctance to spend, lay at the bottom of many a disaster which might have been averted. Most impru- dently, while taking counsel of their own poverty, the authorities wholly failed to take into account the old soldier at Quebec.

Frontenac had only postponed his purpose of taking Pemaquid at all hazards. Everything was carefully planned at Quebec, and Villebon, at St. John, was ready

---

[1] For this reason since called Breakfast Hill ; between Rye and Greenland.

to lend his assistance.   In July, 1696, a second expedition was despatched against the English fortress.   There were two war-ships, commanded by Le Moyne d' Iberville and de Bonaventure, and a mixed force of Indians, picked up on the way at St. John and Penobscot, com-

IN THE BAY OF FUNDY.

manded by the younger St. Castin.   In the Bay of Fundy, Iberville fell in with two English ships-of-war, sent there to intercept Villebon's supplies.   A sharp combat at once took place, in the course of which one of the English vessels, the Newport, was dismasted and taken. The other made her escape in a fog.

Having thus rid himself of what might have proved

the ruin of his attempt then and there, Iberville, after refitting his prize, made sail again, and on August 14th the ships cast anchor before the fort.

Pemaquid is a peninsula. The fort stood at the shore, facing the sea. Castin immediately broke ground in the rear of the fortress, where the cemetery now is, thus cutting off communication on the land side. Batteries were also thrown up on the adja-   Pemaquid
cent islands, with so much industry that   taken.
the investment of the place was quickly completed, both by land and sea.

Captain Chubb was still in command of the fort, with less than a hundred men to defend it. Incapacity or indifference, it matters little which, had left it in this weak state.

The besiegers worked so diligently that their batteries were ready to open fire on the afternoon of the next day after landing.[1] The fort was then summoned. Chubb retorted defiantly enough, but lost courage upon the explosion of a few shells inside his works, reinforced by a savage threat from Castin to give no quarter, and threw open his gates to the elated besiegers, who were far from expecting so easy a conquest.

Once more the victorious enemy dismantled the works and threw down the walls, constructed with so much labor, yet defended with so little spirit.

By the terms of the surrender Chubb and his men were paroled and sent to Boston. So incensed were the Indians against him that the whole garrison, doubtless, would have fallen victims to their fury, if Chubb, who knew only too well what he might expect from them,

---

[1] M. Thury, who seems to have been more at home among such scenes than in his mission, with Father Simon, assisted in this work, each doing his very best.

had not stipulated for a safeguard until his men could
be embarked. When they reached Boston Chubb was
Chubb put
in arrest. promptly put in arrest and lodged in gaol,
where he lay until the next spring, by
which time the feeling against him had so far cooled
that his imprisonment was deemed a sufficient punish-
ment, and he was allowed to go to his home at Andover,
and there hide his disgrace in retirement.

Meanwhile, another expedition was forming at Boston, under Church's command, to go and clear the eastern frontiers of enemies again. Before it was ready to
move news came that Pemaquid had fallen. That disaster redoubled the exertions to get Church to work, for
it was thought that the victorious enemy might come to
the westward as far as Portsmouth, that place being
nearly defenceless against an attack from sea.

It was soon learned, however, that Iberville's squadron had set sail for the eastward instead, after com-
pleting the destruction of Pemaquid; so that fears of an
attack were removed, only to give place to apprehen-
sions that he and his savage allies might now make
their escape unscathed.

It chanced that three men-of-war were then lying idle
in Boston harbor. These ships, with two armed merchant vessels, and some few land forces, were hurried
off in pursuit of Iberville's squadron. It was sighted,
but lost again among the intricate passages of the eastern coast, with which the French pilots were much better acquainted than the English.

Church's expedition proved an even worse failure.
With their usual fatuity the authorities had seen fit to
release an Indian prisoner from gaol while Church was
getting ready. News of his coming had thus every-

where preceded him, with the result that wherever
Church went, the Indians had buried themselves deeper
in the woods.   In vain he tried every means known to
his experience to conceal his presence or   **Church goes**
throw these wily foemen off their guard.   **out again.**
All was of no use.   His ill-fortune dogged him like his
shadow.   In order to be able to move his men at will,
and undiscovered, he had provided himself with whale-
boats, in the handling of which his Cape Indians were
thoroughly at home.   The better to hide his intended
movements from the vigilant savages Church steered
first for Monhegan Island, ten miles off the mainland at
Pemaquid, where his vessels were securely hid from
prying eyes.   Then, manning his whaleboats at nightfall, he rowed across into Penobscot Bay, and, after
concealing the boats among the bushes at daybreak,
ranged the woods up and down in search of the savages.
In this way the western shores and islands of the bay
were scouted from Owl's Head to Bangor, without getting sight of more than four or five wandering savages
in a region usually much frequented by them.

Finding the seacoast deserted as far as Mount Desert,
Church now sailed over a long course, landing next at
Chignecto or Beaubassin, in Acadia, which place he
plundered and burned.   The inhabitants,   **Chignecto**
both French and Indians, fled at his com-   **burned.**
ing, but some of the former returned upon promise of
good usage.   After reading them a sharp lecture upon
the barbarities practised by the savages upon the English, and forcibly contrasting it with his own magnanimity in now keeping his Indians from knocking them
all in the head, Church took his departure for the St.
John River.

Here there was a trifling skirmish with some workmen, who were building a new fort at the mouth of the river, in which affair one Frenchman was killed and one wounded and taken. From the wounded man it was learned where the great guns, intended for the fort, had been buried **At St. John River.** below high water mark. These were secured. Church now called a council to decide whether an attempt should be made on Villebon's fort, situated still higher up the river. It was thought impracticable, as the river was so low, and Church accordingly turned homeward.

While on the way back, Church fell in with a reinforcement, under Lieutenant-Colonel Hathorne, who, besides superseding him in the command, to his great chagrin, promptly ordered him back to St. John again. Villebon's fort was reached and attacked this time, but to no purpose, as the English were beaten off without much effort. And so this expedition ended, like the others that had gone before it, in disappointment [1] and disgrace.

Meanwhile, Iberville, after eluding the squadron sent in pursuit of him, had gone to Newfoundland, where he virtually possessed himself of the whole island, by taking St. John's, its chief port. Bonavista and Carbonière Island remained in the hands of the English, only because the cold weather put a stop to further operations. This conquest, so important in every way to French interests, from its bearing upon the control of the Bank fisheries, was thrown away as quickly as it was made,

---

[1] CHURCH, justly offended at being superseded, is silent about this affair. Hutchinson, II., 94, gives some details, not found elsewhere, perhaps taken from Hathorne's journal of the expedition. Charlevoix confuses the part taken by the English squadron with that acting under Church and Hathorne.

because no measures had been concerted to hold what
had been gained. Iberville, therefore, burned St. John's
and went back to Placentia, where the French had a
poor establishment, placed there more with an eye to
covering the French half of the island than for its ad-
vantages as a port of commerce.

Though Newfoundland was the more remote, New
England had far more at stake there than she had in
Acadia, which was, at best, little more than an incum-
brance, saddled upon her by the new charter. Indeed
to shut the ports of Newfoundland against her would lit-
erally have taken the bread out of the mouths of thousands of New England fishermen and their families,
besides seriously crippling many other branches of industry closely depending upon these fisheries. It was
not accident, but its conceded appropriateness, therefore, which first made the codfish the chosen symbol of
Massachusetts, as it continues to be to this day.

In so far, therefore, as these operations threatened to
cripple the resources of New England for carrying on the
war, as they undoubtedly would have done if turned to
better account, they should not be lost sight of; for the
cutting off of its water-supply, at its source, from a
beleaguered city could hardly have proved more ruinous to the besieged than the cutting off of the Newfoundland fisheries from New England; and it was not
to be believed that England would permit France to
exclude her from these fisheries without a struggle.

For the English this had been a year of disasters,
with hardly one redeeming feature upon which to build
hope for the future. At its close the advantage rested
wholly with the enemy. East and west, the hostile

tribes were now acting together as one man. Acadia had been lost, Pemaquid demolished. Much had been expected from the expeditions of Church and Hathorne; nothing realized. It is well, therefore, to turn over a new leaf of the sombre tragedy, now happily drawing toward its close.

XIII

ONSLAUGHT AT HAVERHILL

March 15, 1697

DURING this war the newer settlements, forming a second line between the Merrimac and Piscataqua, and thus becoming so many outposts to the old sea-coast settlements, suffered much by reason of their exposed situation. Yet the careless settlers do not seem to have realized their danger overmuch, or else long familiarity only served to render them indifferent to it.

Of all these villages little Haverhill, with its thirty odd houses, was perhaps the most exposed, because the Merrimac offered such a short and easy route of attack. Moreover, the Pennacooks, of this river, were well acquainted with every nook and corner of the place.

There was the village, nestling close along the bank of the Merrimac for its own protection, and there was a hamlet boldly thrown out on the hills rising behind it. Village and hamlet were a long mile apart, with a sluggish stream, Little River, crawling between them. In the village there were three block-houses, conveniently placed for its defence, to which the inhabitants might fly in case of an alarm; and it is not unlikely that some of the scattered farm-houses were expected to serve the same purpose at need; but those families who, in such unsettled times as these,

Haverhill in 1697.

thus ventured to live apart from neighbors, were sure to bear the brunt of a hostile onset.

It was on the 15th day of March, 1697, when the hills are bleak and bare, the woods yet streaked with snow, and the raw north wind sweeps over the frozen earth in fierce and fitful blasts, that the war-whoop sounded the onslaught so long remembered.

It so chanced that Thomas Dustan, husbandman, rode out that morning to his field, which lay at some distance off from his house. He saw the Indians coming. He had that morning left his wife, Hannah, lying on a sick bed, with Mary Neff, her nurse, and his eight children, whose ages ran from two to seventeen years, wholly unprotected. There was not a moment to lose. Dustan rode hard, with the Indians whooping and yelling behind him, like so many demons let loose. By outstripping them, he gained a few precious moments in which to prepare for instant flight.

Thomas Dustan.

First telling his frightened children to run for their lives to the nearest garrison (a weary way for those toddling little feet to travel), Dustan's next thought was to rescue his helpless wife from the clutches of the savages. Throwing the bridle on his horse, he ran into the chamber where she lay, pale and trembling at the appalling sounds now heard close at hand. If Dustan had dreamed of carrying her off with him, he was too late. Every moment's delay was putting all their lives in jeopardy.

Distracted between the thoughts of abandoning his wife thus, and of saving the lives of his children, Dustan rushed from the house, threw himself upon his horse, and galloped off after them. As he rode away the marauders were at his doors, tomahawk in hand.

Fortunately for him, the greedy wretches stopped to
rifle the house. This gave Dustan a start of a few minutes, which was improved to the utmost; yet so quickly
had all this happened that the terrified children were
not more than forty rods from the house when the distressed father overtook them. As his eye ran over the
forlorn little group, his heart may well have sunk within
him. To save all seemed out of the question. The
whole could travel no faster than the youngest of them
all, while the shouts of his pursuers announced that
they were already on his track, and would soon be up
with him. What was to be done?

For just one moment Thomas Dustan thought of
snatching up the youngest and most helpless one of all,
putting spurs to his horse, and leaving the rest to their
fate. It was a horrible temptation, prompted by the
instinct of self-preservation, but repented of on the
instant. The thought of what that fate must be might
well have made the strong man shudder. Scattering
shots from his pursuers hastened his decision. Come
what would, Dustan resolved to live or die with his little
family. Better fall, like a man, defending them to the
last, than live to be pointed at as the coward who had
saved his own life by the sacrifice of his own flesh and
blood.

Yet it was necessary to act with all prudence and skill.
Dustan well knew that the savages would not venture
within gun-shot until they had first drawn his fire.
Urging his little flock to quicken their pace, he wheeled
his horse and levelled his gun at the nearest of his pursuers, who instantly halted, expecting a shot. Dustan,
however, knew better than to throw his only chance
away. He kept the Indians covered with his gun until

the children had widened the distance between them, then coolly rode back to rejoin them. By repeating this manœuvre the savages were kept at bay, the stout-hearted father fortunately escaping the bullets fired at random in the hope of knocking him off his horse. And in this manner the flight and pursuit continued until the savages had been drawn so far from their band that they gave over the chase in disgust. With unspeakable relief Dustan, at length, saw his little family safe and sound within the shelter of a stout block-house, from which, on looking backward over the ground he had just traversed, he could see his own house in flames.

Meanwhile, those savages who had not joined in the pursuit were hurriedly ransacking Dustan's house, for, by this time, the alarm had spread to the village, which was now up in arms. The nurse had been seized in the attempt to fly with the new-born infant before she had gone many rods from the house.

Upon entering the room where Mrs. Dustan was lying the greasy redskins roughly bade her to get up. With the fear of instant death before her eyes, the poor woman arose, and with trembling hands began to put on her **Mrs. Dustan taken.** clothes, while her captors were busy loading themselves with all the plunder they could carry away. This done, she was led from the house, which was immediately set on fire, and was soon blazing fiercely.

Smoke and flames were now bursting forth from all the houses in the little neighborhood, which, one after the other, had been, in like manner, assaulted and plundered. Twenty-seven settlers lay dead or dying among the smoking ruins of their own peaceful dwellings. Thirteen miserable captives, shivering with cold and

fright, were huddled together, benumbed by the blow
that had so unexpectedly fallen upon them. These were
now being hurriedly loaded down with the
spoil of their own houses. The savages   Slain or taken.
then plunged into the woods, driving their prisoners before them like so
many beasts of
burden.

Mrs. Dustan and
Mrs. Neff, who still
held the baby in
her arms, marched
with the rest. No
mercy was shown
to laggards. One
miscreant, not yet
sated with slaugh-
ter, tore the help-
less infant from
its nurse's arms
and dashed out
its brains against
the nearest tree.
Among the pris-
oners some were

DUSTAN MONUMENT.

old and feeble. Whenever one showed signs of giving
out he was instantly despatched by the blow of a tomahawk, and his load given to another. By this means
the retreat was pressed to the utmost.

Though in hourly expectation of meeting with the
same fate, Mrs. Dustan succeeded in keeping up with
the band during the rest of the day, notwithstanding her
extreme bodily weakness. The halt for the night brought

with it a short respite. She saw that none of her loved ones were among the little knot of captives. And with that knowledge, reviving hope gave her the strength still to bear bravely up against her cruel sufferings of mind and body, as in the deepening gloom she threw herself upon the bare earth, there to live over again in speechless misery the woful tragedy of the day.

Upon resuming their march, the hostile band separated into small parties, the better to throw their pursuers off the scent. To each one was parcelled out its share of the prisoners and plunder.

The party whose property Mrs. Dustan and Mrs. Neff had thus become took a wide circuit through the wilderness of woods, hills, and waters, stretching away to the north. After travelling for several days longer, all fear of pursuit now being at an end, a more westward course was steered, which, at length, brought them out of the woods, on the shores of the Merrimac, some sixty odd miles, as the river runs, from their starting-point. In a few short hours the friendly current would have carried the wanderers to their homes again.

The camp, to which the prisoners were now conducted, was pitched on a pleasant little island, lying at the mouth of the Contoocook River. Here they were given to understand that they would remain, until such a time as their captors should be ready to start for Canada. Should they ever reach it alive, a long and lingering captivity awaited them. Should they perish by the way, who would ever know their fate?

The Indian family, of whom the captive women now formed part for the time being, consisted of two stout warriors, three women and their seven children. Having nothing to fear from two such helpless beings, no

very strict watch was kept upon them, nor did they meet
with ill-usage beyond what commonly fell to the lot of
captives in their situation, namely, to be the submissive
and uncomplaining drudges of their tawny masters.
Their masters already were counting upon getting a
handsome sum for them in Canada, so it would never
do to unfit the captives for the long march before
them.

Besides these twelve Indian men, women, and children
already mentioned, there was also domesticated among
them a captive English lad, one Samuel Leonardson,
who already had been a year and a half in their hands,
in the course of which he had mastered their language,
fallen in with their way of life, and was looked upon
and treated as one of themselves. Upon this half-
savage stripling the last hopes of a desperate woman
now rested.

The captive women could not help showing by their
looks something of the despair in their hearts. Whenever they could steal away by themselves, they prayed
fervently for deliverance. Sometimes their Indian
master would say to them, in mockery of their haggard
looks, " What need you trouble yourself? If your God
will have you delivered, it shall be so."

Not long before the time set for the long march to
Canada to begin, the captives were told that, on arriv-
ing at a certain Indian town, they would have to run
the gantlet. That is to say, that they would first be
stripped of their clothing, and then made to run through
a lane formed of all the men, women, and children of
the place, all armed with clubs, sticks, or tomahawks,
with which each Indian would strike the terrified victims as they ran. To add to their terror, they were also

told how the weak or faint-hearted often fell senseless to the ground under the blows of their brutal tormentors.

The knowledge of what was in store for them seems to have nerved the unhappy captives to an act of desperation. Then, there was the deep-flowing Merrimac, always whispering "home! home!" as it swept by them.

Mrs. Dustan knew that after this journey began all hope of escape would be over. She therefore laid her plans to fly before it should be too late. To attempt this with two stout warriors alive was not to be thought of. There was but one other way. They must die by her hands and those of her companions.

Hannah Dustan was no delicate flower of the city, ready to faint at the pricking of her finger with her needle, but the sturdy helpmate of a sturdy yeoman, whose will to do and dare had been strung to the highest tension by the knowledge that there was one way of escape, and but one.

This settled, the next thing was to gain over the nurse and the boy, Leonardson, to her plan, which was to kill all the Indians without distinction of age or sex, except one boy, who was to be taken away alive. There could be no paltering with the situation. They knew that to let any escape would endanger their own safety.

From this moment, Hannah Dustan pursued her determination with Indian sagacity, and almost savage ferocity.

Young Leonardson was charged to find out just where and how to strike with the hatchet, so as to kill at one blow. There must be no bungling here. The lad seized his first chance to do so. "Strike here," replied the unsuspecting savage, laying a tawny finger upon his temple. Then drawing the same finger rapidly around his shaven crown, he showed the lad how the knife was used in taking a scalp, and how the scalp was torn from the victim's head.   The lesson was well learned.

The prisoners now knew what they had to do, and

HANNAH DUSTAN SLAYS HER CAPTORS.

how to do it.   The time for the attempt was fixed for the very next night.

In the dead of night, when the Indians lay fast asleep in their wigwam, three dusky forms rose noiselessly and stealthily up from their midst.   Each grasped a hatchet.   Each had marked a victim.   Bending over the prostrate bodies of the sleepers, blow followed blow in quick succession.   Mrs. Dustan's weapon was buried in the brain of her master; Leonardson's in that of the

same Indian who had directed him where to strike.
None escaped, save a squaw, who, though sorely wounded, ran out into the thickets, where she hid
herself, and the boy whose life they had
agreed to spare. He got away, unharmed, in the darkness and confusion of the moment.

The Escape.

Arming herself with her dead master's gun and tomahawk, Mrs. Dustan led the way to the place where
the canoes were beached. All these were stove and
sunk, except the one in which the fugitives now pushed
out upon the broad river, with no other thought than to
hasten away from the scene of slaughter. Two of their
destined victims had saved themselves by flight. They
knew that the next encampment was not far off, and
would soon be alarmed.

The shore had scarcely been left behind, however,
when Mrs. Dustan suddenly recollected that, in the hurry
of their flight, they had neglected to take off the scalps
of the slain. In this woman an iron will seems united
with cool courage and rare presence of mind. She would
not leave the accursed spot without carrying away with
her the bloody evidences of their exploit. These, at
least, could not be called in question. The canoe was
again headed for the shore, and not until the bloody
trophies of that fearful night's work were secured did
the fugitives again embark on their perilous voyage.

It was beset with dangers. Many a hideous fall or
treacherous shallow lay between the fugitives and their
destined haven. Not far below their starting-point,
the bed of the river is heaved up, from shore to shore,
in huge masses of jagged rock, through which the pent-
up waters boil and plunge with indescribable fury.
Here the canoe had to be unloaded and carried around

the falls, before it could be launched into smooth water again.   Below these again, the free course of the
river is much broken by rifts and shallows, where only
a skilful handling of the paddle could keep the canoe
from oversetting.   Hardly was one danger surmounted
before the distant roar of angry waters told them of another ahead.   Down this perilous road the fugitives
held their steady course, hope rising higher and higher
as the long leagues of wooded
shores swept majestically by
them. They took turns at the
paddle, keeping a sharp lookout for lurking enemies.   In
the night two slept while
the third plied the paddle.[1]
Half-starved, worn out with
unceasing labor and watchfulness, the feelings with
which the weary wanderers
saw at last the familiar shores

DUSTAN TANKARD.

and cottages of Haverhill rising before them can only
be guessed.   They were welcomed home as beings risen
from the dead.

The story of the exploit soon spread throughout the
length and breadth of the colonies, and was everywhere
the theme of mingled wonder and admiration.   After recovering from the effects of their captivity, all the actors
in this remarkable tragedy went to Boston,[2] taking with

---

[1] It is said that the fugitives were hospitably received and entertained by Jonathan
Tyng, at his house on Wickasuck Island.

[2] " May 1, 1697.   Hannah Dustan came to see us ; I gave her part of Connecticut
flax.   She saith her master, whom she killed, did formerly live with Mr. Rowlandson,
at Lancaster.   He told her that when he prayed the English way, he thought that was
good, but now he found the French way was better."—*Sewall Papers.*

them the ghastly trophies that Hannah Dustan would not leave behind her. The Massachusetts General Court being then in session, a reward of twenty-five pounds was voted to the Dustans, and twelve pounds ten shillings each to Mary Neff and Samuel Leonardson. Besides this gratuity, doubly welcome to those who had lost their all, Governor Nicholson, of Maryland, sent Hannah Dustan a pewter tankard, as a mark of his regard for her remarkable heroism. This token is still in existence.

Monuments have been raised to commemorate this exploit, both at Haverhill, where the savage onslaught began, and at Dustan's Island, in the town of Boscawen, N. H., where the maternal vengeance overtook some of the actors in that day's work. Yet, strange to say, even to this day the site of Thomas Dustan's house is not positively known.

XIV

TO THE PEACE OF RYSWICK

UNKNOWN to the people of New England, during the winter of 1696-97 a blow was impending by the side of which Indian raids were trifles indeed. And when it was known, the danger itself had passed away, like the storm-cloud, watched in doubt and dismay, until it has drifted far down the darkened heavens, and light and sunshine have come again.

Canada being a royal colony, its affairs were really directed from Versailles. For years Louis had been importuned to lay Boston in ashes, as the only means of securing the tranquillity of Canada. Hitherto, more weighty affairs at home had kept the project in abeyance, but at last Louis was ready to act. At the ports of Brest and Rochefort a formidable squadron, consisting of ten heavy ships, two fire-ships and a galliot,[1] was being fitted out, first to destroy Boston, and afterward to lay waste the New England coast as far as Portsmouth. New York and Albany were to be served in the same way, provided all went as it was hoped and expected. A good deal of other work was cut out for the Marquis de Nesmond, who was to command; but these were the leading objects with which he was charged. So much pains was taken to keep the project a profound secret that orders were sent to Fron-

Fleet sails to burn Boston.

---

[1] A SMALL open, vessel, using both sails and oars and intended to chase. The crews were usually soldiers, laying down their oars to take up their muskets.

9

tenac to have fifteen hundred men in readiness by a
certain date, without letting him know for what service
they were wanted.

News that this powerful armament was at sea reached
Boston some time in the summer, and its object was so
easily guessed that the whole country, far and near, was
stirred as never before. At that time the reliable Major
March was out scouting with five hundred men, at the
eastward. Boston, as well as all the seacoast towns, was
in a state of feverish excitement. The old fortifications
were overhauled and repaired, new ones built, and heavy
guns mounted along the water-front, and at the castle.
For weeks the provincial militia were held in readiness
to march to the threatened points. These measures are
a sufficiently clear indication of public feeling.

Fortunately for New England, the whole enterprise
fell through. De Nesmond had been saddled with so
many orders, his passage across the Atlantic was so long,
that when he arrived at Placentia (July 24th), it was too
late in the season to bring the coöperating land forces
down from Quebec, where they had been
held to prevent news of the intended descent from getting noised abroad. To this puerile
attempt to combine the operations of a fleet and army
three thousand miles away, New England owed her
escape from a great danger. Old as he was, Frontenac
would have managed the affair much better.

The project fails.

In all probability, the holding of so many men inac-
tive in Canada had a tendency to diminish the number
of Indian raids during the summer. There were, however, more than enough to show what a handful of creeping savages could do among thousands of unguarded
husbandmen. In June a large war-party placed them-

selves in ambush outside of the village of Exeter, N. H.,
meaning to make an assault early on the next morning. Against the advice of their friends,
some women and children of the village   Exeter visited.
went out into the fields to gather wild strawberries.
In order to frighten them back, some alarm guns were
fired. This quickly brought all the people together
in arms, and thereby frustrated the intended attack, as
the Indians supposed themselves discovered, and after
firing a few random shots made a hasty retreat. One
person was killed, another wounded, and a child carried
off.[1]

How death lurked on every side is strongly emphasized
by the following incident. One quiet Sabbath afternoon,
early in July, Major Charles Frost, with several of his
neighbors, was returning home from meeting in Eliot,
Me. The road on which they were riding had been
ambushed in a retired spot by an outlying party of savages looking for scalps. To make sure of their prey, the
lurking assassins had stuck some bushes in   Major Frost
the ground, at a turn of the path, behind   slain.
which they crouched, armed and ready. The Major's
two sons were permitted to pass the ambuscade in safety,
but the worthy Major, against whom the savages had
nursed their revenge ever since the kidnapping affair at
Dover, eight years before, was shot dead in the road.
Dennis Downing and John Heard's wife, two of Frost's
companions, were also killed on the spot, and Heard was
wounded. "The good Lord keep us in these perilous
times!" exclaims pious Joseph Storer, in giving an account of the affair. "The good Lord sanctify it to us
all!"

[1] BELKNAP'S *New Hampshire*, I., 279, 280.

In a day or two after, three men carrying the mail were waylaid and killed as they were leaving Wells. Storer warns his brother, Captain John Hill, at Saco, against travelling in the daytime. Indeed, the ways had now become so dangerous for men, that dogs were trained to carry the mail between exposed points. Frost had been a tower of strength to this weak corner of Maine, and it is no wonder that his death should be mourned as a pub-lic calamity.

After commit-ting several more murders in this vi-cinity, the Indi-ans next made their unwelcome appearance among the Saco settle-

DOG MAIL-CARRIER.

ments. Of a party of five belonging to the garrison of Saco fort, who were chopping wood on Cow Island, in the Saco, three were killed, and three more, posted as sentinels, but keeping careless watch, surprised and car-ried off.[1] In going down the river the marauders were fired upon from the shore, and some of them hurt.

One tradition of this descent deserves to be preserved. Captain Humphrey Scamman's garrison stood on the bank of the river, about two miles from the sea. He was at work that day, mowing in his meadow, the house being left in charge of his wife and children. The day was sultry, and the labor fatiguing, so goodwife Scam-man presently sent their little ten-year-old boy to his father with a mug of ale, probably charging him to be

[1] THESE were Lieutenant Fletcher and his two sons.

careful not to spill it by the way. Soon after starting on his errand the lad caught sight of the Indians approaching the house. He instantly turned back, still carrying the mug in his hands, but it **Saco raided.** was now too late, as the Indians quickly took possession of the house, and made prisoners of the whole family, including Scamman, all of whom were carried off to Canada. At the end of the war they were released and returned home. Their house was found in the same condition as when they had left it, even to the beer-mug[1] which the frightened boy had hastily set down on the dresser, when he ran back home to warn his mother of the approach of the terrible redskins.

SCAMMAN'S JUG.

In September, bloody notice was served on the inhabitants of Lancaster, Mass., that safety was only to be purchased at the price of unremitting vigilance. This town, which had suffered so severely **At Lancaster.** in former wars, was again completely surprised, nearly twenty persons killed, one of whom was the Rev. John Whiting, the young pastor of the church there,[2] and five more carried away into captivity. Two

---

[1] THIS interesting relic, a brown earthen jug, evidently of Dutch make, decorated with an equestrian figure of William III., is now in the possession of Joseph Moody, Esq., of Saco.

[2] THE meagre account of this affair is taken from Mather. Hutchinson loosely places

or three houses were burnt with their occupants, too
decrepit to fly, in them. The raiders were pursued for
two days without coming up with them.

The long wished for peace of Ryswick was proclaimed
at Boston, on December 10, 1697. At between three
and four in the afternoon, eight or ten

Peace at last.

drums and trumpets sounded out the glad
tidings to the citizens. Hostilities with the Indians did
not, however, cease for some time to come, or not until
they found out that the French no longer dared to give
them open support.

The winter of 1697-98, was the coldest within the memory of his generation, Mather says. Moreover, the settlers along the Merrimac were destined to feel once and
again the rage of their old enemies before the day of
trial was passed. Proclamation of peace, by sound of
trumpet in the streets of Boston, could not stay the
stroke of the tomahawk, or turn from their bloody designs those who had a debt of vengeance yet to pay.

In the latter part of February[1] a war-party made a
fierce onslaught upon Andover, Mass. They had apparently singled out two of the foremost citizens for
their prey. The house of Captain Pascho Chubb, late
commandant at Pemaquid, was assaulted, and he and

Killing at Andover.

his wife were slain on the spot. At the
same time the house of Lieutenant-Colonel Dudley Bradstreet[2] was attacked, the inmates
dragged out of doors, one of them brutally tomahawked,[3]

the number killed at twenty or thirty. Mr. Whiting was the successor of J. Rowlandson.
It is said that quarter was offered him by the Indians, but that he preferred to fight
for his life and lost it. He was only thirty-three.

[1] THE double date given by Sewall and Pike, February 22, $\frac{1797}{1798}$, corresponds with
March 4, 1798.

[2] STILL standing in North Andover.

[3] MAJOR WADE'S son, of Medford, a guest and relative of the family.

and the rest, strange to say, after a short detention, set at liberty. Besides rifling Colonel Bradstreet's house, the marauders burned some of his neighbors' houses and barns, with their contents, but only two persons, besides those already reported, are known to have been killed by them. Mather relates that the Rev. Thomas Barnard, the minister of the place, narrowly escaped their

BRADSTREET HOUSE, AT NORTH ANDOVER, MASS.

fury; and Sewall adds that the pulpit cushions were taken away and burned.

While making off toward Haverhill, the same party fell in with Jonathan Haynes and Samuel Ladd, of that town, driving their teams homeward, and killed both of them. A son of each was taken at the same time.

Occasional outrages of this sort, continued during the spring months, served to signal the expiring efforts of the war, like the random shots fired after the main battle is over. Deprived by the peace of the means of carrying on the war, the hostile tribes quickly realized that since they had been abandoned by their friends, the only course left was to make terms with their enemies. Finding them in this temper, Major Converse and Captain Alden held a conference with some of the chief sachems at Penobscot, in October; the Indians, as usual, throwing all the blame of their past acts upon the French. Treaty of Casco. There was no doubt, however, that they were now sincerely desirous of peace. A meeting was therefore arranged for this end, which took place at or near Mare Point in Casco Bay, in January, when articles of submission were signed by Moxus and many more chiefs, representing the different tribes.

By this treaty the Indians freely acknowledged their past misdeeds, set forth in the strongest colors by the English, and once again pledged their worthless honor for the performance of the same old threadbare obligations. Next to the cessation of the long reign of arson, pillage, and murder, the rescue of English captives was the chief object to be attained. Some hundreds of these were scattered far and wide among their brutal captors. They were to be restored, but the inclemency of the season Captives given up. prevented this merciful act from taking effect at once. Many had perished miserably of ill treatment or starvation, but all who were able to bear the fatigues of the long march homeward, and who, themselves, wished to return to their friends, were permitted to do so. Strange to say, not a few preferred to remain among the savages, thus furnishing a homely, but apt illustration of the ease with which so-called civilized beings relapse into barbarism. We may take comfort in the belief that not one of these renegades would have made a useful citizen, had he remained true to his color and teachings.

Various estimates of the loss of life in this war are to be met with. But it is evident that none were carefully compiled, as they run all the way from 500 to 700 killed. The latter number is probably the more accurate. Asacumbuit alone claimed to have slain one hundred and fifty persons with his own hand. In view of the length of the war, the highest **Losses by the war.** figure does not seem large, but when we reflect that the losses mostly fell upon the agricultural population, and in many cases virtually wiped out of existence entire towns or villages; that hundreds of dwellings and barns were burned to ashes, with their contents; and that progress, as measured by pushing forward the frontier, was beaten back twenty years, the true nature of this conflict stands out in strong relief. The weakness of the English plan seems to have been in the attempt to hold an untenable line, more as a point of honor than from the dictates of a sound policy. It has been seen that the effort severely taxed the entire resources of Massachusetts and New Hampshire, both in men and money.

Though no estimate of the losses to the Indians is possible, it may be measured somewhat by its visible results. Many of their best warriors had fallen in fights. As many more, perhaps, had died from the effects of disease or starvation, occasioned by the destruction of their winter supply of corn, which put them to the most cruel privations. It was now become a matter of difficulty to raise fifty warriors, where it had been easy to raise a hundred and fifty. In some cases only fragments of tribes remained, and in others the remnants had joined their nearest neighbors for mutual protection.

The hard, uncompromising fact, which stared this doomed people in the face, was that they could not afford even trifling losses, impossible to be repaired; and repair them they could not so long as they were being hunted like wild beasts. At the close of the war they held nothing that they could call their own within sixty miles of the sea-coast, between the Merrimac and Penobscot rivers. That, surely, was a visible sign of their impending doom.

QUEEN ANNE'S WAR

XV

THE NEW OUTLOOK
1702-1703

WAR broke out again between England and France in 1702.[1] In Europe it was called the War of the Spanish Succession; in the colonies, Queen Anne's War; as that princess had succeeded to the throne of England, made vacant by the death of her great brother-in-law William III.

Two dramatic incidents preceded the formal declaration of war. In taking leave of his grandson, a boy of seventeen, whom he was seating on the throne of Spain, in the teeth of Europe, Louis XIV. had made use of the picturesque and significant expression, "*Il n'y a plus de Pyrénées.*"[2]

This act gave birth to the formidable coalition meant to curb the ambition of the brilliant despot of Versailles.

The other event took place at the death-bed of the exiled James II. According to his biographer, Louis approached the bedside of the dying man, and after desiring those present to remain, *Death-bed of James II.* as if to give greater solemnity to what he was about to do, he said, "I am come, sir, to acquaint you, that whenever it shall please God to call your majesty out

---

[1] WAR was proclaimed at Westminster May 4, 1702.
[2] "THERE are no longer any Pyrenees."

of this world, I will treat your son, the Prince of Wales, in the same manner I have treated you, and acknowledge him, as he then will be, King of England." [1]

As an example of studied insolence this declaration is almost without a parallel in history. The insult stung Protestant England to the quick. In a few short months William followed James to the grave, but his spirit still survived, the resort to arms was fully accepted, and war declared on May 4, 1702.

Willing or unwilling, the colonies of the two great belligerents were none the less to be dragged into the

QUEEN ANNE.

quarrel, though under conditions widely different from those existing in Europe. The coming ordeal was indeed one to make men thoughtful, yet there are no signs of faltering.

There were in all New England about 120,000 persons of all ages. Although New England had the most men, Canada invariably had the better leaders.

[1] JAMES died at St. Germain, September 16, 1701, at the age of sixty-seven.

Military men were chosen there to conduct military enterprises. There were none such in New England. Border warfare was the only school in which her rude yeomanry had been trained up, and as soon as the exigency was over they returned to their farms or workshops. The Canadian yeomanry, on the contrary, being mostly hunters, boatmen, or wood-rangers, and always in the woods, were about as well skilled in forest warfare as the savages with whom they fraternized; so that disparity in numbers was by no means the true measure of the ability of the combatants.

Canada and New England compared.

There was, however, an enrolment of the colonial militia into regiments, troops, and companies. But with only an annual muster to bring them together their discipline stood small chance of being improved. The truth is that the spirit of the people was unalterably opposed to a permanent military establishment of any sort whatever. Their fathers, in their wisdom, had fixed the tradition that a standing army was a standing danger, and so the sons would have none of it. Hence the career of arms, with its twin incentives, thirst for glory and hope of promotion, was as good as shut to the ambitious young men of the day. Unlike the young Canadian nobility, they took the field from a stern sense of duty, not from choice, having it always in mind that they were soldiers only for the time being. Citizen soldiers are good for little until they have lost their identity as citizens in the soldier. Consequently, great enterprises had turned to great failures during the last war, not so much from faulty conceptions, as from the want of organization, discipline, command, and of that kind of confidence

Militia system.

which comes with them. For mere bush fighting raw
levies had indeed proved sufficient, but for such operations as laying siege to Quebec, something more than a
courageous rabble was needed.

This enrolment of the fighting strength of the colony
into troops and regiments, which, by the by, seldom
took the field as such, did, however, facilitate the mus-
tering of such bodies as were called out upon emergencies, when each regiment was required to furnish its
quota, either by voluntary enlistment or by draft.
Here we find the germ of that antiquated militia system
which endured well into the present century. More
curious still it is to note that the methods in force in
our own time, with all their abuses, were in full opera-
tion in what a later generation has been taught to look
back upon as a model of civic virtue. There were those
who slipped out of one colony into another to avoid
military service or, worse still, the tax-gatherer. In
order to put a stop to wholesale desertions from the
Its abuses. frontier towns, a law had to be passed
prohibiting all persons of sixteen years of
age from leaving them. Yet fear of the law was less
potent than fear of the scalping-knife. There were also
bounties and bounty-jumpers ; and there was falsifica-
tion of names and ages, as well as fraudulent raising of
provision returns, muster-rolls, and the like. And, finally, there was also the same eager buying up of sub-
stitutes by those whose courage or patriotism failed
them at the pinch. Such was the system and such were
its defects.

If the military arm was thus weak, the civil administration was powerless to strengthen it, because no soldier
had ever been put at the head of the government. Al-

though captain-general by virtue of his commission, only here and there one in the long line of governors was possessed of more military knowledge than could be picked up on the annual training-field, **Civilian leaders.** where the martial exercises were usually opened with a prayer.   Not that men who pray will not

fight, and fight well, but there is evidence that by this time the spirit that had prompted the fathers always to seek the Lord before unsheathing their swords, had grown somewhat weaker with the sons. In Vaudreuil, Dudley was going to be pitted against an adversary of experience in active warfare, and fare accordingly. And as events move on, it

LOUIS XIV.

will be seen that the English were driven to adopt the tactics of their enemies. In diplomacy, however, the two distinguished adversaries were more evenly matched.

In this war, as in the last, the colonies had for an adversary Louis XIV., surnamed the Great. If he had been as blind to the wants or perils of his transatlantic subjects as England was to hers, the contest would have

10

been more equal. Such, however, was not the case.
The whole situation on this side of the water was about
Louis XIV.   as well understood at Versailles as at Que-
guides the War. bec; so well indeed that in most cases
the movements of war-parties upon our frontiers were
generally first ordered or sanctioned or suggested by

GOVERNOR SIMON BRADSTREET.

Louis himself.
Though it may
seem strange that
this monarch, with
half Europe
leagued against
him, should thus
find time to turn
from great affairs
to little, it is no
less true.   While
he lived, Louis not
only insisted upon
ruling everything,
but upon knowing
everything.   It
was really there-
fore with him

that the English colonists were now measuring their
strength.

England's policy, briefly stated, like that of the savage
toward his offspring, was to leave her colonies to shift
for themselves. If they survived the ordeal, well and
good; if not, it would be because nature had not well
fitted them for the battle of life.

In the brief breathing time allowed from the ravages
of war, the wheel of time had moved relentlessly on-

ward.   Many of the chief actors had disappeared from
the stage.   Frontenac was dead at seventy-seven.   Bradstreet, one of the last survivors among the first-comers,
had died at the great age of ninety-four; so had Lord
Bellomont, after a brief rule of only two years; and so
had Stoughton, who had borne the burden of govern-

THE EARL OF BELLOMONT.

ment since the death of Phips.   Madockawando, the
father-in-law of St. Castin, had also succumbed to the
dread destroyer, with many more whose names once
struck terror to the hearts of their enemies.   In view of
its probable murderous character, it would perhaps be
too much to say that the war was popular in New England.   But the people were intensely loyal to the cause

of Protestantism, of which William was the recognized champion, and intensely partisan, too. They resented, as warmly as all Protestant England did, the insult put upon the nation in challenging William's right to the throne. Canada was wholly Catholic. Those in authority there took their cue from their royal master in declaring William a usurper. So that there was no want of antagonisms to fan the old embers into a fiercer blaze than ever.

The short administration of the Earl of Bellomont covered a season of recuperation from the exhaustion of war. He died in office on March 6, 1700. Stoughton, the lieutenant-governor, having died the next year, the government devolved for the first time upon the Council, a cumbrous body of twenty-eight persons, of whom a majority constituted the executive for the time being.

Joseph Dudley succeeded Lord Bellomont as governor. He came into office with a war on his hands, which, for ten years, taxed all his resources to the utmost, and the fact stands out in strong relief that his worst enemies, whom he took no great pains to conciliate, were forced to admire his abilities, much as they disliked him as a ruler and a man. Although the son of a Puritan of the sternest type, Dudley's own leanings were strongly toward absolutism. By the old Puritan party he was looked upon as the degenerate son of a noble sire ; but even they had the wisdom to see that the times had altered, since they made their own rulers, and were not indisposed to give Dudley a trial, thinking him perhaps, on the whole, better than a stranger. But they never could or would forget his having taken office just after the vacating of the old charter. That wound still rankled.

Dudley arrived at Boston, June 11, 1702. He was well received even by those members of the Council who had sent him to prison in the time of Sir Edmund Andros. In the face of political changes such as few men have experienced (and in his limited sphere of action Dudley was a consummate politician) the new governor could well afford to let bygones be bygones. No doubt his late opponents were more than pleased with the unlooked-for proffer of a general amnesty, and so for the present there was a truce to the old quarrels.

There was certainly need

GOVERNOR JOSEPH DUDLEY.

enough for united support from all parties. Dudley found his province assailed at once by war and pestilence. During the winter no less than three hundred inhabitants of Boston were carried off by the small-pox, a disease which had periodically scourged the larger towns since their first settlement, almost unopposed.

Looking abroad, for the most part the Indians remained in the same situation in which the close of the

war had left them, their villages being equivalent to
outposts guarding the main avenues to Canada, or
covering their lines of supply or retreat. And they
were situated just far enough from the English border
to make it difficult to attack them by surprise. Some
of the more wary among them, however, keenly realizing
the dangers to which they were exposed in time of war,
were easily persuaded by M. de Vaudreuil to withdraw themselves to Canada, ostensibly for their own
protection, but really as a defence against the Iroquois.
These seceding Abenakis were located at Becancour,
a little river flowing into the St. Lawrence, midway between Montreal and Quebec ; and at St. Francis, on the
river of that name, flowing into Lake St. Peter. They
were thus placed within supporting distance of each
other, under the keen eye of Vaudreuil and the watchful care of the Jesuit missionaries![1] Still others had
withdrawn from the Kennebec to Penobscot.

Dudley fully realized how much the peace of New
England depended upon holding the lately hostile tribes
Council at   firm to their professions of friendship. If
Casco.   they could be kept quiet the war would
be shorn of its terrors. It was therefore all-important
to know their present disposition, and to meet their
grievances, if such they had, in a spirit of conciliation
and just dealing. To this end he summoned them to a
council, which accordingly met at Casco,[2] June 20, 1703,

[1] THE seignory of Becancour was granted in 1647 to Sieur de Becancour. The Abenaki
village was on the east side of the river Becancour, at some distance from its mouth.
The seignory of St. Francis was granted in 1678 to Sieur de Crevier. The Indian
village lay on the east side of the river St. Francis, which communicates by a branch
with Lake Memphremagog, and so opened a practical route to New England, often
traversed by war-parties.

[2] THIS was New Casco fort, built at Falmouth in 1700 ; so called to distinguish it
from Old Casco (Fort Loyal) destroyed by the enemy in 1690.

and was largely attended by delegates from the different tribes. Hither came the old, seasoned, war chiefs
of the Penobscots, Norridgewocks, Androscoggins and
Pennacooks, armed and painted for the ceremony, accompanied by a numerous retinue of their wild followers.

When the council opened Dudley saluted the grave
sagamores present as his friends and brothers, and said
that he was come to reconcile whatever differences had
happened since the last treaty. After the usual pause,
the Indian orator who spoke for the rest assured the
governor that "as high as the sun was above the
earth," so far were their thoughts from breaking the
peace between them. In proof of sincerity they first
presented him with a belt of wampum, and then invited
him to go with them to the two heaps of stones, erected
to commemorate a former treaty at this place, affection-
ately called The Two Brothers.[1]   Still further to
strengthen the bond between them, both parties added
more stones to the piles before them. A little later, the
noted chiefs Bomazeen and Captain Samuel came in to
declare that they, too, were "as firm as the mountains,"
and should continue so "as long as the sun and moon
endured."

So far everything had gone smoothly. But something now occurred which disturbed the white men not
a little. The council was breaking up with the usual
noisy demonstrations of joy. When it came the turn of
each party to fire a salute, in ratification of the treaty,
upon being asked to do so the English fired first, without hesitation. But when the Indians fired, it was no-

---

[1] THIS name has since been taken by the two little islands lying off the Falmouth
shore.

ticed that their guns were loaded with ball.[1] Treachery seemed lurking in the air.

A round of festivities succeeded the deliberations of
the council. The Indians danced, sang, and shouted to
their hearts' content. Many presents were given them,
which were thankfully received ; and the assembly
broke up with fair promise that the harassing warfare
of former years would not be renewed. In this belief
the scattered settlers along the seaboard prepared to
stand their ground, all unconscious of the storm about
to burst upon their devoted heads.

[1] DUDLEY afterward wrote to Subercase, governor of Nova Scotia, laying bare the
treachery of his predecessor, Brouillan. Subercase had accused the provincial troops
of committing a sacrilegious act in digging up the heart of Brouillan from the place
where it was buried. Dudley responds in these terms : "About five years since I
had gone to Casco Bay to make an agreement with the Indians of my government.
There came to that place two Frenchmen of Port Royal, to whom M. de Brouillan had
promised two hundred pistoles to kill me. These Frenchmen came to Casco Bay dis-
guised as Indians, and were present when I was making my agreement, but their hearts
failed them in what they had undertaken. Some time after, one of the two, being a
prisoner, and brought here, acknowledged it to me, in my house, on his knees."

XVI

SIX TERRIBLE DAYS

August, 1703

WHILE Dudley was congratulating himself upon having brought the Indian tribes so emphatically to commit themselves in favor of peace, Vaudreuil, governor of Canada, through his agents, the missionaries, was doing his utmost to prevail on them to renew the war. Even while the conference at Casco was in progress, it is asserted that the Sokokis, of Pigwacket, were only waiting for a French reinforcement to begin their march for the border.[1]

Under the late treaty[2] the French claimed to the Kennebec. The English denied this claim in toto. It was no very difficult matter to bring the tribes living to the east of that river, who had suffered in the past from the encroachments of the English, into full and entire accord with the French upon this question. Boundary question. It was plain enough, even to the dullest perception, that, unless prevented, the English would move back into the disputed territory, from which they had so recently been driven, without loss of time. Already there was talk of rebuilding Pemaquid. Vau-

---

[1] PENHALLOW.

[2] THE treaty of Ryswick restored Acadia to France, without fixing its boundaries. The English still insisted that the St. Croix was the true dividing line, but in 1700 both parties agreed upon the St. George, the English having no settlements beyond that river, while the French had.

dreuil thus had ample material with which to work upon the fears or prejudices of the eastern tribes, and he hastened to improve it.

As soon as hostilities had actually ceased many of the fugitive settlers had gone back to their deserted homes between Wells and Falmouth. If his plans should succeed, Vaudreuil aimed at nothing short of making a clean sweep of all the settlements in Maine. If those in the west were destroyed, he argued that there would be less danger of the English renewing those in the east. So the work was to be thoroughly done, by making a combined attack on all the settlements at once. In this way one would be prevented from helping the other, the panic would become more widespread, and the conquest probably be all the more easy. But first of all the Abenakis of Maine must be worked up to the proper pitch of fury against the English.

A pretext was soon found. It chanced that while St. Castin was away from home, some lawless Englishmen had plundered his house. He being an Abenaki chief, the Penobscots instantly resented it as an insult offered to the whole tribe. The two missionaries, Bigot of Penobscot, and Rale of Norridgewock, seized the opportunity thus offered still further to inflame their wrath; so that what ought to have been equitably adjusted, without provoking ill-blood, was wickedly used to plunge the nations into war again. This, at any rate, was the assigned cause. But the other fact that in **Pretext for war.** less than eight weeks a general assault began on all the settlements of Maine, denotes more preparation than so trivial a provocation would seem to imply. Be that as it may, on August 10th, several bands of French and Indians, clearly act-

ing in concert, and estimated at not less than five
hundred in all, suddenly fell upon the reviving villages
of Maine with fire and slaughter.

The blow seems to have fallen first upon Wells,[1] and
thence have been taken up all along the shore as far as
Falmouth. Not one hamlet escaped. At Wells thirty-
nine persons were either killed or carried away into
captivity.

There is a local tradition touching an adventure of
one Stephen Harding, who kept the ferry at the Kenne-

ANCIENT FERRY-WAY, KENNEBUNK RIVER, ME.

bunk River, where all travel passed at that time. The
story has probably lost nothing in being handed down
through several generations, yet its main incidents are
believed to be true.

At this early day the only travelled ways closely
hugged the seashore, taking advantage of the hard sand
beaches, passing the intercepting streams by fords or
ferries, and cutting across the gray, old, rock-ribbed
headlands by strips of half-worked roads, practicable

[1] WELLS then included what is now Kennebunk. News of the attack reached
Boston on the 11th. This was followed on the next day by exaggerated accounts of
the affair. "August 12, at night, news comes from Wells that they have buried 15—
durst not go to bury their uttermost (outermost). Lost, as they fear, 60." *Sewall
Papers.*

only for the two-wheeled carts then in use, yet dignified by the sounding title of the King's Highways.[1]

Harding's log-house stood on a swell of ground enclosed between Gooch's beach, the main river, and a tidal creek making in from it toward the west. From here the view is clear and open across the beach for a mile toward Wells, so that no one could approach the house that way unseen in the daytime, if the occupants were on the lookout.

Tradition reports Harding to have been a man of uncommon physical strength and courage—in fact, a veritable giant. The Indians knew him well, and he knew them of old.

One morning, on going out of the house, Harding saw quite a large body of some sort of people coming over the beach from the direction of Wells. He was at first undecided whether they were friends or foes, but their wary movements soon satisfied him that they must be Indians. They were, in fact, the raiders who had ravaged Wells the day before, returning with their prisoners and booty.

It was now Harding's turn to be alarmed. Fortunately the redskins were still a good way off; but there Harding's was not a moment to lose. Hurrying escape. back to the house, Harding told his wife to take their little year-old infant, make haste with it across the creek, and hide herself at a certain oak-tree, until he should join her. The terrified woman snatched up the child, and ran off with it, as she was told; while Harding, more bold than prudent, remained behind to protect his property, should his fears prove groundless.

Meantime, the thought struck Harding that more

[1] IN some localities in Maine these ancient roads may be traced to this day.

Indians might be lurking about his premises. If so he would inevitably be caught in the toils.

It turned out as he thought, for upon going into his blacksmith shop, and giving a loud whoop, four stout Indians started up from the ground where they had lain concealed, and made a rush for him. Harding now thought only of making his own escape. His cornfield offered the only cover at hand, so into it he

SCENE OF HARDING'S EXPLOIT.

plunged, making rapid strides for the creek. But while running at the top of his speed, who should he see but his wife lying prostrate among the corn? Overcome by terror, the poor woman had sunk down helpless, after going only a few rods from the house.

Harding's extraordinary strength was now put to the test. Taking his wife under one arm, and her babe under the other, he dashed on again for the creek, plunged in, waded through mud and water, to the opposite bank, and dived into the woods beyond, while his

baffled pursuers stood looking at him from the shore he
had just left.

Harding's faithful dog had followed close at his
master's heels. The animal was killed for fear that his
barking would betray the route the fugitives had taken.
They then plunged deeper into the woods. All that
night they lay hid. Late on the next day they reached
Storer's garrison, at Wells, weary, footsore, and famishing. It is more than probable that the Indians wished
to take Harding alive, or he would hardly have got off
so easily. They showed great admiration for his prow-
ess in this affair, often saying, when speaking of him,
" Much man Stephen; all same one Indian."

After rifling Harding's house, pulling up his corn,
and killing his hogs, the savages crossed the river to
William Larrabee's, whose wife and three children were
inhumanly butchered, while the husband and father
was a horrified witness of the deed from a place where
he had concealed himself.

From here they moved two miles farther up the river
to Philip Durell's house, at Kennebunk Landing. They
found no one at home here but the women and children,
Durell himself being absent. When he did get back,
at nightfall, it was to a desolate home.[1]

Cape Porpoise, being inhabited by only a few fishermen, was wholly laid waste, and, for the second time in
Maine beset.   its history, depopulated. Upon the ap-
                pearance of the enemy at Winter Harbor [2]
the inhabitants took refuge in Fort Mary. Here the

---

[1] BRADBURY, *History of Kennebunkport*, further relates that the Indians carried
off, at this time, Mrs. Durell, her two daughters, Susan and Rachel, and two sons, one
of whom, Philip, was an infant. The prisoners were taken as far as Pigwacket (Fryeburg, Me.) when Mrs. Durell was allowed to go home with her infant. Both daughters
married Frenchmen, and refused to return after the war.

[2] THOUGH locally preserved, the name is now merged in that of Biddeford Pool.

attack was repulsed,[1] but that made on the stone fort[2] at the falls, above, was more successful, thirty-five persons being killed or taken there. At Scarborough, the garrison bravely held out until assistance reached them. At Spurwink,[3] a neighborhood of Cape Elizabeth, inhabited almost exclusively by families of the name of Jordan, no less than twenty-two persons of that name were killed or taken. At Purpooduck, another little fishing hamlet of Cape Elizabeth, finding no men at home, the marauders murdered twenty-five and carried off eight of the women and children.

It only remained to dispose of the fort and settlement at Falmouth. The veteran Major John March was then in command of the fort. Stratagem was first resorted to. While the main body of assailants kept out of sight, three chiefs boldly advanced to the gate with a flag of truce. At first, March paid no attention to the flag, but finally went out to meet it, taking with him two others, all three being unarmed. His men were, however, warned to be watchful against treachery. Only a few words had been exchanged, when the Indians drew their hatchets from under their blankets, and fell with fury upon March and his companions. March being a man of great physical strength, succeeded in wresting a hatchet from one of his assailants, with which he kept them off until a file of men came to his rescue. Luckily he escaped with a few slight wounds.

---

[1] WILLIAMSON, *History of Maine*, following Penhallow, errs in saying that this garrison was taken. It was then commanded by Captain Turfrey, who writes to Governor Dudley under date of August, 1703, to the above effect. See *Massachusetts Archives*. Under date of August 16th, Dudley wrote to Winthrop, saying that the forts at Saco, Blackpoint, and Casco were assaulted, but were yet safe. *Winthrop Papers*.

[2] THIS fort stood on the river bank, just below the falls, in what is now the Laconia Company's premises.

[3] THE attack here was known in Boston on the 12th.

His less fortunate companions, Phippeny and Kent, both old men, fell under the blows of the other savages. One of his guards was also shot down from an ambush near by, probably placed with the view of rushing into the fort if the attempt to surprise March's party had succeeded.

Having failed to gain the fort by treachery, the savages next fell upon the scattered cabins outside; which were soon blazing on all sides. This done they returned to attack the fort. For six days the weak garrison defended itself unflinchingly. During this time the besiegers were joined by the confederate bands, **Falmouth holds out.** who had been destroying all before them at the west. Beaubassin, the French leader, now pressed the siege with greater vigor and skill. Covered by the bank on which the fort stood, the savages set to work undermining it on the water side. For two days and nights they steadily wormed their way under the bank toward the palisade without any hindrance from the garrison, and were in a fair way to have carried the fort by assault, when the arrival of the provincial galley compelled them to give over their purpose in a hurry, as that vessel's guns raked their working party. On the following night they decamped. Two hundred canoes were destroyed, and an English shallop retaken by the relieving galley.[1]

One hundred and thirty persons were either killed or taken during this bloody onset. At night the sky was lit up by the fires kindled by the Indians. Maine had nearly received her death-blow. Throughout her en-

---

[1] JOHN MARCH was a native of Newbury, Mass. He was immediately made a lieutenant-colonel for his gallantry in this affair, the General Court afterward voting him £50, in consideration of his brave defence and the wounds he received.

tire border nothing was left standing except a few isolated garrisons, and it was a question if even these
could hold out much longer. The deception had been
so complete, the onset so sudden, that organized resistance was out of the question. The English, heedless
of the signs of the gathering storm, had been lulled
into a state of false security, and the awakening was
terrible indeed.

11

XVII

THE WAR GROWS IN SAVAGERY

1703

THE preceding chapter closed the record of six terrible days which had left a track of blood for fifty miles along the stricken seaboard of Maine. How fared it with the exposed frontiers of New Hampshire after this new outbreak? We have scarcely patience to continue the sad recital of indiscriminate slaughter, which cast the silence of death over so many desolated hearthstones in this ancient province.

On August 17th a war party, led by Captain Tom, set upon Hampton Village. Five of the inhabitants were killed, one of whom, a widow Mussey, was a noted Friend. They also plundered two houses here before a general alarm brought the people together in sufficient numbers to drive the assailants away.

Fear and dismay now spread on the wings of the wind. It could never be known where the subtle enemy would strike next; hence the widespread alarm which at once turned every man's thoughts to his own means of defence. Little enough could be done where **Steps for defence.** the enemy possessed every advantage— particularly that of choosing his own time and place of attack. Still, the usual measures were resorted to. The people were ordered into the garrisons. Only the most necessary labor was performed, and that

went on under the protection of an armed guard. The
women and children were ordered to be sent out of the
Maine garrisons to a place of safety. Wadleigh's and
Somerby's troops were quartered at Wells to prevent
the discouraged inhabitants from deserting the place in

ANCIENT SEAT OF THE PIGWACKETTS, FRYEBURG, ME.

a body ; while a foot company of a hundred men was
ordered to man the remaining garrisons there, the horse
being designed to keep the roads well scouted and patrolled.

But for these prompt and efficient measures it is
doubtful where the panic would have ended.

Dudley had thus met the outbreak firmly. In August he was making up a marching force of five hundred men, soon increased to nine hundred, and by September to eleven hundred, half of whom, however, were quartered in garrisons, leaving his disposable force still too small for emergencies. He therefore turned to his neighbors for help, though it must be admitted with no very marked success. Connecticut, indeed, sent a troop into Hampshire County, but Rhode Island held aloof.

It was well understood that the enemy after striking their blows would retreat into their own fastnesses, and Dudley had determined to follow them there.

In October, Colonel March marched at the head of three hundred and sixty men for Pigwacket. Long disuse had so obliterated the old trails that the guides became bewildered and could not find their way, compelling March to return empty-handed. Nothing daunted, Dudley immediately fitted out a second expedition.

All was to no purpose. Long before these forces could be gathered together the enemy had fled beyond reach, and from safe coverts his scouts were no doubt watching the futile efforts of the pursuers as they floundered on through the wooded defiles of the great northern wilderness, where range rises upon range until the great White Hills break upon the sight in all their majesty.

Worse still, while these forces were out the savages, like so many wasps, brushed away for the moment, began their depredations in Maine again. At Black Point, Captain Hunnewell and nineteen more belonging to the garrison there, were waylaid as they were going out to work in the neighboring meadows, and all but

one man either killed or taken.[1] This bloody affair took
place on October 6th. Emboldened by their success, by
which the force there was greatly weak-   **Black Point
ened, the savages next assaulted the gar-   harried.**
rison itself. Eight men under Lieutenant Wyatt, with
the help of two vessels then lying in the harbor, held
out until they were able to make good their retreat on
board the vessels, when the triumphant enemy quickly
set the fort on fire ; and so that link in Dudley's chain
of defence was broken apart.

After performing this exploit the Indians renewed
their outrages in and about York and Berwick, seemingly intent upon destroying every white settlement in
Maine. At York the wife and five children of Arthur
Bragdon were slain, and Mrs. Hannah Parsons and her
daughter carried into captivity.

It being worse than useless to play at hide and seek
with these vigilant foemen, who first showed themselves
in one place and then in another, far distant, the authorities persevered in the plan of hunting them down
in their own villages. Usually, it was next to impossible for white men to approach them undiscovered,
and after long and frightful marches a few deserted
wigwams would be all that the disappointed rangers
could find. This autumn, however, Colonel March was
more fortunate. During a second march to Pigwacket
his men killed six Indians, and took six more. That he
should have travelled so far to effect so little, or that
so trifling a result should be hailed as a great success,
is a telling commentary upon the peculiar character of
Indian warfare. Nothing more discouraging or more

[1] THE spot where this affair occurred is on Prout's Neck, in Scarborough, and has
ever since been known as Massacre Pond.

exasperating can well be imagined, yet there was no help for it.

This success induced the Massachusetts government to offer a bounty of twenty [1] pounds for every Indian scalp, taken by volunteer ranging parties, thus bringing into the conflict the new, and to this later generation repugnant, incentive of private gain. This was treating Indians and wolves alike. It was even more; for thus to authorize the forming of scalping parties was to put those engaging in them on a level with the savages themselves. Yet public feeling had reached a point when no more was thought of killing an Indian than a wolf. Penhallow, who is by no means a bloody-minded writer, says that this bounty prompted some and animated others to "a noble emulation." The Rev. Solomon Stoddard, minister of Northampton, venerated for his virtues, who lived in the midst of hostile alarms, declared that the Indians should be looked upon only as "thieves and murderers," and he proposed hunting them down with dogs "the same as we do bears," as the best and only way of tracking them to their dens.[2] He says, what is quite true, that the same thing had been done with success in Virginia, and goes on to quiet any qualms that might arise on the score of inhumanity by the plea of an inexorable necessity. There is no doubt whatever that he spoke the general opinion. At that very moment his own flock were anxiously discussing the chances of having the Indians come down upon them without a moment's warning. Then again the

Scalp bounty.

---

[1] HUTCHINSON and others say forty, but the Act of September 7, 1703, now before me, says twenty.

[2] LETTER to Governor Dudley, October 22, 1703. Dr. Dwight says he was held "in a reverence which will scarcely be rendered to any other man."

atrocities of the last war were now freshly recalled with
fear and trembling ; and where hardly one family could
be found, along a wide extent of border, not mourning
the loss of a relative or a friend, the morality of any ef-
fectual method of retaliation was not likely to be called
in question.

It resulted that no less than seven companies of
rangers were engaged in scouring the woods for scalps
during the winter, under the bounty act—a stroke of
policy relieving the authorities of the expense of main-
taining an equal force of enlisted men. In their
marches these rangers made use of snowshoes, as the
Canada Indians had done in their de-   Snowshoe
scents, for which reason they were styled   men.
snowshoe men. Thus equipped, they were able to
reach the farthest haunts of the savages in the depth of
winter, without more fatigue than the same march
would have caused them in summer.

One company only succeeded in finding any Indians.
This was the one commanded by Colonel William
Tyng, of Dunstable, who went to the headquarters of
" Old Harry," so-called, at Lake Winnipesaukee, where
five Indians, including " Old Harry " himself, were
slain.[1]

All could not prevent the daring enemy from molest-
ing the settlers when and how they pleased, and Indian
cunning was often more than a match for English wit.
Thus, on December 20th, three out of five Saco men,
who were bringing home wood, were found slain.
Seven more, who were also out of the garrisons, luckily

---

[1] BESIDES the bounty, the heirs of the actors in this affair were subsequently
granted a tract of land at first called " Harry's " Town, then Tyngstown, then Derry-
field, and lastly Manchester, N. H.

made their escape to Wells. Shortly after four men belonging to Captain Gallop's sloop were killed at Casco Bay, after landing from their boat.[1] Within a week, a
Berwick assailed. most desperate attempt was made to destroy Berwick,[2] the border town of Maine. It was on the morning of January 28th, when the ground was covered with snow, that a war-party, small in numbers but great in daring, fell suddenly upon Neale's garrison. Fortunately the sentinel discovered their approach in season to give the alarm, but a young girl, and a young man who happened to be at some distance off, had to run for their lives. The girl was quickly overtaken and knocked down with the blow of a tomahawk, but the lad still kept on and had almost reached the garrison when his pursuers, seeing him likely to escape them, fired at and shot him down. Believing him dead, they kept on toward the garrison, and were come close up to it when a well aimed shot from the flanker laid the leader dead on the ground. While his comrades were busy trying to drag the body away, the young man came to himself again, and got safely into the garrison. The assailants then fell upon Smith's garrison, but the inmates there being ready to receive them, they were soon beaten off and one or two of their number wounded. Meantime, the firing had aroused the people at Brown's garrison. Captain Brown, with about a dozen good men, made all the
Captain Brown's bravery. speed he could to the relief of his neighbors. He came upon the Indians as they were engaged in binding up the plunder they had found in some out-houses, bravely ran upon them and put

[1] Sewall's *Diary*.

[2] Often called by its Indian name of Newichewannock in the accounts of the time.

them to flight. Brown's party fired briskly at the fugitives as they ran off through the snow, wounding several, as afterward appeared by the bloody tracks in the snow, and making them leave all their plunder behind, besides some of their own hatchets and blankets. The want of snow-shoes prevented the English from pursuing until the next day. In this raid the savages burned two houses and killed about seventy cattle, besides a good many sheep.[1]

A little later in the season, on February 8th, a small party of the enemy made a more successful descent upon Joseph Bradley's garrison, situated in the northerly part of Haverhill.   Here the inmates had gone about their usual employments, so thoughtless of danger that the gates of the garrison were left standing wide open. Bradley's wife, Hannah, who had been made a prisoner at the same time as Mrs. Dustan, was busy **Mrs. Bradley** stirring a kettle of boiling soap, over the **taken.** fire, while Jonathan Johnson, a soldier, was loitering about the house, when a small party of savages, rushed in upon them, tomahawk in hand. Mrs. Bradley instantly flung a ladleful of boiling soap into the face of the foremost savage, putting him *hors de combat*, but his companions seized her, killed Johnson on the spot, and hurried the rest of the inmates off into the woods before an alarm could spread to the village.

Thus this heroic woman became for the second time a captive. She was now obliged to travel on foot in the deep snow, carrying a burden that would have been heavy for a strong man to bear, with no other food for days together except some tough scraps of dried skins

[1] CAPTAIN JOHN MARCH's letter to Governor Dudley, dated the day after the attack; and probably the same affair mentioned by Penhallow, who makes the Indians lose nine killed, though March knew of but one.

or a few ground nuts, or the bark of trees, wild onions and lily roots—in fact, the proper sustenance of wild beasts. To heighten her misery, a child was born to her during the long and weary march to Canada. With a mother's devotion, Mrs. Bradley sought to save its life at all risks, but this was next to impossible in the face of such hardships as her condition imposed. Her captors seemed to take a fiendish delight in torturing the hapless little waif of the wilderness, and at length put it to death by throwing hot embers into its mouth to stop its crying.[1]

During this winter Massachusetts and New Hampshire together had 890 men in service, New Hampshire turning out every fourth man fit for military duty. The exigencies of the times called for the most arduous labors on the part of the civil authorities, whose sessions often reached far into the night. Communication was painfully slow. What can now be done in a few minutes then required as many hours, days even. The startling words "Haste! post-haste!" affixed to the cover of an important despatch, shows, at most, a rider galloping up hill and down at the top of his speed. Relays could not always be arranged for in advance. There were no bridges over the great rivers. A drowsy ferryman, knocked up in the middle of the night, would not be apt to hurry himself overmuch. Arrived at his destination, his despatch delivered, the courier would snatch a few hours' sleep, while the orders were being got ready for his return. This was the day of alarm guns, beacons and bonfires. Yet death moved as swiftly then as now.

---

[1] Mrs. BRADLEY was sold to the French, and redeemed by her husband in the spring of 1705.

Late in January, as the council was breaking up at Boston, Colonel Schuyler walked into the chamber, accompanied by a young man of soldierly port, known to a few there as Colonel Samuel Vetch. Few thought of him as destined to play so conspicuous a part in the near future as subsequently turned out to be the case. Yet Vetch was no less destined to make his mark in these unquiet times, because they were exactly suited to his genius and his ambition. And in the years to come Vetch was sure to appear in every important crisis.

Samuel Vetch.

Vetch is first heard of as one of the survivors of the memorable Darien colony of 1688–89, he being then a young Scotch captain attached to that ill-fated and ill-conceived expedition. From Darien Vetch came to New York, where his energetic character and natural abilities soon won for him friends and social position, as is evinced by his marrying into the Livingston family soon after.[1] Never very scrupulous, he seems easily to have fallen into the loose notions, too prevalent among a certain class of merchants of that day, for we presently find him charged with carrying on an illicit trade with Canada. He is next heard of in Boston, seeking employment in the wars.

---

[1] HE married the daughter of Robert Livingston.

XVIII

THE SACKING OF DEERFIELD

February 28, 1704

HAVING struck a benumbing blow at the sea-coast settlements of Maine, and thrown all that frontier into a
state of unspeakable terror and confusion, and while
the colonial forces, hurried to that quarter, were vainly
scouring the woods in pursuit of the insolent raiders,
the enemy was getting ready to repeat the blow at a
point so remote that little preparation had been made
to receive it.

The village of Deerfield, the frontier settlement of
the Connecticut Valley, had been singled out for swift
destruction.

As the outpost covering all of the settlements lower
down the valley, it was important to hold it at all
hazards, since their safety demanded that the enemy
should be met and checked at the threshold.

Moreover, as this group of thriving settlements was
practically isolated from the sea-coast, but within supporting distance of the river towns of Connecticut
colony, Dudley saw that help should come from there in
case of need. Nothing, in short, could be plainer. Besides, these half dozen towns which were
the object of Dudley's warm solicitude,
actually covered Connecticut from invasion. This also
was undeniable. Dudley pressed these facts home upon

Connecticut Valley.

Governor Winthrop [1] with considerable warmth, until
a sort of tacit understanding was reached that Connecticut should aid in defending that part of the valley in
question, upon the appearance of danger. [2]

Dudley, who had so many irons in the fire, was compelled to be satisfied with these half measures, simply
because he could do no better. He knew—everybody
knew—that to repel an Indian attack forces must be
on the spot, not at a distance. The moral effect, however, was good. Including the promised aid, there
were in the four towns of Northampton,   Fighting
Hadley, Hatfield, and Deerfield about five   strength.
hundred fighting men. By adding Springfield, the
whole valley probably could muster at least six hundred
and fifty men. [3] But not more than half of these could
be put in the field without leaving the towns to which
they belonged unguarded, and that was not to be
thought of.

The physical defences were of the rudest kind.

Some years before, all or most of the houses in Deerfield had been enclosed by a stout timber stockade ; but
with the growth of the place, both old and   Deerfield
new settlers were forced to build outside,   alarmed.
where their farms lay. [4] Inside and out, there were
forty houses, or, as some say, forty-one. Warned by the
kidnapping of two persons belonging there that Indians

[1] USUALLY called Fitz-John, the prefix being used to distinguish him from his father
and grandfather, John Winthrop.

[2] THE correspondence between the two governors on this head is in the *Winthrop
Papers*.

[3] ACCORDING to a report made by Colonel Samuel Partridge, who had military
charge over the valley settlements, Hatfield had 100 men of its own, Hadley the same
number, Northampton 150, and Deerfield 25 just after the raid. Springfield is omitted
from the list. Adding the sixty from Connecticut, and allowing Deerfield only the
same number as Hatfield, the six towns could muster not less than 650 fighting men.

[4] LETTER of Rev. John Williams to Governor Dudley. *Massachusetts Archives*.

were lurking near them, aware that their village was greatly exposed to attack, the alarmed settlers had now taken refuge inside the stockade, where they were over-crowded, restless, discontented, and as time wore on without anything further occurring to excite their fears, too much disposed to regard the whole affair as a false alarm.

Most of the old stockade having rotted away, it was dangerous to let it remain in that condition, and also dangerous to go into the woods after the timber to re-new it. ' In fact, the imperilled settlers hardly knew which way to turn. They were afraid to remain, yet forbidden to remove. Many were on the point of leav-ing, probably some did leave, but as their fears abated, pride or a careful eye to their own, kept them mostly steady at the post of duty. This was the situation in the autumn of 1703.

Meantime, Colonel Schuyler of Albany had learned from some friendly Mohawks, who were returning from a visit to their Canada relations, that an attack on Deer-field was actually in preparation. Schuyler lost no time in notifying Governor Dudley. In the valley the news caused a panic. All occupations save those of watching and scouting were laid aside. The Connecticut horse came up at a gallop. But as time wore on and no enemy appeared, the panic subsided. Like the old cry of "wolf!" it failed, at last, to arouse even a languid in-terest. So the autumn passed away and the long winter set in.

It was in the depth of winter, and the snow lay deep along the peaceful valley, and high up the rugged mountain sides. The river, now solidly frozen over, formed an ice-bridge from bank to bank. The nearest village lay some miles below. There was little for the husbandman to do, except to watch the slow lengthening of the days, as the morning sun climbed the eastern hills, or note his brilliant setting behind the darkening mountains on the west. So he woke, and dozed and slept again without care and without fear.

But while these settlers were thus resting in the most profound security, all unknown to them the Governor of Canada was launching one of his murder- **Rouville's war-** ous expeditions against them. The his- **party.** torian, Charlevoix, says it consisted of two hundred and fifty men, commanded by Hertel de Rouville; other writers place the numbers much higher. It matters little; there were enough and more than enough for the terrible work cut out for them here. Perhaps the Jesuit historian forgot to include the Indians who joined De Rouville later.

It was a frightful march to look forward to; though in some respects, perhaps not so difficult as if made at a different season of the year, the party being equipped with snow-shoes, on which they could move with ease and rapidity over the frozen crust. Streams could be passed on the ice; swamps were no longer to be avoided; rough or broken ground offered no hindrance. Yet was the march long and painful. At each halting-place, sheltered only from the cutting blasts by burying themselves in the depths of the forest, these hardy rangers would scrape out shallow burrows in the snow, in which they lay huddled together around a few fagots, like so many shaggy dogs, until roused to begin the march again. And like dogs they would have only to shake themselves to be ready. The bearded Canadian and the painted savage shared this wretched bivouac together, spurred on by the thirst for booty and slaughter.

This winter of 1703-4 was one of unusual severity. The cold was intense. Indeed, the elements themselves seem to have conspired against this lonely outpost among the mountains. Cold had bridged the streams; had smoothed the way over the deep snows, which in falling had so drifted up against the stockade as to make scaling it in one or more places from the outside an easy matter. Yet, instead of redoubling their vigilance, the heedless settlers seem to have thought the severity of the weather their greatest safeguard.

One man only could not shake off the feeling of impending danger. This was John Williams, minister of **Rev. John** Deerfield, a man of much force of character, **Williams.** learning and piety. So strongly had the presentiment of evil taken possession of him, that he preached it in his sermons. Finding this time thrown away, he applied for and obtained a reinforcement of twenty soldiers just four days before the murderous assault, about to be related, took place. Williams was now undoubtedly easier in his mind, thinking that a more strict watch would be kept. There were wooden watchtowers, called flankers, set up along the stockade, in which the sentinels took up their posts at nightfall, remaining till daybreak. The night of Monday, February 28th, came.

At the hour when the mothers of Deerfield were hushing their little ones to sleep, little dreaming it was to be that sleep from which there is no waking, De Rouville's cut-throats were going into bivouac, only two miles from the village. Not daring to light fires, they shivered through the long hours as best they could, while warmth and comfort reigned in the happy homes so soon to be made desolate.

Finding all quiet, shortly after midnight De Rouville aroused his men for the assault.

Like shadows they stole out of the woods, where they had lain huddled together for warmth. As the crust had grown hard enough to bear a man's weight, snow-shoes were left behind. Great caution was taken in approaching the stockade. There were frequent halts to listen. It was needless. The faithless guards had left their posts, and the sleeping village lay wholly at the mercy of the invaders.

It was about two hours before day when Rouville's vanguard approached the stockade, unseen and unchallenged. Quick to act, the foremost assailants lightly mounted over the snowdrifts, let themselves drop down on the inside, and ran to unbar the gate to their companions, who rushed into the stockade, screeching and yelling like so many fiends incarnate. They then scattered themselves right and left, so as to let none escape, and the work of slaughter began.

Savage onset.

The pen is powerless to portray the fright and bewilderment of that moment. To the suddenly awakened inhabitants it must have seemed like the dawning of the Judgment Day.

The experience of one was the experience of all, and Mr. Williams has told his own in a most graphic way.[1] His house was one of the very first to be attacked. Leaping out of bed in his shirt, Williams ran for the door, just as the Indians had forced their way in. Two

---

[1] In *The Redeemed Captive Returning to Zion*, of which many editions have been printed.

soldiers lodged with him. Shouting to them to get up, Williams darted back to his bedside for his pistol, **Williams taken.** snatched it up, levelled it at the foremost Indian as he was entering the room, and pulled the trigger. Luckily for Williams it missed fire, or his life, probably, would have paid the forfeit on the instant. He was instantly seized, disarmed and bound, and kept standing for near an hour in the cold, without a rag of clothes on except his shirt. Meantime, two of his young children, with his negro woman, were dragged to the door and despatched; while Mrs. Williams, brutally turned out of a sick bed, with five more of her children, was reserved to share her husband's captivity. The house was then ransacked from top to bottom.

While the Indians were thus employed, John Stoddard, one of the two soldiers who lodged with Williams that night, was aroused by the uproar. Only one avenue of escape was open to him, and of that he hastened to avail himself. It was the work of a moment to jump out of bed, throw up the window, leap to the ground, and make for the river, over the snow, all undressed and in his bare feet. The snow was three feet deep, and the nearest settlement several miles away. At the **Stoddard's escape.** moment of making his hasty exit he had the presence of mind to snatch up his cloak. This was quickly torn into strips and wrapped around his benumbed feet, sandal-wise. In this wretched plight he continued his flight to Hatfield, where he arrived more dead than alive, to give an account of the bloody work going on above.

Ensign John Sheldon's house stood near the northwest angle of the stockade. It was well for him that

he was not at home. Mrs. Sheldon was startled from a
sound sleep by the din of blows, raining down against
her door. The poor woman could only sit up in bed
and listen in an agony of terror and suspense. The
door, being barred, re-
sisted every effort made
to force it. Failing in
this, the assailants then
set to work Sheldon's house
chopping a   pillaged.
hole with their axes,
and when they had suc-
ceeded in doing so, a
savage put his eye to it
and peered in. Someone
was seen stirring in the
dim light within. In-
stantly a musket was
thrust in and fired.[1] The
fatal bullet struck poor
Mrs. Sheldon, as she
was in the act of ris-
ing from her bed, and
she fell back upon it a
corpse.

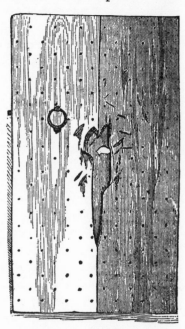

DOOR OF SHELDON HOUSE, WITH MARKS OF
AXES.

Meantime, her son John and his wife Hannah, who
slept upstairs, and were also awakened by the tumult,
sought to escape by jumping out of the window. The
snow broke the force of the fall somewhat. Young
Sheldon quickly scrambled to his feet unhurt, and made
for the woods, which he fortunately gained, and by

---

[1] THE house was torn down in 1848, but the door is still preserved in the museum at
Deerfield.

keeping well under cover succeeded in reaching the village below, spreading the alarm as he went. His wife, less fortunate, sprained her ankle in the fall, and being thus disabled, the marauders soon laid hands upon her.

This house was one of two left standing inside the stockade, besides the meeting-house. All the rest were set on fire, to burn along with the ghastly evidences of the morning's work. Death, in its most terrible form, thus overtook many who, to escape the tomahawk, had hid themselves in their cellars, only to be stifled beneath the ruins of their burning dwellings. When all was over, forty-seven of the unresisting inhabitants lay dead in or around their own homes. A hundred and twelve more, half dead with cold and fright, were crowded into the Sheldon house, spared for the time being for their reception.[1]

The only resistance that the marauders seem to have met with came from the house of Benoni Stebbins, just mentioned, in which seven brave men and a few courageous women successfully defended themselves during all the time that the carnage raged fiercest around them. Mr. Williams, himself an eye-witness of the determined efforts to capture this house, saw the same Indian whom he had failed to shoot shortly before, shot dead from it. Although the gallant Stebbins had fallen, and two of his brave companions were badly wounded, in spite of coaxing, promises, or threats, to all of which the heroic defenders turned a deaf ear, this one house continued to stand firm as a rock in the midst of the storm of fire and blood surging

Benoni Stebbins.

---

[1] COLONEL WHITING puts the loss at 49 killed, and nearly 100 taken. *Letter* to Governor Winthrop. Secretary Addington to Winthrop says 57 killed to 90 captives.— *Winthrop Papers*.

round it long after the enemy were masters of the rest
of the village.

It was somewhere about eight o'clock [1] when the
enemy's main body moved off toward their last camp,
guarding their long train of captives, and loaded down

ENSIGN SHELDON'S HOUSE, DEERFIELD, MASS.

with booty. After passing the river a halt was made to
recover their packs, as well as to prepare the prisoners
for the long march before them, by making them take off
their own shoes and put on Indian mocassins brought
for the purpose. Not all the marauders, however, had

[1] ACCOUNTS vary ; some make it earlier, some later.

marched off with their elated companions. A certain number of stragglers lagged behind, looking for plunder among the smoking ruins. Rouville dared not delay his retreat longer, well knowing that the country below would soon be up in arms. In fact, the glare of the burning buildings had been seen far down the snow-bound valley, spreading its tale of blood before it in the heavens, and calling every able-bodied man to the rescue. Among others some sixty mounted men from Hatfield were early on the road, but the snow was deep and the pace slow.

But the first to reach the ground were some scattered settlers, or fugitives, who rallied at the stockade of Jonathan Wells, situated at the lower end of the village, until some thirty or more eager and determined men had collected there, ready for action, when, under the lead of Wells, they charged on into the stockade, driving out the enemy's stragglers and rescuing the living inmates of the Stebbins house, which was still hard beset. Indeed, they were reduced to the very last extremity when this timely aid appeared on the scene.[1] The women and children who had been cooped up there instantly ran back to Captain Wells's garrison, while the men joined their rescuers in hot pursuit of the retreating enemy.

Meadow fight.

The pursuit was kept up for a mile and a half through the meadows, the exasperated English even throwing off hats and coats in their eagerness to overtake the fugitives. Wells, more prudent, vainly hallooed to them to halt. They were too much carried away by the chase to hear him.

---

[1] It took fire while its valiant defenders were fighting in the meadows, and was burned to the ground with its contents.

All at once a rapid discharge of musketry scattered them in confusion. They had run headlong into an ambuscade which Rouville had cunningly laid for them, upon hearing the firing. A swarm of infuriated savages now sallied out upon the little band of reckless white men, who, breathless with their previous exertions, sought safety in flight, keeping up a running fight, however, until the protection of the palisade was gained, when Rouville, satisfied with having cooled the ardor of his would-be pursuers, resumed his march the way he came. Nine of the English and five of the enemy fell in this rash encounter.

By midnight eighty well-armed, resolute men were assembled at Deerfield. Word was brought in by an escaped prisoner that the enemy had encamped not more than five miles off. By two o'clock of the next day the Connecticut men began to come in, when the question of making a further pursuit was put to a vote and decided in the negative, as being a thing too hazardous to attempt without snow-shoes, the snow being so deep that the pursuers would have to travel in the enemy's track, exposed to being flanked or ambushed at every step.

Much fault was found with the failure to pursue, and there can be little doubt that the check sustained on the previous day had something to do with it. Dudley gave vent to his disgust in his usual emphatic way. "I am oppressed," he declares, "with the remembrance of my sleepy neighbors at Deerfield, and all that came to their assistance, could not make out snow-shoes enough to follow a drunk, loaden, tyred enemy of whom they might have been masters to their honor."

Words fail to describe the horrors of that dreadful

march as day by day the wretched prisoners toiled on through the deep snows or up the steep mountain sides, staggering beneath the weight of their burdens. To fall behind was certain death. One blow of the tomahawk put a speedy end to the sufferings of those who failed to keep up with the rest. Poor Mrs. Williams was one of the first to meet this fate [1] at the hands of her inhuman master, while her anxious husband, after being roughly refused the privilege of helping his wife up a steep ascent, was vainly waiting for her at the van of the forlorn procession.[2]

At West River, sledges had been left, to which the wounded and young children were now transferred, thus enabling the marauders to move on more expeditiously. At White River, fears of a pursuit having abated, they separated into smaller parties, the better to subsist by hunting. Part kept on up the Connecticut, part struck off into the valley of White River, and across the Green Mountains to Lake Champlain. With these went Williams. Once, when his savage master roused him to begin the day's march, Williams found his feet so swollen and bruised that he could hardly stand erect. In vain he pleaded his inability to keep up the killing pace his master required. The savage significantly fingered the

March to Canada.

Williams's hardships.

---

[1] HER body was recovered, and her grave may still be seen in the old graveyard at Deerfield.

[2] HUTCHINSON, II., 128, strangely defends the murder of these helpless prisoners, as an act necessary to the safety of the captors. But this sort of reasoning would as easily justify the slaughter of prisoners by civilized as by uncivilized combatants. As a matter of fact, under the savage code, a prisoner ceased to have any rights whatever. His captor might kill or keep him, just as he saw fit. Enough were killed to glut his thirst for blood, and enough saved alive to satisfy his avarice. Nineteen persons were thus sacrificed during the retreat.

tomahawk in his belt, and Williams found his strength wonderfully revived by the threat of instant death. After forty days passed in the wilderness, the weak, haggard, and footsore captive reached the French fort at Chambly, bowed down under the most acute distress of mind and body, having been separated from his children, of whose fate he was wholly ignorant.

After suffering untold hardships, the surviving captives straggled into the Indian villages on the St. Lawrence. Some sixty were eventually restored to their friends, a few at a time, either by ransom or exchange. By a sort of irony Williams, himself, was exchanged for a noted freebooter, called Baptiste, October, 1706. Eunice, his ten-year-old daughter, was adopted by the Caughnawaga tribe, embraced the Catholic faith, and eventually married a full-blooded Caughnawaga Indian Eleazer Williams. named Amrusus, who thenceforth appears to have taken his wife's family name of Williams. From this marriage came a grandson, Eleazer Williams, who achieved considerable notoriety rather more than a generation ago by pretending to be the son of Louis XVI. Eleazer, however, became a Protestant, and in 1822 went to establish an Episcopal mission among the Menomonees and Winnebagoes at Green Bay, Wis., where he was married to Miss Madeline Jourdain of that place.[1]

[1] I FIND the following memorandum concerning him among my fathers MSS. "Williams came to Boston several times and used to visit me. He was short and stout and spoke with a strong French accent. His errand was begging, in which he had pretty good success. His figure was not unlike that represented in the prints of Louis XVI., hence somebody started the ridiculous story that he was the dauphin of that king. Williams himself was evidently willing that people should believe the story. He said to me, in conversation, 'that he could say nothing about it, as he knew nothing, but that there were strange and unaccountable things in the story, especially respecting a scar on his person, which agreed 'with a similar one on that of the dauphin.' Williams died at Hogansburg, N. Y., August 28, 1858."—See the Appendix to Dr. S. W. Williams's edition (1853) of *The Redeemed Captive*.

One feature of this raid, related by Penhallow, is worthy of mention, if true, if only for its singularity. He says that some of our captives, then in Canada, who knew that this expedition of Rouville's was on foot, took advantage of it to send letters to their friends, the bag in which they were carefully put being afterward found hanging to the limb of a tree in the highway. And he adds that these letters gave comforting intelligence to those who before were ignorant whether their friends were living or dead.[1]

Charlevoix puts Rouville's loss at only three Frenchmen, and a few savages (as if their losses were of small account); but adds that Rouville himself was wounded. Others make the number forty or fifty, judging from the dead bodies seen before the enemy had time to hide them under the ice of the river.

---

[1] PENHALLOW'S account seems to differ little from the others. He says he had it from the Rev. Mr. (Solomon) Stoddard, minister of Northampton, Mass., who was not likely to have been misinformed as to leading facts. Much valuable information is contained in the *Winthrop Papers*, which were not accessible to earlier writers. Through Hoyt's and Sheldon's histories of Deerfield, the sacking of that place has become one of the best known chapters of local history.

XIX

THE ENEMY CUTS OFF BOTH ENDS OF THE LINE
1704

THE tragedy of Deerfield sent a thrill of horror into every New England hamlet and home. What might not the daring enemy next attempt?

After the first shock was over, the authorities bestirred themselves to guard against a repetition of such disasters. This was something like shutting the stable-door after the horse had escaped. Bitterly was the parsimonious policy condemned that had laid the whole valley open to attack. But it was now too late to indulge in vain regrets. The enemy must first be reckoned with.

Unfortunately there was no longer that concert of action that had existed under the old confederacy of the New England colonies, by means of which the forces to be furnished by each in time of war were duly apportioned. Old feuds and old dislikes prevented any cordial understanding with Rhode Island. Winthrop, of Connecticut, seems to have made up his mind to do just enough to save himself from the charge of indifference, and no more, let the demand be ever so pressing.[1] But Deerfield seems to have stirred even his sluggish blood somewhat. In April he sent off sixty troopers to be posted at Hatfield until further orders. As re-

[1] SEE the correspondence in the *Winthrop Papers.*

gards the eastern frontier, Dudley now succeeded in
obtaining a hundred Pequots, Mohegans, and Niantics,
wards of Connecticut, to serve on that exposed front, on
the theory that Indians could be pitted against Indians
with advantage. He had first meant to post them at

GLIMPSE OF LAKE WINNIPESAUKEE.

the foot of Lake Winnipesaukee, as a cover to the New
Hampshire settlements, but had finally yielded to their
fears of being cut off there, and had left them posted at
Berwick instead. These Indians were under the command of Major Samuel Mason, of Stonington. They

were furnished with subsistence by Massachusetts, and a *per diem* allowance of twelve pence by Connecticut, but were actually volunteers, or more accurately speaking, guerrillas. In this employment of those fragments of tribes, whom the English had once crushed with iron hand, against their own race, the moralist of to-day might find food for reflection, but the exigencies of those times were such as to require the prompt use of every available weapon within reach, regardless of what posterity might say.

These arrangements enabled Dudley to withdraw an equal number of men for the expedition, now fitting out under Church, without weakening too much the vulnerable points of the frontier. That expedition will be treated of in another chapter.

But all could not prevent the skulking foe from striking at both points, so carefully guarded, at nearly the same time. They first broke in at the weak eastern corner, just out of reach of Dudley's Indian contingent. On May 11, 1704, as Nicholas Cole, of Wells, with Nicholas Hodgdon, Thomas Dane, and Benjamin Gooch, all three soldiers belonging to Wheelwright's garrison, were out looking for some stray cattle, they were attacked by a party of twelve Indians, **Wells men killed.** who killed Cole and Hodgdon, took Dane prisoner, but failed to secure Gooch, who made his escape to the garrison. A party immediately set out in pursuit of the marauders, but failed to come up with them.[1]

At the extreme western corner of the line a war-party of French and Indians, eluding the vigilance of the scouts, surprised a garrison in the lower part of North-

---

[1] BOSTON *News Letter*, May 15 to 17, 1704, where Gooch is called Gough, probably owing to the habit of pronouncing it as if spelled Googe to this day.

ampton,[1] May 13th, before day, killing or taking all the inmates. In all twenty persons were slain. After re-

Northampton struck. treating for some distance, the raiders sent back a wounded prisoner to warn his friends that if they followed in pursuit the rest of the prisoners would be instantly despatched. The unfortunate messenger was met on the road, alone and unarmed, and slain by Indian stragglers. Colonel Whiting chased this party for two days without coming up with them—"a weary march to no purpose," sighs Samuel Partridge.

The people of Hatfield were aghast at the audacity of the thing. Partridge writes : "We are so surprised that we day and night stand upon our guard, and most of our men keep watch every other night, and spend our whole time in the day fortifying, so as to be in a posture of defence."

Meanwhile, trustworthy intelligence had reached the valley to the effect that the enemy was building a fort and planting corn at a place high up the river, called in the Indian dialect Cowass or Cowassuc,[2] and now known as the Great Connecticut Oxbow.

If true, this piece of news boded no good to the English settlements below. But, first of all, it was necessary to know whether it was true or not.

To this end, a scouting-party of six was sent out from Northampton early in June to clear the mystery up. After a fatiguing tramp of nine days through the wilderness they came to the river not far from the supposed site of the fort. While debating what move to make next two Indians came in sight paddling a canoe.

---

[1] THEN called Passacomuc, now Easthampton.

[2] BETWEEN the towns of Haverhill, N. H., and Newbury, Vt.

This was taken as a sign that they were on the right
scent. Until sunset they lay close. As it grew dark,
smoke was seen curling up above the tree-   **Lyman's**
tops about half a mile off. With all the   **exploit.**
care requisite to conceal their approach, it was two
o'clock in the morning before the assailants could reach
the spot aimed at, when it was found that the smoke
had come from a wigwam which stood in plain view a
few rods before them. While hesitating how to approach it without waking the inmates, rain began falling, and presently a " smart clap of thunder " sent, as
the pious narrator [1] relates, by " God and his good
providence," drowned the noise made by the assailants
in forcing their way through the surrounding thickets.
Then, after creeping on their hands and knees to within three or four rods of the wigwam, the eager scouts
rose to their feet, ran up and fired a volley into it, instantly flinging down their empty guns and rushing in
upon the astonished savages to finish the work with
clubs and hatchets.

Two escaped ; seven were killed on the spot. Six
were scalped, the victors leaving the seventh unscalped
at the ironical suggestion of one of their number, who
said that inasmuch as they now had a scalp apiece, they
could well afford to give one to the country.

Not venturing to remain longer in the vicinity, the
scouts immediately made the best of their way home,
without, however, obtaining the information they had
come for. Being in constant fear of pursuit, they were
nearly starved to death before reaching the settlements,
having eaten nothing for four or five days except young

---

[1] CALEB LYMAN'S account in Penhallow.

buds, strawberry leaves, and even grass, to alleviate the pangs of hunger.

The actors in this bold exploit bitterly complained because they received only thirty-one pounds reward from the government, when, in fact, the scalp bounty had risen by this time to thirty-two pounds a head in Massachusetts, to which New Hampshire added enough to make the whole bounty forty pounds. Dudley wrote that he had 1,900 men and twenty vessels in service at this time. The people were loudly groaning under the burden of taxation, which this state of things imposed. If, therefore, as was claimed, every Indian killed by the regular forces cost a thousand pounds, the payment of forty pounds to a volunteer who took a scalp without expense to the government would, of course, be looked upon as an economical measure from every point of view. And the mutilation of a dead body was considered essential to establish the equity of a claim to the bounty—nothing more.

XX

CHURCH'S LAST EXPEDITION

May, 1704

THE tragedy of Deerfield so stirred the blood of the veteran Church that, although now grown corpulent and getting on in years, he mounted his horse and rode seventy miles to Boston to offer his services to Governor Dudley again. After some exchange of views as to the proper method of crippling the enemy, which Church always insisted could only be done by carrying the war to their own doors, he was put in command of a new expedition, designed to make a clean sweep of the coasts of eastern Maine and Nova Scotia. This done, he was directed to pay a visit to Norridgewock on his return, should it be found practicable to do so, and lay waste that standing menace to the peace of the Maine frontier. Governor Dudley would not sanction an attack on Port Royal, though Church strongly desired to destroy that nest of contraband traders, among whom, it was whispered, some New England merchants might be found, base enough to turn the enemy's wants for carrying on the war against them to their own profit.

CHURCH'S SWORD.

While these preparations were on foot, in the month

13

of April, 1704, there appeared in Boston the first number of the first newspaper published in the English colonies, *The Boston News Letter*.[1] Strangely enough this diminutive sheet, not larger than a modern hand-bill, contains no reference whatever to the war then raging, or for that matter to anything else that should stamp it as the destined progenitor of the great newspaper of the present day. Indeed, the history of that period could never be written from the columns of the *News Letter* alone.

With his usual activity, Church soon succeeded in raising a mixed force of English and friendly Indians, chiefly in old Plymouth colony, to the number of five hundred and fifty men, a few Indians being allotted to each company of whites. Church boasted that there was not a pressed man among them. Like the previous ones, this expedition was provided with enough whale-boats to move half the command against any given point at once. Celerity and secrecy of movement were thus secured. Two armed vessels of the royal navy, and one sailing under the province flag, were to act as a convoy to Church's fleet of transports.

Queen's arms.

In short, the expedition in all respects was as well, if not better, equipped as any that had been sent out on the same errand. One step in advance may be noted here. A certain number of improved muskets, recently imported, were distributed among the new levies, and thus came to be known as Queen's Arms. Dudley had certainly acted with vigor, and Church had seconded his superior to the best of his ability.

---

[1] A SINGLE number, of a similar sheet, had been issued nearly fourteen years before (September 25, 1690), under the title of *Public Occurrences*, but summarily suppressed for circulating "doubtful and uncertain reports." The matter is largely made up of news of the war then raging,

In the main, the same old programme was marked out for this expedition.   Church was too old a cam-

ANCIENT CHART OF PENOBSCOT BAY.

paigner not to know that the prospect of coming upon the hostile Indians unawares was poor indeed.   Burning their deserted wigwams might be compared with

burning so much old brushwood.   They were almost as
easily rebuilt as destroyed; and it was too early in the
season to lay waste the Indian cornfields.   Church
therefore had proposed to himself the rooting out of as
many of the French trading and fishing stations of
Nova Scotia as he should have the time to visit, satisfied in his own mind, as he was, that it was there he
could do the enemy the most harm.   It being impracticable to reach Canada, he argued that the next best
thing to do was to strike where the enemy was most
vulnerable—that is through Nova Scotia.   This was
rude strategy, to be sure, but it was the only means left
of making reprisals for such murderous raids as that of
Hertel de Rouville.

After seeing his fleet under sail, Church accompanied
Governor Dudley to Portsmouth, where a company of
New Hampshire soldiers reinforced the expedition.
Leaving the ships of war behind as a blind, on May 15th
the transports made sail direct for Matinicus Island,[1]
where active operations may be said to have begun.

Next day a small party, sent off on a scout to the
nearest group of islands,[2] was lucky enough to capture
three Frenchmen and an Indian, before they could make
good their escape, from whom, under threats of torture,
Church obtained some reliable information as to the
numbers and positions of the enemy in this quarter.
He then pretended to relent.   In gratitude for having
their lives spared, two of the prisoners piloted Church
to several small habitations of the French in Penobscot Bay, that of St. Castin among the rest.   St. Castin,

---

[1] MATINICUS lies out in the open ocean, seventeen miles southeast of Owl's Head ; the
lonely outpost of Penobscot Bay.

[2] GREEN ISLANDS of the Fox Islands group are probably meant.

himself, was luckily gone to France, but his wife and
children fell into Church's hands. All of the enemy met
with here, whether French or Indians, were either killed
or taken, though the actual numbers are unknown.

Mount Desert was next visited. On the way there
every nook and corner of the coast was thoroughly explored, every possible precaution taken to waylay any

ENTRANCE TO MOUNT DESERT HARBOR.

of the enemy's war - parties who might be coming
westward on one of their destructive raids, and for
whom Church was now so sharply on the lookout. Failing to make any discoveries of this nature, Church's
flotilla rowed on into what is now the Southwest Harbor
of Mount Desert, a primeval solitude of wild sublimity,
suddenly turned into a scene of unwonted activity by
the presence of the ships-of-war and transports, lying
there at anchor.

The expedition had now traversed something like fifty leagues of coast without effecting anything of consequence, while the labor involved in making these

AT MOUNT DESERT ISLAND.

night excursions was excessively arduous, the men being either constantly at the oars or kept scrambling over rocks and through thickets, loaded down with their arms and packs. Still Church would not be disheart-

ened.   After taking some provisions out of the transports, he once more set his face eastward, leaving the
ships to follow him later, while he resumed his careful
examinations along shore, as one wild headland opened
upon another before him.   Machias Bay was thus
reached and explored from top to bottom, but even in
this noted rendezvous of the redskins neither tracks nor
fires were discovered.   The place was wholly deserted.
So again, Church pushed on into Passamaquoddy Bay,
where he had been constantly told he would find plenty
of Indians; so that here, at least, he had hopes of effecting something that should redound to the credit of
the expedition.

The first landing in this fine bay was made upon the
island where Eastport stands to-day, June 7, 1704.
One or two French families, probably   At Eastport,
petty traders, were then living on this isl-   Me.
and.   Church forthwith seized and questioned them
closely; and upon the strength of a story invented by
an old woman on the spot to mislead him, to the effect
that there were Indians lurking in the woods about
them, Colonel Gorham was left here to look after them,
while Major Hilton crossed the bay to scour Campobello
Island.   With the rest of his force Church then pushed
on up the bay, the same night, coolly braving the perils
of whirlpools or tidal eddies that make the passage difficult enough in the daytime, but seldom attempted at
night even by the best pilots.   But Church knew that
a single hour's delay would render all chance of success
hopeless.

At a little before day a landing was made at another
French habitation [1] on the St. Croix River, so noted in

---

[1] CALLED Gourdan's in Church's account.

the early annals of New England. The people here
were surprised, and taken without resistance. After
In the St.   looking to the disposal of these prisoners,
Croix.   Church followed on after his men, who
were industriously looking about them for more enemies.
They were under standing orders to advance only in
open order, so that if suddenly fired upon the fire would
do as little harm as possible. By the dim light Church
saw some of them crowding up around a solitary hut,
nearby. Angry at so flagrant a violation of his orders,
Church called out to them to know what they were doing there. They answered that there were some of the
enemy in the hut who would not come out. " Then
knock them in the head!" shouted back the choleric
old man. This order, given in haste, and repented of at
leisure, was promptly executed by the excited soldiers.[1]

Finding nothing more here the English pushed on
up the river to the falls,[2] where still another French
trader was living on a spot always much resorted to by
the Indians on account of the fishery, and now cleverly
turned to account as a rallying point from which to set
forth on the war-path.

The advancing force being discovered, nothing could
be effected here except to destroy some dried fish, which
the enemy had been curing for winter use on the bank
of the river, and the exchange of a few harmless shots
with the owners, who ran howling into the woods.

Having united all his detachments below, and being
joined by the shipping there, a descent was next
planned against the French posts in Nova Scotia, in

---

[1] CHURCH himself justifies the act by a reference to the atrocities committed by the
enemy at Deerfield and elsewhere.

[2] PROBABLY at Calais.

pursuance of which the armed ships sailed to blockade Port Royal, and Church, in his transports, to Mines, or Grand Pré, on the basin of Mines. Having arrived before the place when the tide was low, Church was forced to lie out in his whaleboats all night, waiting for the flood. Next morning the English, upon landing, had a harmless skirmish with some of the enemy, who were simply making a show of resistance to cover the driving off of their cattle. In pursuing these too eagerly the English lost the only men killed during the whole expedition—a Lieutenant Barker and one private of Church's own company.

That night Church set fire to the place; in the morning the dykes were cut by his orders, so as to flood the farms rescued by the Acadians from periodical inundation, with such great labor to themselves.[1] The work of destruction being completed, the English returned on board of their transports with the prisoners taken either here or in the neighborhood. It should be said in explanation of Church's acts here that he merely carried out the express orders of Governor Dudley, conceived, it must be admitted, rather in a spirit of savage barbarity than of fair and honorable warfare. Yet it was but a foretaste of what the future had in store for the doomed Acadians of this romantic region. Enough of them were now carried off to offset the number of English captives held in Canada.

Grand Pré burnt.

The transports next sailed back to Port Royal, where the whole fleet was once more united, but not, it seems, ready for action. Thus far Church had been laying

[1] THEY made the mistake of cultivating the low meadows instead of the uplands, to avoid the labor of felling the timber.

waste undefended places, where little risk was run. Here an opportunity for more brilliant action offered itself, as Port Royal was defended by a fort in which a permanent garrison was kept. It was also the chief port of Acadia. In short, if Port Royal fell, Acadia would be rendered both harmless and helpless. Yet, with a force at hand fully competent to the task before it, nothing whatever was attempted. The invaders contented themselves with a mere idle demonstration— with lying off in the basin out of cannon-shot. The fort was not even summoned. It is hard to understand **Port Royal** the true motives of this ridiculous affair. **looked at.** If, as Church alleges in his narrative, he was restrained by peremptory orders from making an attack at all, why was he there? If, again, these orders were as imperative as he makes it appear (and his truthfulness is not called in question), why should he have submitted the question of an attack to a council of war, which decided against it, on the ground that the place was too strong for them? Thus, instead of being an exhibition of strength, the expedition had only shown its weakness. Yet Church still had nearly 400 men fit for duty, with three ships carrying almost a hundred guns at his back.[1]

Church, therefore, leaving Port Royal unscathed, sailed away to Chignecto (Beaubassin) at the head of the Bay of Fundy. The inhabitants having received timely warning had carried off their effects out of **Chignecto** Church's reach. But this did not prevent **laid waste.** their making a feeble opposition to his landing, though they ran away as soon as the invaders

---

[1] THE French accounts make it appear that an attempt was actually made and repulsed. Nothing is found in the English accounts to support this claim.

were drawn up ready to charge them. After destroying the settlement Church turned homeward, calling
again at Passamaquoddy, Mount Desert, and Penobscot, without seeing an Indian at either place.

At Casco, where he next put in, Church found orders
awaiting him, directing him to march up to Norridgewock before returning home. Finding his men strongly
opposed to making
the march, now that
their minds were bent
upon a speedy com-
ing home, Church
readily found an ex-
cuse for disobeying
the order. Thus end-
ed Church's fifth and
last expedition. A
wide extent of terri-
tory had been trav-
ersed, a few insig-
nificant villages de-
stroyed, and a num-
ber of prisoners,
equal to those taken

RUINS OF CHURCH'S HOUSE.

at Deerfield, brought away. The expedition was looked
upon in the main as a failure, and if the adaptation of
means to ends be looked to, it was one. So far from
suffering loss, the Indians had been merely frightened
away from their old haunts, like birds of prey before the
fowler. When he had passed on they came back again.
Nothing was more true or more certain than that the
geographical position of Port Royal was a constant
menace to the New England fisheries. And as its re-

duction had been the professed object of the expedition, the failure to attack it easily provoked suspicion that all was not as it should be. And when Dudley's agency in the matter became known, as it eventually did, his motives were severely impugned. In fact, Dudley had not taken the public into his confidence. His alleged reasons, as stated by Church, failed to satisfy an increasing number of political and personal enemies, and indeed were puerile in the extreme.

XXI

NEGOTIATIONS FOR NEUTRALITY
July, 1704—April, 1706

THE scene of Indian depredations now shifts for the moment from the harassed frontier to one of the older settlements.   On the last day of July, 1704, some four hundred French and Indians fell upon Lancaster, Mass.   It was rather more than half the force which had set out from Quebec, under the command of Beaucour, boasting to lay waste the Connecticut Valley with fire and slaughter. When it had reached the Connecticut, a disgruntled Frenchman seized the opportunity of deserting to the English, thus frustrating the original plan of a surprise, and causing part of the invading force to turn back disheartened, while the rest struck off into the woods toward the Nashua.   Our scouts, perplexed by these movements, were at a loss to penetrate the enemy's designs, nor was it possible to tell where the blow would actually fall next, though the valley settlements, guided by their own fears, thought there might be some snare to entrap them.

Lancaster being a frontier town, Captain Jonathan Tyng was posted there with a company of soldiers. The enemy's first onset was made in the west part of the village, near Lieutenant Wilder's garrison.   Wilder himself and three more persons were killed here dur-

ing the day. Tyng rallied what men he could, and with
the aid of some Marlborough men, under Captain How,
made a resolute attempt to save the village, but being
greatly outnumbered, he was at length driven into the
shelter of the garrisons, leaving the rest of it in the
possession of the exultant enemy, who then set about
the work of wanton destruction unopposed. In a short
time the meeting-house and several dwellings were in
flames, and all burned to the ground. The marauders
also butchered a great part of the live stock belonging
to the inhabitants.

Meanwhile the alarm was rapidly spreading throughout the neighboring towns, whose inhabitants, seizing
their weapons, flocked to the assistance of their distressed friends in such numbers as to enable them to
renew the fight upon more equal terms, when the marauders, seeing only blows were to be had by remaining,
beat a hasty retreat, carrying their dead and wounded
along with them.[1]

Yet, notwithstanding that the English were now
everywhere on the alert, the savages continued to
strike first in one place, and then in another, keeping
up their petty, but irritating, warfare of small parties
against isolated farms or neighborhoods all summer.[2]

In the beginning of August one of these prowling
bands waylaid a small scouting party, going from
Northampton to Westfield, killed one man

Petty warfare.   and took two more prisoners. There being
more of the English coming up in the rear, the assailants,

---

[1] During this winter a story was current in the Connecticut Valley that Vaudreuil
had first imprisoned Beaucour and then degraded him and taken away his sword.
Letter of William Whiting.

[2] Under date of May 8, 1705, Sewall records that several " persons killed and carried
away last Friday " from York and Spruce Creek.

in their turn, were unexpectantly assailed and quickly routed, with the loss of two killed and all of the prisoners just taken. Groton, Amesbury, and Haverhill in Massachusetts, and Exeter, Oyster River, and Dover in New Hampshire, all suffered more or less from the visits of these small scalping parties.[1] In October their reappearance in the neighborhood of Lancaster[2] was the cause of a fatal mistake by which the Rev. Andrew Gardiner, minister of the place, lost his life. It seems that a scout had been out the day before looking for the enemy. The soldiers composing it came back worn down with hard travelling. Out of consideration for those whose turn came to stand guard that night Mr. Gar-   Rev. Andrew diner volunteered to mount guard himself,   Gardiner. and did accordingly take his post in the watch-box, over the flanker, when the time came to man the walls, remaining there until a late hour, when, as he was coming down from his post, he was seen, shot at, and mortally wounded by a soldier of the garrison, who took him for an enemy. The unfortunate clergyman lived only long enough to forgive the man who shot him, and to take a last leave of his sorrowing friends.

Winter having set in, it was fairly hoped that the Norridgewock village might be surprised by a sudden dash, while the enemy were off their guard. In the very heart of winter, with the snow lying four feet deep, so that the frozen wilderness stretched out before

[1] At Oyster River they wounded William Tasker, and at Dover laid an ambush for the people returning from public worship, but happily missed their aim.—Belknap. August 11th they wounded Mark Gyles of Dover (with his son), who died a few days after. Another party fell on York, where they slew Matthew Austin and then went to Oyster River, where they killed several while at work in their fields.—Penhallow.

[2] October 15, 1705, three men are carried away from Lancaster, from Mr. Sawyer's windmill.—Sewall's *Diary*. They were Thomas Sawyer, his son Elias, and John Bigelow.

them one vast sheet of dazzling white, Colonel Hilton
set out with two hundred and seventy hardy borderers
for the distant Kennebec village, where more mischief
Hilton's   had been hatched against the whites than
march.   in any other place short of Canada.   The
long march was expeditiously made on snow-shoes, the
onset duly arranged, but when the village was reached
not a soul was to be found.   The birds had forsaken
the nest.   After setting fire to the deserted wigwams
and to the chapel,[1] which stood at one end of the village,
the baffled rangers marched back the way they came.
And so all this expense, hardship, and fatigue went for
naught.

These two examples, one of a successful, the other of
an unsuccessful, raid, tell the whole story of this war.
The Indians knew that they could always find the English, while the English were never sure of finding them.

Spring brought with it a brief respite from a conflict
which never seemed nearing its end, and which it was
realized that the enemy might protract indefinitely;
yet a respite of any sort was thrice welcome to those
who lived in constant fear of death by violence.   Most
unexpectedly a ray of light pierced through the surrounding gloom.   It was learned that steps had been
Exchange   taken looking to an exchange of prisoners.
of captives.   Of all the trials arising from the war, perhaps the hardest to bear was the suspense relative to
the fate of friends or relatives.   That innocent women
and children should be held for ransom was perhaps
one of the penalties attached to carrying on a war with
barbarians, but that a people like the French, professing to represent in themselves the highest type of

[1] THIS chapel had been built by English carpenters in 1698, at the conclusion of peace.

Christian civilization, should, either openly or covertly, sanction such a practice, was not only fostering one of the worst features of the war, but to all intents it was descending to the level of the savages themselves.

The history of these negotiations affords a welcome relief from the relation of one murder after another.

In October, 1704, a letter was received at Wells from Captain Samuel Hill,[1] announcing the safety of several of his neighbors who had been mourned by their friends as dead.   Later, in December, John Sheldon and John Wells applied to Governor Dudley for leave to go to Quebec, with the view of opening the way for the release of their friends in captivity there.   Agents go to Quebec. The application was approved, and it was decided that Captain John Livingston, of Albany, should be employed to conduct Sheldon and Wells on their journey to Canada.

Early in May Hill himself arrived at Boston, he having been paroled by Vaudreuil, with the same general object in view.   Hill reported a hundred and seventeen persons, old and young, in the hands of the French, and seventy more scattered about among the Indians. The boys and girls were kept apart from their parents ; the adults were put to work, either as domestics or at such occupations as they had followed at home.

Within a week or two Livingston and the other messengers returned, bringing with them Captain Courtemanche, a French officer, whom Vaudreuil had commissioned to conduct the negotiations   Counter-proposals. on his part.   Better still, the messengers brought back with them two of Sheldon's children, his son's wife, Hannah—the same who had sprained her

[1] TAKEN at Wells, August 10, 1703.

14

ankle at the time she was taken—besides one of the children of Mr. Williams.[1]

Courtemanche was handsomely treated by Dudley, but his demand for the release of one Baptiste, a notorious freebooter, then lying in Boston jail, charged with piracy, proved a stumbling-block to the negotiations, as Dudley, who fully intended to hang Baptiste, plumply refused to include him in the exchange. Livingston declares this refusal to have been the only thing that hindered the parties from coming to an agreement then and there.

Nothing being settled, Courtemanche was sent back by sea early in the summer, in company with Vetch, Hill, and young William Dudley, the governor's son, to continue the negotiations at Quebec.[2] They took with them the draft of a treaty of neutrality drawn up by Dudley, which was submitted to Vaudreuil soon after their arrival in the autumn. This important step, which seems to have been kept very quiet, put an entirely new face upon the situation, and in view of possible results had need of being conducted with the greatest secrecy and delicacy on both sides.

Neutrality tendered.

Dudley's agents got back to Boston in November, having been detained by Vaudreuil until the homebound fleet had sailed from Quebec, as a matter of precaution. They brought with them counter-proposals

[1] In a letter to Mrs. Livingston, dated at Quebec, April 21, 1705, Williams warmly acknowledges his debt to her husband.

[2] VAUDREUIL was afterward mildly reproved for the freedom allowed the negotiators while in Quebec. The Minister writes as follows: "The illness which obliged your envoy, Sieur de Courtemanche, to return in an English brigantine, has much the appearance of having been assumed as a cover for trade, etc." He further declares that Vaudreuil ought to have had young Dudley and Vetch duly "attended," meaning watched, while they were in Quebec.—Ponchartrain to Vaudreuil, June 9, 1706.

from Vaudreuil, providing for the cessation of all hostile acts between the two governments, a general exchange of prisoners, besides guaranteeing the shipping of each party from capture by the other, but forbade New England vessels from fishing on the coasts of Acadia. The limit for concluding was fixed in the following February. The envoys also brought home with them five or six English prisoners,[1] one of whom was Stephen Williams, the young son of Rev. John Williams,[2] taken at Deerfield.

As the people of New England would rather have fought ten years longer than to give up the rights they had always claimed in the fisheries, after submitting Vaudreuil's proposal to the General Court, Dudley despatched another messenger to Quebec in the winter by land. Up to this time Vaudreuil had been acting under instructions from the King's minister, Ponchartrain, whose feelings of magnanimity had at length revolted at the useless barbarities practised by his savage allies, but Vaudreuil now believed he saw through Dudley's motives in protracting the negotiations under the flimsy pretext that the proposed treaty must be ratified by all the English colonies, and, piqued at the discovery that he was being played with to gain time, he made preparations calculated to force matters to a definite issue.[3] Meantime the negotiations reverted to the question of exchange, which was now pressed to some purpose. It will be easily understood that while these mysterious messages were passing between the two governors, the

---

[1] "TAKEN at the eastward."—Dudley's *Letter*.

[2] AFTERWARD minister of Longmeadow, Mass.

[3] THE time fixed having expired, "I permitted several small parties of our Indians to recommence hostilities in his (Dudley's) government, in order to force him to declare himself."—Vaudreuil to the Minister, April 28 (N. S.), 1706.

prisoners and their friends were enduring the most cruel suspense.

In the winter (1705–6) John Sheldon, whose activity in behalf of his old friends and neighbors is worthy of high praise, went a second time to Canada, as Dudley's messenger. By this time Dudley had made up his mind to yield the point with regard to Baptiste, which he had said he never would do. Sheldon now brought back forty-four released prisoners, chiefly taken at Deerfield. In the same summer the brigantine Hope took a number of French prisoners to Quebec,[1] for whom fifty-seven English were received in exchange, the minister Williams being given up for the pirate Baptiste. Some few more were not obtained until the following year.

Sheldon's good work.

The inside history of these negotiations sheds light upon the dilatory motions of the contracting parties. In fact, complications arose at the very outset. Vaudreuil, for instance, insisted that the English must treat with the Indians for the captives held by them, as he, Vaudreuil, disclaimed all authority over them. This brought from Dudley a point-blank refusal to negotiate on any such basis, pointedly styling it "an Algiers trade," and to still another person, who had vainly worked upon his sympathies, declaring his fixed resolve "never to buy a prisoner of an Indian, lest we make a market for our poor women and children on the frontiers." For his final word he assured Vaudreuil that he, Dudley, " would never permit a savage to tell him that a Christian prisoner was at his disposal."

Ransom refused.

All this had a very heroic sound indeed, and in

---

[1] PENHALLOW says seventy.

theory was excellent, but in practice it did not work well with Indians who had only refrained from knocking their prisoners on the head for the sake of the ransom. To Vaudreuil it simply meant that he, instead of Dudley, would have to pay the price demanded.

But more difficult than all the rest to deal with was the act of those who, unable to resist the temptations held out to them, had voluntarily sundered all ties binding them to home or kindred. Some had turned savages, others had embraced the Catholic religion. In either case the separation was full and complete. In its way the work had been as thoroughly done in the smoke and dirt of the wigwam, **Seceding captives.** as in the seclusion of the convent, for when the time came to claim their children the grief-stricken parents were told by those having them in their keeping, and with apparent candor too, that their son or daughter no longer owned their authority. Indeed, in some cases, children actually had to be kidnapped by their own relatives and carried off by force.

It is safe to say that this method of enfeebling an adversary had not been foreseen in New England. But bad as it was, a relapse into savage life was less deplored, perhaps, than a relapse into Catholicism, so to speak, for not death itself could have cast such a dark shadow over a sorrowing household as the knowledge that one of its members had abjured the faith of his fathers for one he had been taught to look upon from his cradle as the way of perdition.[1] Some even became eminent members of the Roman Church. Among others, Esther Wheelwright, who had been carried away from Wells when a child, became the Mother Superior of the Ursulines of Quebec.

[1] IN proof of this, see p. 33 of this work.

These incidents, so peculiar in themselves, and so far-reaching in their results, belong to what may be called the psychic phenomena of these wars. They go to show that their horrors were by no means confined to the work of the axe or the gun, but also included other, yet no less effective, methods of disintegration suggested by a policy as deep as it was unassailable. No more touching incident meets the eye of the student of these wars than that of the aged parent vainly watching for the one who, though living, never came back.

To make an end of the matter of a neutrality, each party accuses the other of double-dealing. It is certain that Dudley employed all his art to keep the negotiations open as long as possible. It is equally certain that Louis approved of the treaty. But with this brilliant despot the point of honor was supreme. Even as late as June, 1707, when the treaty was practically dead, he strictly charged Vaudreuil to take care that it should not be made in the name of Queen Anne, as he did not recognize her as the Queen of Great Britain.

But the proposal came many years too late. Too late Vaudreuil put before Dudley the absurdity of their cutting one another's throats without in the least affecting the result as between the two great belligerents. There was now but one sentiment in New England among high or low, and that sentiment had become so embedded in the popular mind as to be ineradicable. In a word, the conquest of Canada was become as much the settled policy of the future as the "*delenda est Carthago*" of the Roman senator.[1]

In Canada there was much grumbling because young

---

[1] DUDLEY claims to have urged this upon the queen ever since the beginning of the war, or for "these seven years past, by all the offices proper."—*Letter to Lord Sunderland*, August 14, 1709.

William Dudley, the governor's son, had been allowed to remain so long in Quebec about the business of the negotiations. It was even asserted that he and his companions had been detected in the act of examining and measuring some of the fortifications.[1]   But here neither party had the advantage of the other. Vaudreuil's agents had been instructed to do the same thing.

Although there was a truce to active hostilities while negotiations were going on, several persons lost their lives at Kittery during the summer.[2]   The winter was quiet, perhaps because the frontier garrisons were now well provided with snow-shoes, so making the Indians more cautious.

[1] CHARLEVOIX : Vetch was also accused of taking soundings of the St. Lawrence, in going and returning.

[2] AT Spruce Creek (Kittery) five were killed and five more taken.   Among the slain was Mrs. Hoel, a gentlewoman of birth and education.   Enoch Hutchins lost his wife and children.   John Rogers was afterward dangerously wounded, and James Toby shot still later.—Penhallow.   See *ante*, for mention of this war-party.

XXII

HOSTILITIES RESUMED

April, 1706—October, 1706

HOSTILITIES were resumed in the spring of 1706. In April the Indians attacked the house of John Drew, at Oyster River. Eight persons were killed and two wounded here. There was a garrison-house near at hand with nobody in it, except some of the women who, **Durham assaulted.** nothing daunted, let down their hair, put on men's hats, and fired away so briskly from the loops that the enemy fled without even securing the booty found at Drew's house. A townsman, John Wheeler, who fell in with the party, was killed, with his wife and two children. Four of his sons made good their escape by taking refuge in a cave near the shore of Little Bay. After looking for them in vain, their pursuers gave over the search.

In June Dudley was warned from Albany that another war-party would soon be upon him. He at once applied to Winthrop for one hundred men to reinforce the valley garrisons without loss of time; these to be followed by a much larger force. His letter closed with this Parthian shaft: "The first is necessary to save their lives till the last comes. Otherwise, I only expect your people to come to their funeral, as has been done sometimes before."

Dudley's advices made this war-party, said to be mission Indians from St. Francis, two hundred and seventy strong. Piscataqua was its supposed destination. The people were at once ordered into close garrison, scouting parties set in motion along the frontier, patrols organized in the villages, and one-half the militia directed to be in readiness to march at a minute's warn-

ANCIENT GARRISON, DRACUT, MASS.

ing.[1] Indeed, the emergency was such that in July Massachusetts had one thousand men under pay for the defence of her frontiers.[2]

This time the enemy had shrewdly chosen the most remote settlements on the Merrimac as the point of attack. They were not, however, left unguarded. The

[1] THIS seems about the earliest mention of the subsequently famous minute-men.
[2] LETTER of Secretary Addington.

blow fell first upon Dunstable.[1] On July 3d a garrison
in which Captain Pearson of Rowley with twenty
troopers was posted was assaulted by this band. It
chanced that the soldiers had just returned from a
scout without making any discovery, and after turning
their horses out to graze in the meadow, taking off
their equipments, and laying aside their
arms, were indulging in a carousal in true
barrack-room fashion, to make amends for the fatigues
of the day. Worse still, no sentinels were posted. At
sunset John Cummings and his wife went out to milk
the cows. Meantime the Indians had quietly surrounded the house, and when Cummings and his wife
came out of it they were fired upon. Mrs. Cummings
fell dead on the spot, and her husband was taken. With
loud yells the Indians then rushed through the open
gate into the house before the astonished soldiers could
have time to seize their arms or get themselves into a
posture for defence. A furious hand-to-hand fight took
place, in which such of the soldiers as had not lost their
heads laid about them with chairs, clubs, or whatever
else they could lay hands upon, with such effect as
finally to clear the house of their assailants.

Fighting at Dunstable.

---

[1] DUNSTABLE first included Tyngsborough. It was settled before 1697.

[2] SEWALL refers to this affair as follows: " You will too soon hear of the sorrowful
news of one of Captain Nelson's sons being killed in a garrison at Dunstable, this last
summer, where my sister Dorothy's husband, Northend, narrowly escaped."—*Sewall
Papers*, October 15, 1706.

The account given in Farmer and Moore's *Historical Collections* is substantially
followed, though it is there erroneously referred to the time of Lovewell's War, and
contains other very apparent discrepancies. For instance, it is hard to understand just
why the Indians should not have discovered the presence of the soldiers if their horses
were turned out to pasture, or have shut their ears to the sounds of the carousal, if one
was really going on at the time. The main incidents, however, are vouched for by
Hutchinson, Penhallow, and Dudley, though the whole story smacks of embellishment.
Dudley says that nine English were killed to seven Indians, thus disproving the statement that only the trumpeter was killed on the side of the English. He also confirms
the fact of a surprise, or rather of criminal negligence.

From here the savages went to Daniel Galusha's, about two miles distant, on Salmon Brook, where they quickly despatched Rachel Galusha, but luckily missed another woman who had **Galusha's garrison.** the presence of mind to hide herself underneath an empty cask in the cellar, until the intruders had gone. But, after plundering the house, the savages had set it on fire, and the poor woman, imprisoned in the cellar by the flames, only effected her escape by tearing away the loose stones from around a small hole with her naked hands, until the opening was large enough for her to crawl out through it.

On the same day the Indians forced the garrison of Nathaniel Blanchard, killed him, his wife, and also a Mrs. Hannah Blanchard. They then scattered themselves through the contiguous towns as far as Wilmington,[1] Mass., where, on the night of July 8th, one party forced an entrance into the house of John Harnden, while he was absent, killed his wife and three children, and carried off five more. These last are said to have been recovered by a pursuing party of Harnden's neighbors.

On the next day some forty of the marauders fell upon Amesbury, where eight of the inhabitants were killed. Two others, who were at work in the fields, took refuge in a deserted gar- **Murders at Amesbury.** rison, in which two unserviceable old guns had been left, without powder or ball. These were, however, pressed into service, and when the savages ventured near the house the guns were thrust out of the loopholes at them; while the men, whose lives were staked upon the success of their clever ruse, called out to each other, " Here

---

[1] THEN part of Reading.

they are, but don't fire till they come nearer!" These two brave white men had the satisfaction of seeing their cowardly assailants slink away to cover again.

Still another band, who had marked Major Hilton for their especial prey, lay in wait for him around his garrison at Exeter, where they could see all who went in or out of it, without detection. One morning ten men came out of the house with their scythes, and went away into the fields to mow. After they had laid aside their guns to begin mowing, the crawling savages suddenly rose up and rushed in between them and their fire-arms, killed four, wounded one, and captured three more. The two others made their escape. Two of the prisoners, Hall and Miles, afterward came in, in a deplorable state, having lived for three weeks on roots and the inner rind of trees.

Chelmsford, Sudbury, Groton, Hatfield, and Brookfield also suffered more or less during this incursion, the subtle enemy, as usual, inflicting much loss and sustaining little themselves. Indeed, it was fairly reckoned that so far every Indian killed or taken in this war had cost the English a thousand pounds.

Dudley had complained to the queen of the backwardness of Connecticut in furnishing men, and Winthrop had received the queen's commands on the subject. This drew a tart letter from Winthrop to Dudley, who still insisted that Connecticut had not furnished her proportion. The relations of the two men had long been strained and this incident did not tend to diminish the friction between them.

An exposure took place this summer which made a great noise at the time. It was an open secret that the Albany merchants were getting rich by trading with the

Canada Indians ; but this was being done under cover of a *quasi*-truce, which no doubt was sufficient to quiet the consciences of those engaged in thus giving aid and comfort to the enemy. No such state of things, however, existed in New England. With the enemy at their doors, such conduct on the part of her merchants was altogether too flagrant to admit of any such miserable subterfuge as that.

A certain number of English prisoners were known to be in the hands of the French at Port Royal. The authorities at Boston having fitted out a small vessel to go there for the purpose of procuring an exchange, the opportunity was seized by some well-known merchants of Boston to open a contraband trade there and elsewhere, along the coast, under the cover of a flag of truce. William Rowse, master of the vessel, was a party to the scheme. So was Samuel Vetch, who had figured so prominently in the negotiations of the year before. All the parties to the plot were no doubt reasonably certain of the connivance of Bonaventure,[1] the French commandant, in *Illegal trading.* their schemes, for Bonaventure subsequently entered into a labored attempt to clear himself from the charge. In doing so he implicates still another Boston merchant.[2] Des Goutins, king's commissary, confirms the general charge in a letter to the Minister of the following year, in which he says that there were " no pots, scythes, sickles, knives nor iron in the country. They

---

[1] BROUILLAN having returned to France, Bonaventure, *lieutenant du roi,* was left in command, but was not made governor at Brouillan's death, as he expected, the post being given to Subercase instead.

[2] " MR. NELSON, merchant at Boston, being indebted to me in the sum of 5,000 livres, which I had lent him at the time of his imprisonment in France, wishing to make payment, had sent me by the packet-boat, for 1,300 livres, goods consisting of cloth, scythes, and pots."—*Letter to the Minister.*

would be lucky," he adds, "if the enemy would sell
them goods again for their beaver, but Subercase is opposed to it."

Rowse made two trips on this business. On the
first he brought back only seventeen prisoners, and on
the second but seven more. His long stay at Port
Royal to accomplish so little excited suspicion, and at
his last returning he was charged with having spent his
time in trading with the enemy in goods contraband of
war, instead of attending to the business for which he
was sent. Being unable to clear himself, he was sent to
prison. Besides Vetch, John Borland, Roger Lawson,
John Phillips, Jr., and Ebenezer Coffin, all merchants
in good standing, were also apprehended and put under
bonds on a similar charge. What came· to light, as a
result of these proceedings, caused a general burst of
indignation, particularly against Vetch. Some of the
more clamorous ones even wanted him confined "in
the stone cage " for fear he should get away.[1]   Even
Dudley himself came in for a share of the popular indignation, as being a party to these underhand transac-
tions.

There being no court of competent jurisdiction, the
offenders were tried before the General Court.[2]   Paul
Dudley, son of the governor, was the prosecuting attor-
ney. All were found guilty and sentenced to pay various
sums—Rowse, £1,200 ; Borland, £1,100; Lawson, £300 ;
Vetch, £200 ; Phillips, £100, and Coffin, £60. These
fines were, however, remitted by order of the queen, on
the ground that the General Court had exceeded its

---

[1] LETTER of J. Winthrop to Fitz-John Winthrop.

[2] UNDER date of August 16th, Sewall makes this entry in his diary : "Captain Vetch
was brought to his trial in the court chamber." August 17th, he notes down that " Mr.
Borland pleads that he was a factor in the affair."

powers. Dudley was exonerated, the matter charged
against him being of too trivial a nature to be pushed,
much to the disgust of his many enemies, who had
hoped for a different result. In fact a petition was forwarded to the queen praying for his removal. In answer
to this prayer, reiterating the charges of corruption,
both branches of the General Court passed votes of confidence in the governor. His assailants then resorted
to printing anonymous pamphlets.[1] But in the end
Dudley prevailed over both open and covert attacks,
chiefly, it would seem, by reason of his address in the
management of men. At court Dudley was looked upon
as representing in his own person the principle of royal
supremacy, as opposed to the old Puritan doctrines of
popular rights. So long, therefore, as the complaints
against him emanated from that source, Dudley was
reasonably sure of being sustained at London. For
the rest, he was not the man to give an inch to his opponents. They might worry him, but they could never
put him down.

[1] REPRINTED in *Massachusetts Historical Society Collections*, 5th Series, Vol. **VI.**
Hutchinson, Vol. II., prints the petition and answer.

XXIII

FUTILE SIEGE OF PORT ROYAL
May, 1707

EVERY such raid as that recounted in the last chapter only made the impossibility of protecting either life or property in open villages, whose inhabitants were farmers, more and more manifest. When one of these war-parties was abroad no man's life was safe outside of a garrison. It may well be conceived that to men, strong, robust, inured to labor, and accustomed to the freedom of outdoor life, nothing could be more irksome than to be shut up within the four walls of a garrison. Hence, in spite of warnings, orders, or entreaties, fatal risks were taken, and many valuable lives thrown away. This species of assassination was draining the life-blood of a few struggling frontier villages drop by drop.

On the other hand, few Indians were killed in these sudden encounters. In the quiet of a summer's day a distant gunshot would be heard, and its meaning easily guessed. Nine times in ten, before the scattered neighbors could be rallied the marauders would be beyond pursuit. Could the Indians have made good even their small losses the war might have dragged on in-
Indians losing ground. definitely; but unfortunately for them, continued attrition was wasting them away without the power to recuperate, so that their numbers were steadily diminishing. A more efficient means to

their destruction than the edge of the sword was the
wasting of their crops, thus often reducing them to the
verge of famine.

In January Colonel Winthrop Hilton, with two hundred and seventy men, made a scout eastward as far as
Casco without meeting with an enemy. But when come
near Black Point, on his way back, a small band was
tracked, four of them killed, and a squaw
taken prisoner. The woman, who had a
papoose at her breast, was either compelled by threats,
or prevailed on by promises, to lead the English to a
camp of eighteen more Indians, all but one of whom
were slain while asleep.[1]

Dudley had been kept in a state of alternating hope
and suspense in regard to his favorite project of sub-
duing Canada, by reason of the heavy demands that
the war in Europe was making upon England. It
was only by returning again and again to the subject
that the queen's ministers were induced to fall in with
it at all; but even then it was treated as something
that could wait; so that Dudley's patience was sorely
tried.

All hope of receiving effective aid this year (1707)
having failed, and smarting under the wounds his reputation had suffered at the hands of his enemies, who
boldly charged him with having sent Church off to
Port Royal on a fool's errand, Dudley seems to have
resolved upon making one more attempt, single-handed
and alone, trusting to its success to retrieve his reputation and silence his defamers. It proved another

---

[1] It is this affair to which the following curious entry refers: "Gave thanks for
the news of the eighteen Indians killed and one taken last Tuesday."—*Sewall Papers*,
II., 181. In February, 1706-7, a strong scouting party went to Monadnock, another
noted rendezvous for war-parties.

15

wretched exhibition of aggregated incompetency, ignorance, and pulling at cross-purposes.

But before anything could be done the popular feeling must be worked up to the fighting point. And here traces of the deeply rooted faith that they were God's people, guided by His almighty hand, are clearly manifest in the acts of those who then gave direction to public opinion. Honest Samuel Sewall, our Pepys, records that " several ministers pray'd (at the desire of the **Praying against** court) that God would speedily, by some **Port Royal.** Providence or one way other, let us know what might doe as to going against Port Royal." Just how this manifestation of the divine wisdom was expected to appear is not so clear ; but it is evident that the barbarous dictum that God is on the side of the strongest artillery would have found few followers in the Puritan capital.

Meantime, the practical side of the question was being earnestly discussed at the council board. In this instance, a regular fortification, built on a hill-top, mounted with heavy cannon and garrisoned by regular troops, was to be taken either by siege or assault. **New England** Here was no question of mere bush fight- **militia.** ing, such as the rustic New England soldiery had been used to. The best soldiers were none too good for this sort of work. It is no less to the credit of the provincial militia that they were ready to undertake the unusual task with some confidence. Yet we find certain fastidious critics speaking of the rank and file as if nothing but failure was to be expected, when, as a matter of fact, the material was precisely the same as that which won Louisburg and defended Bunker Hill.

Two full regiments were raised in Massachusetts, New Hampshire, and Rhode Island.[1] Colonel Francis Wainwright, of Ipswich, commanded one, and Colonel Winthrop Hilton, of Exeter, the other. Colonel March, an excellent partisan officer, whose brilliant defence of Casco had won for him the place formerly held by

COLONEL FRANCIS WAINWRIGHT'S HOUSE, IPSWICH, MASS.

Church in the public estimation, was put in chief command. The two regiments mustered 1,076 officers and men; and there was also a small artillery corps, in charge of Colonel Redknap,[2] an English engineer, which with supernumeraries brought the whole number up to 1,150 officers and men. Will-

Make-up of expedition.

[1] RHODE ISLAND furnished eighty men. She was alive to the fact that her commerce was suffering from the depredations of French corsairs. See what Subercase says at the end of this chapter. Connecticut declined to furnish any men, Winthrop making some very lame excuses. There was one company of Cape Cod Indians, commanded by Captain Freeman, of Harwich. For the roster of the expedition see Vol. V, 3d Series, *Massachusetts Historical Society Collections.*

[2] REDKNAP succeeded Wolfgang Romer, one of King William's appointees, as supervising engineer of sea-coast fortifications. Romer was *persona non grata* to Dudley, who sharply rebuked him for his arrogant deportment.

iam Dudley, the governor's talented son, accompanied the expedition, in the rather anomalous capacity of secretary of war, and there were no less than five chaplains to keep the rude soldiery in touch with home and its influences, while exhorting them to a valiant use of their carnal weapons.

On May 26th[1] the fleet cast anchor in Port Royal basin. A thousand men were landed the same afternoon seven or eight miles from the fort, part on the north shore under Appleton, and part on the south or fort side, under March himself. Fault was found with landing the men so far off, as the long march up to the fort consumed all the rest of the afternoon, besides defeating the important object of cutting off communication between the fort and country at once.

Troops land.

Young John Barnard, one of the five chaplains, has told the story of the preliminary movements somewhat in detail. He was with Lieutenant-colonel Appleton's detachment, which moved off the ground first.

"It being so late ere we landed, we could not reach the place of our destined encampment, but after several hours' travel, partly thro' hideous woods and fallen trees across the way, which we sometimes climbed over, at others crept under, at length we arrived where were two or three houses and barns, and at nine o'clock at night took up our quarters there. There also Captain Freeman and his company of Indians, who flanked our left as we marched along, who also had a warm skirmish with about forty or fifty French, came to us without the loss of a man." Appleton's movement was essential to cover March's advance.

---

[1] THE old style is adhered to for the sake of conforming to the English accounts and records. The dates in Charlevoix are new style.

By their own admission, the sudden appearance of this fleet, the disembarkation of the English in such force, with their prompt advance toward the fort, put the French in such a fright that Subercase had great trouble in restoring their courage to the fighting point.[1] He, however, kept up a bold front, and by throwing out a numerous body of skirmishers, who *Sharp skirmish-* knew every inch of the ground, contrived *ing.* to delay the march of the two attacking columns as much as possible, thus gaining time for the inhabitants to come in from the out-settlements. Appleton had brushed away his assailants. To oppose March an ambush was laid at the crossing of Allen's Creek, a small stream, bordered by copses of thick brushwood, which lay between him and the fort, so that when his van came up, on the morning of the twenty-seventh, there was some sharp skirmishing before the English could shake off their assailants, and move on to the ground they were to occupy. In this encounter five men were wounded.

March now encamped at the foot of the hill on which the fort stood, where a few deserted houses offered some shelter to the weary soldiers. The task before him was by no means an easy one. From the ramparts of the fort forty cannon, some of them thirty-six pounders, frowned upon the hostile camps. A vigorous assault might perhaps have proved successful. March shrank from making it. The other alternative was to bring up his artillery, make a practicable breach in the walls, and then, if the fort still held out, try the fortune of an assault only as a last resort. Upon finding their commander in that disposition, the soldiers naturally

---

[1] " *Ce qui causa une si grande allarme que le gouverneur eut bien de la peine à rassurer le garnison.*"—*Charlevoix.*

came to the conclusion that the place was stronger than it really was.

Everyone was therefore asking why the artillery was not brought up. This duty naturally fell to the naval officers, who now came forward with a positive declaration that the thing could not be done under fire of **Fatal delays.** the fort. The opinion was hotly contested, but the royal officers would not budge. From that moment the fate of the expedition was sealed. It is true that Redknap had begun the work of raising batteries, though his spiteful temper when on shore showed how fully he shared the antipathy of the sea officers for the land officers, which proved the shipwreck of the whole undertaking. But batteries without cannon were seen to be labor wasted. The place, however, was closely invested, trenches opened, and a regular siege begun, which, if resolutely kept up, could hardly have failed of its object, even if the English had confined **Quarrels break out.** their efforts to holding the French cooped up within the four walls of their fort; but at the moment when the battle was half won, the leaders lost heart, they fell to quarrelling among themselves, their disputes spread to the soldiers, and soon all subordination was at an end.

March was at his wit's end. His council advised one thing one day and recalled it the next. On May 31st, only five days after landing, it was decided that the place was too strong to be attacked with any prospect of success. Chaplain Barnard gives an amusing account of an interview he had with March on that occasion.

"When Colonel Appleton went over to Colonel March's camp," the honest chaplain goes on to say, " he took me along with him. After the council-of-war

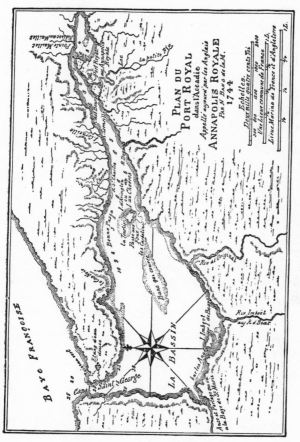

PLAN OF PORT ROYAL, NOVA SCOTIA.

was over, General March, meeting me, took me aside and said to me, 'Don't you smell a rat?' I, who knew not what he intended, said, 'No, sir.' 'Why,' said he, 'Colonel Appleton is for staying to break ground only to have his wages increased.' I said, 'Sir, I am a stranger to Colonel Appleton's intentions.' He then said to me, somewhat roughly, 'I have heard you have said the artillery might be brought' (and indeed I had said so to Colonel Appleton, and even projected a safe method for it). I said to him, 'Sir, I think it may.' 'Well then,' said he, 'it shall be attempted; you shall be the one that shall bring it up.' I replied, 'Sir, that is not my business, as you well know; however, if it will be of public service, and you please to command me to it, I will readily venture myself on it, and find a way to do it.' 'Very well,' said he."

There is no evidence that the youthful chaplain's services were ever brought in requisition, though already he had won a reputation for bravery by marching alone beyond the lines for the purpose of making a sketch of the fort; and while thus engaged a cannon-ball had struck the ground so near him as to cover him with dirt; whereupon Barnard, suddenly realizing that he had no business there, beat a hasty retreat.

Good or bad, Redknap's objections had decided the breaking up of the siege, at what one officer indignant-ly calls "ye fatal council of war." There was no gain-saying a professional opinion, solemnly delivered. Yet there was a stormy time. The decision was re-tracted, then reaffirmed. "I think our general was both fool and boy-ridden," [1] is the tart comment of one disgusted bearer of a commission.

[1] PROBABLY referring to William Dudley. See *Hutchinson*, II., 152, *note*.

Charlevoix relates, with considerable detail, a repulse which he says the English met with on the night before the siege was raised, while making an assault on the fort. The English accounts make this only a demonstration designed to cover the burning of some buildings outside the fort, and close to it, which was successfully done, under a hot fire of cannon and musketry. "Never did men behave more bravely or bolder," is the enthusiastic comment of an eye-witness of this affair.

Siege is raised.

The army was re-embarked on June 6th. Most of the fleet put in at Casco, whence March despatched Redknap, with two other officers,[1] to break the news of his failure to Dudley.

But their ill news had flown before them, and a unique reception awaited their coming. Upon landing they were compelled to elbow their way through a crowd of noisy women, drawn together from the lowest quarter of the town, who saluted the unlucky envoys with mocking cries of "Welcome, soldiers!" One of these viragos, who carried an enormous sword of lath in her hand, rudely thrust it into their faces, at the same time bawling out, "Fie! for shame! pull off those iron spits by your sides; for wooden ones is all the fashion now!"[2]

Cutting taunts.

After running this gantlet, the crestfallen trio walked on under a running fire of the coarsest abuse, with a constantly increasing crowd of children, servants, and idlers following close at their heels, all shouting, "Port Royal! Port Royal!"

Dudley was furious. All his bright anticipations were clouded in disgrace. What was to be done? He

[1] CAPTAIN SUTTON of the Royal Marines, and Holmes of the provincials.
[2] LETTER of John Winthrop, in *Winthrop Papers*.

knew too well that he was the bright and shining mark
at which all the obloquy would be levelled. Again all
the old trumped-up charges would be revived. Many
would rejoice at his discomfiture. It was not in Dudley's nature to sit down quietly under it. He decided
on heroic treatment. The armament was practically
intact. He would send it back. The frame of mind he
was in may be inferred from the following sentence of
a letter to Governor Winthrop, of Connecticut : " They
are returning to that ground where I mean to have them
lye fifty days at least."

It was an unwise decision, yet no doubt had the support of the people. There had been some desertions.[1]
Two additional companies in a measure made good these
losses, but could not restore life to a body already expiring. Three prominent civilians [2] were sent to act as a
council to March, with authority to overrule him, if they
saw fit. Again the fleet sailed. A second
Second landing. landing was made on August 10th, on the
north side of the harbor ; for Subercase had employed
the interval in throwing up field works on the ground
formerly occupied by March, so that the situation was
now wholly changed for the worse.[3]

Though staggered by the unexpected return of the
English, Subercase immediately resorted to his old
tactics of wearing them out by keeping up an incessant
firing upon their camps, waylaying foraging or reconnoitring parties, or cutting off stragglers, so making it
dangerous for them to stir beyond their own line of

---

[1] SOME of the Plymouth and some of the New Hampshire men had gone home.
The rest of the Plymouth men were confined in the Castle at Boston. See Belknap's
New Hampshire, I., 343.

[2] THEY were Colonels Hutchinson and Townsend, and John Leverett.

[3] *Wainwright's letter* to Dudley.

sentinels. In a very short time it was the English who were besieged in their camp.

The rest of the story is soon told. March broke down under the strain, and turned the nominal command over to Wainwright.[1] Meantime the provincial troops were marched a quarter of a league above the fort, with the evident design of making their approach from the rear. Subercase learned from a prisoner of the plan to carry the artillery past the fort, under cover of the night, and cleverly defeated it by lighting fires all along the banks. Wain- **Sharp fighting.** wright then fell back to a point opposite the fort, was cannonaded out of it, moved still lower down, and finally, on the 20th, goaded into attempting something, crossed his whole force over to the fort side and advanced as if to assault it in earnest. Subercase sent St. Castin out to ambush them. There was sharp fighting for a time, with the probable object of drawing out the entire garrison, as otherwise the demonstration was mere bravado; but Subercase would not venture upon so dangerous a step, until he saw the Eng- **English draw off.** lish falling back to their boats. Then a second and third detachment were hurried off to St. Castin's aid. All three were sent back, very roughly handled. The English then re-embarked, unmolested, apparently satisfied with having shown that they could fight, even when nothing was to be gained by it.[2]

[1] COLONEL FRANCIS WAINWRIGHT died at Ipswich, August 3, 1711, within a few days of the date fixed for his marriage, and after a very short illness. Sewall says of it: "'Tis the most compleat and surprising disappointment that I been acquainted with. Wedding Cloaths, to a Neck-cloth and Night-Cap, laid ready in the bride chamber, with the bride's attire. Guests several come from Boston but no bridegroom."—*Sewall Papers.*

[2] ON the English side sixteen were killed, and as many wounded, and three killed and fifteen wounded on that of the French. M. de Saillant, *enseigne de vaisseau*, was among the killed; M. de Boularderie and St. Castin among the wounded.

Boston was thrown into a ferment. Dudley manfully endeavored to extract some consolation from the storm of disaster, but as everybody knew the truth, the effort to disguise it was worse than idle. The three high commissioners were laughed at for their pains; and jeered at in the streets with such stinging remarks as, "The three Port Royal worthies!" "The three champions!" etc. "But what could be done when the very devil had entered into the common soldiers?" is the concluding observation of a distressed looker-on.

All summer roving bands of Indians were infesting the highways beyond the Merrimac, killing, scalping and robbing unwary travellers. To enumerate all the casualties of this nature would be tedious. One, however, may be mentioned. On August 10th some of these lurking assassins fell upon a party of four horsemen, who appear to have been escorting a Mrs. Littlefield from York to Wells. The lady had a considerable sum of money with her. Only one of the party escaped to tell the horrid tale.

Upon the return of the Port Royal expedition the enemy grew bolder. They seemed to bear Oyster River a peculiar grudge, although that place had suffered more than all of its neighbors. In September a party of French Iroquois, hideously painted, suddenly rushed from their coverts, and with piercing yells fell upon **Killing at Durham.** a company of men who were engaged in cutting and hauling timber in the woods, under the direction of Captain Chesley. Seven fell dead, and one was mortally wounded, at the first fire. Chesley, with those left alive, manfully stood his ground, until he himself shared the fate of his companions. He was a brave officer, just returned home from Port

Royal, where he had distinguished himself by his good conduct.

Exeter, Kingston, and Dover, in New Hampshire, and Berwick, York, Wells, Winter Harbor, Casco, and even the inland town of Marlborough, in Massachusetts, suffered to a greater or lesser extent. The winter, however, passed in quiet; but that quiet proved the deceitful prelude of what was coming.

Subercase was in great spirits over his successful defence of Port Royal, and its results. He very reasonably believed this success should be vigorously followed up. In this vein he writes to the Minister[1] that three hundred New England vessels had fished this summer (1708) on the banks and shores of Acadia, all taking an abundant catch ; and asks that a swift-sailing man-of-war be sent out to cruise for their capture. He declares that she would make a million a year in prizes, would probably capture the Boston frigate (probably meaning the provincial cruiser), enable him to fortify La Héve, and if, as he believes, settlers came here in consequence, he would, with these helps, capture Rhode Island, which he says is inhabited by rich Quakers, and is the resort of rascals and even pirates.

Nothing is said of the West Indian corsairs who preyed upon the New England fishermen without mercy, carrying their prizes into Port Royal and receiving whatever they needed in exchange for captured goods. Subercase was boastful, but Dudley refused to acknowledge himself beaten yet.

[1] LETTER of December 25, 1708.

XXIV

HAVERHILL SACKED

August 29, 1708

STRANGE to say, although war raged so fiercely in New England all this time, a kind of truce existed between Canada and the province of New York. Both had their selfish reasons. To provoke the still formidable Iroquois would be to bring down a horde of enemies on the back of Canada. An attack on the Dutch or English settlements would furnish the provocation. Louis, therefore, had given strict orders to Vaudreuil[1] not to disturb the English on the Hudson so long as they kept quiet, and, on their part, the Albany traders found golden reasons for keeping quiet, so long as they themselves were let alone. It was well termed a criminal neutrality, since it left Canada free to throw her whole strength against New England, instead of having to look two ways at once; and while she was being impoverished by the war, the Dutch traders at Albany were actually making money by it.

This anomalous state of things permitted the old channel of communication, so long existing between the seceding Mohawks and their relations in New York, to be kept open, as in time of peace. Both parties came and went freely. The

New York neutral.

Indian go-betweens.

---

[1] VAUDREUIL to Subercase, cited by *Hutchinson*, II., 130, 158.

Albany traders found this arrangement profitable, the French Indians secured cheap goods for their beaver, and the Canadian authorities were only too glad to wink at it for reasons already pointed out. As the French historian, Charlevoix, truly says: "Thus our own ene- mies relieved our most faithful allies when they were in necessity, and while they were every day hazarding their lives in our service."

It is true that this unauthorized neutrality was also a means of getting intelligence of the enemy's plans. Peter Schuyler was indefatigable, as well in his efforts to keep the Massachusetts authorities advised of Vau- dreuil's designs, as in holding the French Mohawks aloof from joining his desolating war-parties. But it is much to be doubted whether this advantage was not more than offset by the $\quad$ Peter Schuyler.
contraband trade which made it possible. Indeed, it would be putting it mildly to say that this sort of secret service did New England quite as much harm as good. On the other hand, the events now to be related go to show that Schuyler's skilful intrigues sometimes bore fruit at a most critical time.

Rumor had for some time been busy with a great war-party that Vaudreuil was said to be forming for a raid into New England. As the destined point of attack could only be guessed, the whole frontier was strengthened, the roads patrolled, and the inhabitants warned to be more than ever vigilant. So the spring passed and summer began.

Late in June, 1708, Colonel Schuyler[1] wrote from

---

[1] SCHUYLER'S letter is dated June 22d. He had been in Boston a short time before. *Hutchinson*, II., 131, credits this information to Colonel John Schuyler. It was Colonel Peter.

Albany to Governor Dudley the cheering intelligence that he had succeeded in persuading several of the hostile sachems, leagued with the French, " to throw down the hatchet at the feet of the governor of Canada," thus signifying their resolve not to go out on the war-path against New England again. He also added that he had great hopes of prevailing with the Indians, lower down the St. Lawrence, to adopt the same course.

At this very hour an expedition was in preparation against New England on a large scale. It had been resolved upon at a great council, held at Montreal, at which the chiefs of all the mission Indians domiciled in the colony were present, and had promised to furnish the warriors demanded of them. One hundred picked Canadians, with a sprinkling of volunteers from the regular troops, were to take part. Besides these, a sufficient number of friendly Abenakis from the New England villages were expected to join the expedition on the march, to bring the whole force up to four hundred strong. St. Ours des Chaillons and Hertel de Rouville were to command the French, and La Perrière the Indians. The better to conceal their march, as well as to hasten it, the different bodies were to take as many different routes to the designated rendezvous, at the foot of Lake Winnipesaukee, where the Abenakis should have preceded them. From thence two short marches would bring them down upon the Piscataqua settlements — Berwick, Salmon Falls, Dover, Portsmouth, Oyster River or Durham, etc.—where the meditated blow was to fall without warning.

A great war-party.

On July 26th this formidable expedition set forward through the wilderness. Fortunately for those against

whom it was directed one party of Hurons and another
of Caughnawagas turned back, the one disheartened by
the accidental death of a warrior, which was considered
an evil omen; the other, among whom Schuyler had so
diligently sown defection, seemingly glad of any excuse
to abandon the enterprise altogether.

Though disconcerted by this wholesale desertion, the
leaders pushed on, under positive orders from Vaudreuil, although their force was now much too small for
the sweeping blow first planned. A further disappointment awaited them at the rendezvous. No Abenakis
joined them there. Instead, therefore, of Haverhill
throwing themselves upon the nearest set- the object.
tlements, the raiders moved off toward Haverhill, some
sixty miles farther west, under the impression that it
would prove a far more easy conquest.

At Haverhill, the Merrimac courses leisurely on between high ridges of land, that slope upward by easy
ascents to moderately level, commanding crests, where
the outlook in all directions was wide and ample. Ex-
tensive as it was, it embraced nothing but one unbroken
solitude, one vast virgin forest, dimpled with shadows
here or dashed with sunlight there. There was not a
white man's cabin anywhere in sight.

Buried in the depths of these forests the enemy was
coming on without fear of discovery.

Just here, at Haverhill, the ridge is broken through
to admit the passage of Little River, coming down out
of the hills, at the east, to throw itself into the Merrimac. This was the open postern through which the
village was easily assailable on that side, weakly guarded by a garrison or two on the heights beyond, where
Thomas Dustan formerly lived. Unless this outpost

16

gave the alarm, Haverhill lay at the mercy of the invaders.

As to the village, it still consisted of no more than thirty houses chiefly grouped near the foot of the ridge, where it is washed by the river, with a few more scattered here and there along the crest above, like watch-houses on a castle wall. In one of these[1] lived Simon Wainwright, captain of the village militia. From his

SITE OF WAINWRIGHT GARRISON, HAVERHILL, MASS.

doorstep Wainwright could look off over the dense forests stretching far and away to the east, could follow with his scrutinizing eye through this labyrinth of aged woods the windings of Little River, from its vanishing point among the distant hills to where it finally breaks through the natural embankment on which he stood; and he could also plainly see if all was well with his lonely neighbors

Wainwright's house.

1 THE house shown in the engraving is opposite Winter Street Church.

over against him on the heights beyond. And this we take to have been his daily habit.

Other garrisons lay to the north and south, that of Jonathan Emerson standing guard over the approach to the ridge from Little River, those of Joseph and Nathaniel Peaslee flanking it in the opposite direction. These simple defences, in a measure, covered the more compact part of the village. **Other garrisons.** In fact, nothing more could be done. Three or four soldiers were posted in each. A certain number also were quartered in the village itself, some houses being designated garrisons and some not. Major Turner, Captains Price and Gardner, all good officers, were in the command of the colony soldiers thus posted.

Only the most sleepless vigilance could have prevented what was going to happen, as in the present case the back of the village, so to speak, was turned to the enemy.

On Sunday, August 29th, at daybreak, or the dusk just before dawn, the savages were discovered just entering the skirt of the village. Of all the days of the week, this one most favored just such a surprise, since, it being a day of rest, the drowsy villagers were still abed. In some unexplained way the outlying garrisons had been passed without giving any alarm. **Village surprised.** One man only, who chanced to be abroad at that early hour, caught a glimpse of the assailants filing silently out of the forest, close upon him. Taking to his heels he shouted aloud the alarm, fired his gun, and ran for his life.

It was too late. The marauders entered the village with him, whooping and yelling, like so many hellhounds, at the complete success of their plans. At this dreadful summons the inhabitants awoke. Smothered noises came from the houses. Presently a woman, bolder than the rest, threw open her door and ran for dear life toward the nearest garrison. A bullet was quicker, and the first victim lay bleeding on the ground. Then the assault became general. Frenchmen, daubed and painted to hide their detestable faces, loaded and fired, and cheered on their no more savage comrades to the work of slaughter. Some houses were weakly, some stoutly, defended. One party made for that of Benjamin Rolfe, minister of Haverhill, in which a few soldiers were quartered. Acting on the impulse of the moment, Rolfe ran to the street door, to keep the savages out. Finding the door securely fastened the assailants first discharged their guns into it, shattering Rolfe killed. the wood [1] and wounding Rolfe where he stood ; then bursting in, despatched the wounded man, brained Mrs. Rolfe with a tomahawk, and dashed out her infant's brains against the doorstone. Paralyzed by fear, the cowardly soldiers were slain while begging for mercy. The house was then ransacked from top to bottom.

Two of Rolfe's children were saved through the presence of mind of Hagar, a negress, who ran with Children saved. them into the cellar, hid each one under a large washtub, and then concealed herself behind a barrel of meat. [2] The marauders searched the cellar, drank milk from the pans, and even helped them-

[1] THE site of Rolfe's house is marked by a monument at Dustin Square. The door, pierced by balls, was afterward nailed up in the meeting-house porch, as a memorial of the event, and was burned in the fire that destroyed that house.—Allen.

[2] ONE afterward became the wife of Colonel Hatch, of Dorchester, Mass.; the other, Elizabeth, of tne Rev. Samuel Checkley, Sr., of Boston. Their daughter became the wife of Samuel Adams, the patriot.

selves to meat from the barrel behind which the trembling negress was crouching, breathless with terror, without suspecting that anyone was concealed there. The
poor fugitives were no doubt favored by the darkness,
as well as the haste these brigands were in to be off
to their bloody work again. Besides Hagar and the
children, Anna Whittaker, who lived with the Rolfes,

PEASLEE GARRISON, HAVERHILL, MASS.

also escaped death by hiding behind an apple-chest
kept under the stairs.[1]

What was true of one was true of all. The French
contingent was quite as active in the house-to-house
slaughter now going on as the savages themselves.
Impious wretches! that had said their prayers, embraced each other, and commended their souls to God,
just before bathing their hands in innocent blood.[2]

[1] SHE also claimed to have saved Rolfe's children.—*Massachusetts Gazette*, September 27, 1764.
[2] *Charlevoix*, II., 326.

Thomas Hartshorne and his three sons were killed in the act of escaping from their dwelling. Mrs. Hartshorne secreted herself and her children in the cellar, closing the trap-door in the floor after them. An infant was left lying on a bed in the garret. Finding no one else, the child was quickly tossed out of the window without ceremony, but fortunately was only stunned, not killed, by the fall. The story goes that this babe was left in the garret for fear that its cries would betray the hiding-place of the others! The trap-door escaped discovery.

Of such sickening details does the story of the sacking consist. Still more remarkable were the events happening at Captain Simon Wainwright's, on the hilltop. As the story has come down to us, the inmates there were getting ready to make a stubborn resistance when a volley, fired into the house at close quarters, killed Wainwright on the spot.[1] One's credulity is severely taxed to believe what follows. It is said that upon her husband's fall, Mrs. Wainwright unbarred the door to the savages, who instantly crowded into the house, weapons in hand. With great presence of mind the wife of the man lying dead there before her, spoke kindly to his murderers, brought them food and promised to do whatsoever they should require of her. Astonished at such treatment, the intruders demanded nothing but money. Telling them it was in another room, the quick-witted woman left them as if to fetch it, but instead of doing so she seized the opportunity to fly with her children, one girl excepted, who was left behind. Enraged at the

Mrs. Wainwright's escape.

[1] PALFREY erroneously identifies him with Colonel Francis Wainwright, late commander at Port Royal.

trick played upon them, the savages set fire to the house
after securing their prisoners.[1]

A still more dramatic incident,[2] if we may believe
tradition, took place at the house of a man named Swan.
This man also had barred his door against the marauders. The Indians first ran against it in a body, but
on finding that it did not give way, one of them set his
back against it, the better to exert his   Mrs. Swan's
whole strength, while the others joined   heroism.
their efforts to his. From the inside, Swan and his
wife opposed their strength to that of the besiegers,
and a desperate tussle ensued between them. As a
result the Indians succeeded in forcing the door partly
open, and Swan gave himself up for lost, when his
stout-hearted wife snatched up an iron spit, collected
all her strength, and ran the foremost Indian through
the body. This house was saved.

In this manner the work of burning, pillage, and
slaughter was going on with little check, when the distant roll of drums and blast of trumpets warned the
invaders that it was time to look to their retreat. By
this time the soldiers, collected from the neighboring
garrisons, were on the march to attack them. The village was immediately deserted. Before leaving, however, the enemy had set fire to the meeting-house, but
the flames were quickly extinguished.

As the invaders retreated, the exasperated settlers
rallied and hung on their rear. Before they could
reach the shelter of the woods, they were   Enemy
furiously attacked by sixty or seventy   retreat.
men, who pressed them so closely that they were com-

---

[1] MYRICK : Chase's *Haverhill*, 222.
[2] IBID.

pelled to halt, throw down their plunder, and face their
pursuers. After a sharp fight, in which they left nine
of their number dead on the ground, superior force
enabled them to shake off their assailants, who then
gave up the pursuit.[1]

In this lively combat, two French officers, Chambly
and Verchères, were killed, and in the various encounters of the day the French admit that eighteen of their
number were wounded. Their accounts add that the
monster Asacumbuit performed prodigies of valor with
a sabre given him by Louis XIV.[2]

Between thirty and forty persons were killed or taken
prisoners in this raid. Sixteen of the slain were inhabitants of Haverhill. The soldiers were
mostly from the towns below. Several
prisoners were retaken during the fight outside the
village. Others made their escape. On the whole the
marauders had little cause for rejoicing. They were so
hard pressed that they lost all their packs, with their

Loss of life.

---

[1] FRENCH accounts speak of this fight as an ambuscade, which was broken through
and put to rout with great slaughter. Though it adds picturesqueness to the narrative,
the English accounts make no mention whatever of such a foolhardy attempt upon an
enemy, probably numbering four to one.

[2] As a mark of the royal favor for having, as he declared, slain one hundred and fifty
of His Majesty's enemies with his own hand. How many were women and children he
did not say. He was wounded in the foot in this raid, and very soon disappears from
view. *The New England Weekly Journal* of June 19, 1727, has the following notice of
his death:

"We hear from the eastward that some days ago died there Old Escambuit, who
was formerly the principal sagamore of the (now dispersed) tribe of Saco or Pigwacket Indians. . . . He, Hercules-like, had a famous club, which he always carried
with him, and on which he made ninety-eight notches, being the number of Englishmen
that he had killed with his own hands. . . . He had formerly made discovery of a very
fine silver mine up Saco River, but could never be persuaded to tell whereabouts it was
till very lately he was prevailed with to promise to carry an Englishman (who had
several times been in quest of it) to the spot, and endeavored to do it. But upon their
way, when they got within a few miles of it, he fell sick, and in a short time died;
having first gave the Englishman all the directions he was able for the finding out of
said mine, who is resolved to prosecute the matter, hoping still to make discovery
of it."

provisions, besides what booty had been secured. The losses on both sides were not far from equal. Had the pursuit been as vigorous as the attack was prompt and well-sustained, the whole party, in all likelihood, would have been scattered or taken.

XXV

INVASION OF CANADA FAILS; PORT ROYAL TAKEN
April, 1709—October, 1710

A CRISIS in the long struggle between New England and Canada was at hand. Early in the spring of 1709 **The queen's** Dudley was notified that the queen was **readiness.** ready to aid the colonies in making one strong and united effort for the final overthrow of French power in America. Vetch, made a colonel for the purpose, came over from England, armed with instructions to set forward the necessary preparations. In company with Vetch came Colonel Francis Nicholson,[1] who had been Governor of Virginia, and more recently of Maryland, and was now seeking a new path to preferment through the medium of the coming campaign. He was well known in New England, through his association with Andros in the government of New York, some years before, but old prejudices seem to have lost their force, now that a common interest brought Puritan and Jacobite to join hands again at the sound of the **Francis Nichol-** war-drum. Moreover, Nicholson was a **son.** man of far more statesmanlike mould than the canny Scot, Vetch, and carried far more weight into the enterprise now on foot than his shrewd, but vehement and irascible, associate. From this time

---

[1] SEE a reference to him in the Hannah Dustan affair. He governed more provinces than any public man of his day. Besides Virginia, New York, Maryland, and Nova Scotia, he was appointed to South Carolina, 1721, having been knighted the year before. He died at his lodgings in Old Bond Street, London, March 5, 1728.

forth the fortunes of the two men were destined to be closely identified.

More welcome news can hardly be imagined. If one-half of what Subercase wrote to the Minister on the subject was true, no sacrifice was too great on the part of the Bostonians, if it promised to put an end to the depredations committed upon their shipping and commerce. These depredations were chiefly the work of French corsairs, hailing either from Martinique or other West Indian ports. Speaking of these free-   French corsairs. booters Subercase goes on to say that "they have desolated Boston, having captured and destroyed thirty-five vessels. They have had during the whole year a scarcity of provisions, because our corsairs captured from them nearly six barques, the greater part of which were laden with cargoes." This refers to the year 1709. The governor adds that "the prizes taken by the freebooters caused a temporary plenty in the colony, and had put it in his power to make presents to the Indians."

In brief the plan of operations was this: The campaign was to be opened by a combined attack upon Quebec and Montreal, both by sea and land. The fall of Canada would, of course, involve that of Nova Scotia, Newfoundland, and all the rest of the   Plan of campaign. French possessions on the continent, which would then come definitively under British rule, once and forever. To this end Massachusetts and Rhode Island were to raise 1,200 men, who were to take part in the sea expedition, while Connecticut, New York, New Jersey, and Pennsylvania should furnish 1,600 [1] for that directed against Montreal.

[1] THE assigned quotas were: New York, 800; Pennsylvania, 150; New Jersey, 300; Connecticut, 350; Rhode Island, 200.

Dudley entered upon the work cut out for him with alacrity. After seeing things in train here, Nicholson and Vetch went round to New York by water, calling at Newport and New Haven on their way, in order to hasten matters to the utmost. Finding everything working to their wishes, they continued their voyage to New York.

TEE YEE NEEN HO GA RON, EMPEROR OF THE SIX NATIONS.

Here they were doomed to meet with disappointment. New York, indeed, no longer hesitated to cast off the trammels of a *quasi*-neutrality, and throw her whole weight into the contest.[1] Well she might. Subjugated Canada would divert the Indian trade of the great Northwest from Montreal and Quebec, to Albany and New York. With New Jersey and Pennsylvania it was different. Recently settled, largely

Pennsylvania and New Jersey hold back. by Quakers, who abhorred the very name of war, the former colony would vote only a money grant of £3,000, while the latter refused aid of any sort. The loss of men in this quarter was, however, made good, in part, by six hundred Iroquois

---

[1] As the treasury was empty, New York for the first time issued bills of credit.

warriors, whose wives and children were maintained at the public expense during the campaign. Nicholson was put in command of this force, reckoned at 1,500 men, which took up its line of march for Lake **Army at** Champlain, cutting roads and building **Wood Creek.** forts as it slowly advanced over ground destined to become the scene of far more momentous events in the future. At Wood Creek the army halted to wait for news of the sailing of the other branch of the expedition, before resuming its forward movement upon Montreal.

Meanwhile, the transports and troops assembled at Boston lay waiting from May to September, in daily expectation of the arrival of the promised squadron and regiments **Royal aid** out of **fails.** England. They waited in vain. It was not until October that a ship arrived

SAGA YEATH QUA PIETH TON, KING OF THE MAGUAS.

with the unwelcome news that the royal troops, destined for America, had been sent to Portugal instead.

Before the receipt of this truly exasperating intelligence, Nicholson had been compelled to break up his camp at Wood Creek on account of the sickly condition of his troops, who were dying off by scores from camp dysentery, contracted by drinking water reeking with the filth of the camps.   Decimated by disease, the enfeebled force retraced its steps to Albany.

ECON OH KOAN, KING OF THE RIVER NATION.

Unwilling to throw away what it had cost so much time, trouble, and expense to get together, the New England governors met Nicholson, Vetch, and Moody at Rehoboth, October 14th, to see what was to be done. It was unanimously decided to send the New England forces to attack Port Royal, provided the queen's ships then at Boston and New York would co-operate. This being refused, nothing remained but to disband the troops, settle the cost,[1] and swallow the disappointment with. the best grace possible under the circumstances.

Nicholson immediately sailed for England to solicit aid for another attempt the next season.   He was ably seconded by Peter Schuyler, who had conceived the shrewd idea of taking over to England some Mohawk

[1] STATED at £23,000 sterling ; reimbursed to the colonies by England.

chiefs, as a means of holding the wavering Iroquois faithful to the English, for that powerful confederacy now had a French, as well as an English, party among them. Schuyler accordingly sailed for **Mohawks in England.** England with five Mohawks, one of whom died at sea. If Schuyler had counted upon making a sensation he was not disappointed. His dusky companions were the lions of the hour. They were shown about London, feasted, flattered, followed about by the common people wherever they went, and caressed by the nobility. They sat for their portraits [1] to a Dutch artist. Honors permitted only to royal personages were paid them. The queen caused them to be clothed at her own expense by a prominent theatrical costumer. Even literary London, in the persons of Addison and Steele, bestirred itself in their behalf

HO NEE YEATH TAN NO RON.

—all this to impress the tawny visitors with a due sense of the might of the British empire. As a fitting climax

[1] THE originals from which engravings in mezzotint were made, reproduced in recent works.

they were given an audience by the queen herself, who graciously listened to the speech spoken for them entreating her royal aid against France in Canada.[1]

Throughout the spring and summer small squads of skulking marauders spread distress and alarm in their track. Mehuman Hinsdale was captured for the second time at or near Deerfield. William Moody, Samuel Stevens, and two sons of Jeremiah Gilman were sur-

Murder renewed. prised on the road three miles out of Exeter, and carried away into captivity. Moody was subsequently the victim of an adventure so remarkable as to be well worth narrating, if for no other reason than to keep alive the memory of what it meant in those days to fall into the hands of the savages.

It seems that a party of ten Englishmen was returning from a successful scout, which had carried them as far into the enemy's territory as Fort La Motte, on the Richelieu River. They were now making all speed homeward, travelling night and day to elude pursuit.

Mr. Moody's adventure. It was necessary to be constantly on the alert, as they were now following the route most frequented by war-parties going to or returning from the Connecticut Valley; and they were most anxious to rejoin six of their companions, who were waiting for them at the mouth of White River, with supplies.

After paddling all night up the Onion River, the scouts left their canoes at the falls, shouldered their packs, and struck out across an elbow, formed by the windings of the stream, until they came to the river again at some distance higher up.

While making a short halt here a canoe was seen

---

[1] THE speech is given by Oldmixon.

coming down the river. There were five persons in
it. On a nearer approach four were seen to be Indians, while the fifth was evidently a white man and a
captive. When the unsuspecting savages came within easy range, the scouts fired with so true an aim that
two redskins were killed outright, one tumbled over,
wounded, into the bottom of the canoe, while the fourth,
upon witnessing the fate of his comrades, plunged head
foremost into the river, and struck out lustily for the
opposite shore.

Leaving two or three men to take care of the swim-
ming savage, when he should leave the water, the rest
followed the motions of the disabled canoe along the
bank, as it drifted down the stream with the current, at
the same time hallooing to the white man to bring the
canoe to the shore. He replied that he could not do
so, because the wounded savage would not let him.
"Knock him in the head then!" shouted back Wright,
the captain of the scouts. This the prisoner attempted
to do with a hatchet, lying in the bottom of the canoe,
but in the struggle which took place the canoe was
overset, plunging both combatants into the water.

The white man swam toward his friends, while the
Indian made for the opposite bank, which he succeeded
in reaching, wounded as he was, and was scrambling off
into the bushes when seven well-aimed bullets pinned
him to the earth.

Meanwhile, the captive was straining every nerve to
reach the shore, but finding his strength leaving him,
he lost heart when within a rod or two of the bank, and
undoubtedly would have sunk to the bottom if one of
the rangers had not ran to his assistance with a sap-
ling, which the drowning man managed to grasp, and

17

was quickly drawn to the land. He proved to be William Moody, of Exeter.

While attention was thus drawn to the captive's struggle for life and liberty, one of the scouts who was looking on from the bank above heard the snapping of dry sticks behind him. He gave one hurried look in the direction of the noise, and instantly shouted out the warning cry of "Indians! Indians!" The cry was scarce uttered when the scout received a charge of buckshot in the face. Another shot dropped Lieutenant Wells, as he was scrambling up the bank after his gun, left there when he went to Moody's assistance.

In a few words Moody then told the panic-stricken rangers that the canoe he had just escaped from was only one of five, two of which the rangers had missed by taking the cut-off, while two more were still above them. Upon hearing the guns the party below had instantly turned back, taking to the woods for a cover, and it was their fire which had just disabled two of the rangers' best men. Dropping shots from the opposite bank also told the rangers that the party from above had now come to the aid of their companions.

Upon finding themselves thus caught between two fires, the rangers scattered in a panic, every man for himself, leaving poor Moody to his fate. Seven succeeded in reaching the rendezvous safely. The eighth man, John Burt, of Northampton, was never heard from.

Moody's tragic end was subsequently learned from some fellow-captives, on their return to the settlements. Upon being so suddenly abandoned by his rescuers he gave himself up for lost. Too feeble of body either to fly or resist, he was driven to choose between starvation or captivity, and nerved by the hope of saving his

life, he called out to the savages from his place of concealment to come and take him. The wretched man
was quickly secured, taken across the river, tied to a
stake and burned alive, in revenge for the losses these
miscreants had sustained in their late conflict with the
scouts.[1]

In June Deerfield was again attacked by a body of
French and Indians, estimated at one hundred and
eighty, led by one of the Rouvilles; but this time the
inhabitants, many of whom had so lately returned from
captivity, met the attack with steadiness, and repulsed
it with the loss of only one man killed and three or four
wounded. In September, at Wells, a soldier was killed
and another taken while passing between the garrisons.

Nicholson came back from England in the summer of
1710 with a small squadron, which, upon being joined
by other ships, then cruising in American waters, sailed
for Port Royal, where so many reputations had been
lost. On board this fleet there was a regiment of royal
marines, and four of provincial troops, or about 2,000
men in all. Captain Martin of the Dragon was commo-
dore of the fleet; Nicholson commanded the land forces,
with Vetch acting as his chief-of-staff. The four provincial battalions were under Colonels Hobby and
Tailer, of Massachusetts, Colonel Whiting, of Connecticut, and Colonel Walton, of New Hampshire. Paul
Mascarene, afterward Governor of Nova Scotia, commanded one of Walton's companies. Besides these,
there was a company of Iroquois Indians attached to
the expedition, under the orders of John Livingston,
who held the nominal rank of major of scouts.

---

[1] CAPTAIN BENJAMIN WRIGHT'S account, abridged by Penhallow, printed in full in
Sheldon's *History of Deerfield.*

To repel this well-equipped force Subercase,[1] the French commandant, could muster only two hundred and sixty men, the greater part of whom he was afraid to trust outside the fort for fear of their deserting. The ramparts were in a dilapidated condition, so that from the first there was little hope of making a successful defence. Indeed, soon after the arrival of the English fleet at the entrance of the basin, Subercase had written to the Minister, exposing his weak condition, and admitting that if the garrison received no succor, there was "every reason to fear something fatal."

As seven or eight deserters had stolen off on board the English fleet on its arrival, the besiegers were no doubt well informed of these facts, and indeed went about their work in a way to show that the result was, to all intents, a foregone conclusion. Little or no opposition was offered to their landing, although in marching up toward the fort a few men were killed by the inhabitants, who fired on the soldiers from their houses and then took to their heels. Colonel Vetch with five hundred men so lined the shore opposite to the fort with his skirmishers as to cover the landing of the cannon and ammunition. By drifting up and back with the tide the English bomb-vessel was able to throw her shells **Port Royal taken.** into the fort, and to draw its fire, thus rendering material service to the besiegers in throwing up their batteries. The fleet had cast anchor in the basin on September 24th. On October 1st the besiegers opened fire from three breaching

---

[1] SUBERCASE was informed by prisoners that the Bostonians were again planning the conquest of Acadia and trying to induce Scotchmen to take an interest in it through Vetch, who had gone to England for that purpose. Mountains of gold were expected from the enterprise. Among other projects was one to seize on La Hève, and make a post there.—*Letter to the Minister.*

batteries at only one hundred yards' distance. It was sharply returned from the fort. The English now being able to reduce it, at will, to a heap of rubbish, a demand for its surrender was complied with as soon as made. Articles of capitulation were signed on the following day. Indeed, in the presence of such an overwhelming force, Subercase had no choice but to submit, yet, with a soldier's instinct, had fought to save his reputation. Strangely enough, his former successful defence was meanly used to convict him of a want of courage in this instance.[1]

A garrison of marines was left in the fort, with Colonel Vetch as military commandant, and the place, now definitely passed under the English flag, was named Annapolis Royal in honor of the reigning princess.

By the terms of the capitulation only such inhabitants as lived within three English miles of the fort were free to go or stay in their old homes upon taking the oath of allegiance to the Crown of Great Britain. Four hundred and eighty-one persons were embraced in this provision. All others were treated as prisoners at discretion, or as subject to such penalties as the conquerors might see fit to impose.

It will be remembered that Church had threatened to retaliate the savage cruelties at Deerfield upon the heads of the Acadians. The threat had fallen upon deaf ears. But Nicholson conceived himself now in a position to enforce it. With this end in view Livingston and St. Castin [2] were sent off overland to Quebec

---

[1] NICHOLSON'S *Journal* of the expedition, with many other documents relating to the siege, is in the *Nova Scotia Historical Collections*, Vol. I.

[2] SUBERCASE before this had warmly recommended St. Castin to the Minister on account of his services during the late siege. He declared that St. Castin was kept out of his estate in France under pretence of illegitimacy, although he had full evidence of

to inform Vaudreuil that Acadia had fallen into English hands. Livingston was further to notify him that if the indiscriminate massacre of innocent women and children by his hired cut-throats was persisted in, then the Acadians would be treated in a like manner. It was hardly worth while making a threat which it is more than doubtful if Nicholson ever meant to put in execution.

After undergoing unheard-of hardships in crossing the wilderness at that inclement season of the year, the envoys reached Quebec in a starving condition.[1] Vaudreuil, probably to gain time, despatched his answer to Boston by the hands of two of his best partisan officers, Rouville and Dupuis, who were secretly instructed to thoroughly reconnoitre the country passed through. In reply to Nicholson's threats, Vaudreuil simply said that if they were carried into effect he should be compelled to do the like by all the English in his hands. And this was all the satisfaction to be had for the attempt to frighten Vaudreuil.

his heirship. " This poor boy has to do with the first *chicanier* of Europe, and lieutenant-general of the town of Oleron, in Bearne, who for long years enjoys this property." —*Subercase to the Minister.*

[1] SEE account in Penhallow.

XXVI

MORE INDIAN DEPREDATIONS
June, 1710—April, 1711

THE operations against Port Royal did not seem in the least to check the wanton destruction of life on the frontiers. On the contrary, the impression that most of the fighting men were away with the expedition seemed to make the savages bolder than ever.

Much the most notable victim of the year was Colonel Winthrop Hilton,[1] of Exeter, whom the Indians bitterly hated on account of his activity in hunt-   **Colonel Hilton** ing them down, and who had long been   **slain.** a tower of strength to the distressed frontier. Hilton had felled a number of mast-trees[2] in the forests of what is now Epping, and was busily engaged with his workmen about them, when the savages stole upon them unperceived, shot Hilton and two more dead on the spot, and captured two others. The rest escaped. On the next day the bodies of the slain were found shockingly mangled, that of Hilton being scalped and a lance left sticking in his breast. The murderers had buried themselves in the woods. This affair took place on June 23d.

On the same day the road in Kingston was ambushed, probably by the same gang, and as some of the towns-

---

[1] HILTON was the kinsman of both Governors Dudley and Winthrop.
[2] THERE were mast-paths cut for the purpose of hauling out the timber to tide-water.

people were passing over it, Samuel Winslow and Samuel Huntoon were killed, and Philip Huntoon and Jacob Gilman carried off to Canada.

Emboldened by these successes, the elated savages showed themselves in the open road at Exeter, where four children were seized while at their play. They also took John Wedgewood, and killed John Magoon on the very spot where he had dreamed that he should meet his death. David Garland was also slain at Dover, while returning home from public worship. Waterbury and Simsbury, two exposed frontier towns in southwestern Connecticut, had several inhabitants killed at this time. The active and ubiquitous enemy then struck swift blows at Marlborough and Brookfield, killing six persons there, and also shooting down the post-rider as he was going to Hadley. They or their confederates Captain Tyng then turned back to the Merrimac, in search slain. of fresh victims, thus throwing their pursuers off the scent; and here, between Concord and Groton, they mortally wounded Captain John Tyng, one of the best and bravest partisan leaders of this war.

Thus the already long death-list was being swelled on all sides at once. Even poor, poverty-stricken Maine could not escape. At Winter Harbor a woman was slain and two men taken prisoners, one of whom, Pendleton Fletcher, had already been thrice a captive. Fortunately, his comrades of the garrison succeeded in redeeming him at this time. A week later, three more were killed and six carried away from Saco settlements.[1]

As usual, the English were powerless to prevent these

---

[1] HUTCHINSON says that Johnson Harmon, a noted partisan in the next war, was one of them.

outrages. Nevertheless, it was necessary to do something to silence the cries of the people. Therefore, in the autumn, when the savages were in the habit of visiting the clam-banks to get their winter supply of food, Colonel Walton made a scout along the Maine coast, looking sharply out for stray parties of clam-gatherers. None were met with, however, until he got to the Kennebec, all having withdrawn to a safe distance after the late raid, as their custom was. But while encamped upon an island here, his smoke   *Walton's* decoyed a small party of savages into his   *scout.* hands. One of the prisoners proved to be a head chief of the Norridgewocks, who, upon finding himself entrapped, maintained to the last a truly Spartan stoicism, steadily refusing to answer all questions put to him, and laughing scornfully in the faces of his enemies when threatened with death. Finding him stubborn, Walton turned him over to his friendly Indians, who quickly despatched him. His squaw proved more tractable. She disclosed the whereabouts of more of their people, some of whom were discovered and slain.

As insignificant as these reprisals may seem they were, nevertheless, hailed with exultation by the whites —a most telling commentary upon the disparity of ends to means in this species of warfare.

At times, however, the Indians themselves seem to have realized that in the long run the battle would go against them. An incident, happening at Saco, shows this to have been the case. It chanced that Corporal Ayres, of the Winter Harbor garrison, fell into their hands. His captors released him without hurt or insult, and very shortly came to the garrison themselves with a flag, professing a strong desire for peace. This, no doubt, was the sincere wish of the old men. But the young men, like wolves maddened by the taste of blood, could not be controlled, and were only waiting for the coming of spring to be at their bloody work again. Four men were slain at Dover while at work in the fields ; one was killed and one wounded at York, the wounded man succeeding in getting into the garrison after being knocked down and scalped; two more were killed at Wells (April 29th) while planting corn; after that John Church was slain at Dover, and the people there were waylaid while going home from meeting, John Horn being wounded, and Humphrey Foss taken, though soon rescued by the determined bravery of Lieutenant Heard.

Upon these alarms Colonel Walton made another fruitless march to Winnipesaukee and Ossipee Ponds, finding only a few deserted wigwams at either place.

XXVII

THE GREAT SHIPWRECK

August 22, 1711

MEANWHILE the indefatigable Colonel Nicholson, who had gone to England immediately after the taking of Port Royal, the more effectually to urge upon the ministry a determined effort for the subjugation of Canada, was now returning successful from that mission. As this result had been rather hoped for than expected, it is necessary to explain just how it had come about. It is explained by the fact that in 1710 the Whig ministers were turned out of office, and a Tory cabinet brought in. Even the great Marlborough found himself out of favor at Court. Changes so sweeping are always significant of a change of policy. The war went on, but secret negotiations were begun with France looking to peace. It was argued that for nine years England had been fighting to cripple the power of the House of Bourbon, only to augment that of the House of Austria. Even Gibraltar, though subsequently ceded to Great Britain, had been captured for the House of Austria. The new ministry, therefore, had adopted a new line of policy, by which England should gain something for herself, to which her allies could lay no claim, should settle the question of dominion in the New World for all time, and finish the war with such a

Conquest of Canada.

Tories in power.

brilliant feat of arms as should lift the ministry to the very crest of the wave of popular favor.[1]

Two things contributed to mask the design. In the first place, the eyes of the allied powers were fixed upon the continent of Europe, where every move was closely watched, and in the next, it was wholly improbable that France should suspect England of playing so deep a game, while professing a sincere desire for peace. Even so consummate a master of the art of duplicity as Louis himself must have been staggered when his eyes were opened to the patent fact that he had been so completely overreached.

To carry out this grand design, a powerful land and naval force was being got ready with all possible despatch, the greatest secrecy being observed as to its destination.[2] Sir Hovenden Walker was put in command of the fleet and Brigadier John Hill of the army. Of the former little is known apart from his connection with this disastrous enterprise; and of the latter not much more than that he went by the nickname of "honest Jack Hill" among his boon companions, and that he was a brother to Mrs. Masham, who, in the general overturning, had succeeded the Duchess of Marlborough as the queen's favorite. Hill's chief recommendation for this command seems to have been hatred for the Churchills, as the duke had no sooner pronounced him good for nothing, and refused him a colonelcy, than the queen pensioned him and made him a brigadier.

Secret preparations.

---

[1] PALFREY (IV., 280–87) says this expedition was the favorite plan of Secretary St. John, afterward Lord Bolingbroke.

[2] ST. JOHN writes to Governor Hunter, of New York, that no one was informed of it except the queen, himself, and his colleague, Lord Dartmouth. Those who were to engage in it were given to understand that its destination was the south of France.

On June 8th, while the council was in session at Boston, discussing matters of routine, the booming of cannon at the castle announced some unlooked-for arrival from sea. The sitting was immediately broken up by the noise of drums in the streets, calling the town regiment to arms, if an enemy to repel his attack, if a friend to show him the proper honors. It proved to be Colonel Nicholson, bringing the queen's orders for the immediate levying of the land and naval forces of the colonies as far south as Pennsylvania. Better still, he announced the speedy arrival of the most formidable armament ever despatched to these shores, destined to lay siege to Quebec, while he himself, with the land forces, chiefly raised outside of New England, should be engaged in attacking Montreal, at the other extremity of the line. This sagacious combination, first devised by some plain colonists in the time of Sir William Phips, now newly renovated and set forth by the queen's advisers, would compel a like division of the enemy's forces to meet it, and it being reckoned that the invaders would still be the stronger at each point, little doubt was felt of the result. The main difficulty lay in getting the English forces up to within striking distance, and, by parity of reasoning, here also lay the strength of the defence.

Thus, at one powerful blow, the colonies were to be forever freed from all fears for the future. Certainly the prospect set before the long-suffering people of New England was brilliant indeed; for, with the downfall of French dominion, all the rubbish of Indian alliances, piratical depredations, contraband trade, and the like, would disappear like water spilled on the ground. Not the least gratifying result, reached by so

comprehensive a plan, was the bringing of New York
into line with New England, for, no longer ago than
March, Massachusetts had complained to Lord Dartmouth of the criminal neutrality maintained by New
York toward the French Indians. Indeed, the selfish
policy pursued by that province in the past had in turn
offended, disgusted, and well-nigh alienated the still
powerful Iroquois, who, from being eager to take up the
hatchet against the French, as they once were, had
grown indifferent or worse in most parts of the confederacy.

As her part in this grand undertaking, New England
was called upon to raise two regiments. Some dissatis-
Summons to faction was felt with the appointment of
arms. Vetch to command them, as he was still
in bad odor with the provincial authorities and people,
on account of former sharp practices of his, but what
would have been resented at another time as a slight
put upon them, now passed off without making any stir.
Yet, considering that Vetch cordially hated the Bostonians, this self-restraint on their part was unusual.

On the 24th[1] the fleet itself entered the harbor under a press of sail. Not having looked for it nearly so
soon, the authorities were taken somewhat by surprise.
Dudley had gone with Nicholson to attend the meeting
of governors called at New London. The assembly,
however, was in session, and with the council it prepared to welcome the distinguished visitors in a suitable
manner.

It was just said that the armament was by far the most
formidable that had ever crossed the Atlantic under the
English flag. Little wonder, then, that the astonished

[1] THIS was Sunday.

Bostonians should have believed it invincible. In all
there were fifteen ships-of-war, first-rates and frigates,
carrying nine hundred guns and manned   The fleet and
by more than five thousand seamen.[1]   army.
There were forty transports and six store-ships, having
on board seven battalions of Marlborough's veterans,
mostly withdrawn from the Netherlands to take part in
this expedition, besides a battalion of marines, and a
fine train of artillery, complete even to the horses belonging to it.[2]

Upon landing, Admiral Walker and Brigadier Hill
were escorted to the town-house by the local militia,
and warmly congratulated upon their safe   Walker and
arrival. The admiral immediately sent   Hill honored.
for John Nelson, who will be remembered for his daring and successful efforts to thwart Frontenac's plans,
while a prisoner at Quebec. No man in New England
was better able to give an intelligent idea of the strength
and weaknesses of Quebec, although Vetch was in the
habit of boasting that he knew more about Canada than
the Canadians themselves. Quebec now was by no
means, however, the Quebec of the last war.

The royal troops were at once landed and went into
camp on Noddle's Island,[3] opposite the town, where
they had a most excellent chance to re-   Camp at
cruit from the effects of their late voyage,   Boston.
and prepare for the unexpected work of the new. This

---

[1] FOR a list of these see *Boston News Letter*, No. 379.

[2] THE following regiments were employed, viz.: Kirke's, afterward 2d Foot; The
Queen's, afterward 4th Foot (King's Own); Hill's, afterward 11th Foot; Desney's, afterward 36th Foot; Windress's, afterward 37th Foot; Clayton's, disbanded in 1712; Kane's,
disbanded in 1713; Churchill's Marines, and King's Artillery. To these were added
the Marines at Annapolis. The strength of the marching regiments was 815 officers
and men, increased in some cases to 900.

[3] Now East Boston.

military camp, thus transferred from the fields of Marlborough's fame, numbered as many men, if not more,
than Boston itself, and no doubt furnished an object
lesson long remembered by all who had perhaps seen
something of the hardships, but little of the "pomp and
circumstance," of war.

Dudley having returned from New London on the
27th, a conference took place between him and the admiral on the next day, during which Walker sharply
complained of the merchants for offering no more than
twenty per cent. for exchange, and ended by threaten-
ing "to be gone somewhere else with the forces."

Councillor Sewall, who was present, remarks that
when the conference broke up, "the governor would
make the general goe out before him, though he much
resisted it." It is presumed that this little breeze soon
blew over, as on the following day the admiral, general,
field-officers, and several of the sea-captains dined with
the governor at Roxbury.[1]

After the exchange of formal civilities was over, the
serious business of the hour was taken in hand. It
now transpired that in their impatience to get the fleet
off before its destination should be discovered, the ministers had come very near defeating the whole enterprise at its birth. It was ignorantly assumed by those
in the secret that Boston could of course furnish subsistence for the royal army for ten weeks.
Trouble begins. So the commanders simply had been instructed to procure it there. Everybody was aghast at a
proposal so absurd on its face, and to many it looked like
a scurvy attempt to throw the responsibility for failure
upon them. This, of course, was equally absurd. It

---

[1] "JUNE 29th, Governor treats the general."—*Sewall Papers.*

was not at all surprising then that only one merchant could be found in the town willing to undertake the truly formidable task of victualling the fleet at so late a day and without one hour's previous notice. This was Andrew Faneuil, uncle to the builder of Faneuil Hall. But for his energy and pluck the expedition must certainly have suffered shipwreck then and there.

The extraordinary demand immediately doubled the price of everything wanted. This advance was met by an act of the General Court fixing prices on the basis of former values. The greedy merchants retaliated by shutting up their shops or removing their stocks to places of concealment. To counteract this an order quickly passed authorizing the seizure of provisions wherever found, and giving the searching officers full power to break into any man's premises if resisted. This high-handed proceeding had the desired effect. Provisions were brought from their hiding-places. The merchants took what was offered them, though not without grumbling at losing so fair a chance of making their fortunes. And it cannot be denied that in their zeal for the good of the service the provincial authorities had stretched their powers to the danger point.

The same thing was true with regard to wages. An embargo was declared on July 7th, both to secure sailors for the expedition and to prevent news of it from getting abroad. Following on the heels of this came an order to impress all bakers, brewers, coopers, and other artisans, who could not or would not supply the public at the stated prices. It seems, however, that the inhabitants could not all at once get over their traditional and habitual reverence for the Sabbath, orders or no

18

orders; for Colonel King notes in his journal[1] that on that day nobody would do any work, although the troops were in want of bread.

It was much less surprising to find it also taken for granted that experienced pilots could be secured at short notice. As a matter of fact, however, the number of seamen in New England acquainted with the rather intricate navigation of the St. Lawrence might be counted on one's fingers. It is true that Vetch had been to Quebec some years before in a small craft and had then taken certain soundings of the river; so had Captain John Bonner,[2] but with rare exceptions the river had remained a *mare clausum* to the English for twenty years past. This difficulty also was overcome by the impressment of several shipmasters, Bonner included, who were known to have some knowledge, more or less, of the dreaded river of Canada.

This done, a new source of irritation was found in the frequent desertions from the army and fleet, which the inhabitants were charged with aiding and abetting. The admiral stormed and fumed. He angrily demanded of Dudley that these losses should be made good by a resort to an impressment, but Dudley knew better than to attempt such a thing himself, and the admiral wisely refrained from doing what wholly exceeded his powers. A law, however, was promptly passed imposing a penalty of £50 for harboring deserters, with a summary process for bringing the offenders to trial. It is only just to say that the people had so patiently borne with all the

[1] BRITISH *Colonial Papers*. But see what Cotton Mather has to say, later on.

[2] " WHEN they (the French) were promising themselves to draw away the English to Popery, news came that an English brigantine was coming up; and y^t ye hon. Saml. Appleton, Esq., was coming ambassador to fetch off the captives, and Capt. John Bonner with him."—*The Redeemed Captive*.

burdens imposed upon them by the queen, which they
felt were quite enough, but also with these unlooked-
for exactions of the royal officers, simply because they
realized of what vast importance the undertaking was
to their own future welfare.

At another time Dudley would have thought that he
had troubles enough of his own, and to spare, without
being burdened with so many complicated   **Dudley's di-**
evils not of his creating, but laid at his   **lemma.**
door all the same. He had his two regiments to raise,
transports to provide, and supplies to purchase, with a
market already swept bare of everything to supply the
royal forces. (In fact, the Bostonians were eating salted
meats in order that the troops might have fresh.) There
was no money. To tide over the emergency £40,000 in
bills of credit were issued. Two full regiments were
raised[1] and put under the command of Colonels Vetch
and Walton, Vetch having come from Annapolis for
that purpose, thus bringing the total land forces up to
nearly, if not quite, 7,000 men.

Ready at last, the combined fleet set sail on July
30th, after a detention of only five weeks in port. The
superb appearance of this truly formidable   **Fleet sails.**
armada, as ship after ship spread its canvas
to the breeze, gave rise to the most confident anticipations of success; yet in view of the domineering conduct of its officers it may well be doubted whether its
arrival or departure was hailed with the more pleasure.

The fleet put in at Gaspé on August 18th on account
of contrary winds. On the 20th it got under way
again, the admiral having now on board the flag-ship a

---

[1] OF the 1,500 provincials, Massachusetts furnished 1,160, New Hampshire 100, and
Rhode Island the rest.

French pilot, called Paradis, picked up by one of the cruisers sent out in advance to prevent news of the fleet from going to Quebec before it.   Vetch, all impa-

Delay at Gaspé.

tience, was in a constant fret over the dila-tory motions of the admiral in not standing on into the river, when the wind was favorable, which course, Vetch did not hesitate to say, would have pre-vented what afterward happened.   But Walker charged the delay, as Vetch contends, to the timidity of Paddon, his captain, and of " Old Bonner," his pilot, about weath-ering the shoals of Anticosti.

Nothing material occurred on the two following days. Some of the vessels had been late in coming out of Gaspé, and had fallen astern.   All, however, had cleared Anticosti, but were making very little headway in con-

Night of Au-gust 22d.

sequence of light winds and a heavy sea. On the afternoon of the 22d the wind worked round to the east or east-southeast, and blew fresh, bringing with it a thick fog.   There being no land in sight, from which to judge of the position of the fleet, with every prospect of a dirty night before them, by the admiral's orders the ships were hove to, heads to the south, in the expectation that they would thus ride out the night at a safe distance from shore.   In plain words, while slowly jogging to windward they were left to drift to leeward.   To anchor in a hundred fathoms was, of course, out of the question.

From this point, up to which they agree fairly well, the various accounts are so conflicting that any attempt to reconcile them would be folly.   One thing is clear: No man in his senses would have handled the fleet in that manner if he had not supposed the land many leagues under his lee.

Darkness enveloped the fleet which was buffeting the rising gale in the way just pointed out, much scattered, and with a growing uneasiness among the officers quite natural to navigators sailing without guide or land-mark.[1]

The admiral's account of what fell under his own observation is sufficiently graphic. He was just turning in for the night when Paddon, the captain of the Edgar, came down to say that land was in sight. Supposing it to be the south shore, Walker merely ordered the signal made to steer in the opposite direction, and then went to bed. Shortly after, Captain Goddard,   **Breakers** of the army, at the solicitation of the   **ahead.** French pilot, rushed into the cabin in great agitation and begged of the admiral at least to come on deck, and see for himself ; but Walker, annoyed at the interference of a landsman, only laughed at his fears and refused to stir. A second time Goddard came down exclaiming, " For God's sake come on deck or we shall all be lost ! I see breakers all around us." " Putting on my gown and slippers," says the admiral, " I found what he told me to be true ; but still I could see no land to leeward." Just then the moon broke through the mist and showed him his mistake. Under his instructions the whole fleet was blindly rushing on to its destruction.

It was midnight, or later, when the alarm was given that the ships were among the breakers. All was instantly confusion, terror, and dismay. Signal guns boomed dismally in the darkness. High above the

---

[1] **THE** admiral laid the blame of this fatal manœuvre upon the pilots, who, to a man, flatly denied having given any such advice. The charts show the fleet at this time to have been actually embayed by the southerly trend of the north shore.

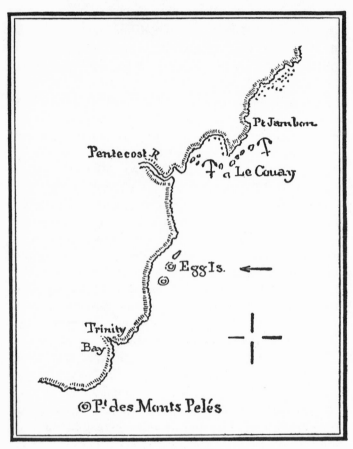

PLACE OF THE WRECK.

shouts of the living rose the drowning shrieks of hundreds of miserable wretches, as one ship after another **Ships go ashore.** crashed bodily upon the hidden rocks of the low-lying Egg Islands. When it was all over, eight transports were seen to have been lost and not far from a thousand persons had perished.

Bad as this was, the wonder is that any escaped to tell the tale. But warned by the signal guns fired by the ships that had struck, some captains wore ship in time to go clear of the rocks, while others, upon finding themselves actually among the breakers, **Narrow** let go their anchors as a last resort and **escapes.** were saved by a lucky shift of wind from the very jaws of destruction. Among others, the flag-ship herself was caught in this perilous plight, from which she only escaped by cutting her cables and crowding on all sail.

The next day was spent in rescuing such of the shipwrecked soldiers and sailors as had survived that dreadful night. The number saved fell only one short of five hundred, but fully nine hundred more lay stretched along the inhospitable shore, victims to incompetency, obstinacy, or neglect.[1]

On the 25th a council of war was held on board the Windsor, at which it was resolved not to make any further attempt to ascend the river. The admiral plainly showed that he was still laboring under the depressing impressions left on his mind by the late disaster. Yet none of the fighting ships had sustained any injury worth mentioning, while the land forces were still strong enough to give a good account of themselves. Though crippled, the fleet was by no means disabled. A commander with the spirit of a Nelson or a Wolfe

---

[1] THE Queen's regiment, afterward the King's Own, lost two hundred and nineteen officers and men and twenty women. These were probably the troops Charlevoix refers to as the queen's guards, etc. Captain Laurence Armstrong, of Windress's regiment, afterward Lieutenant-governor of Nova Scotia, escaped with the loss of his clothes, also his own and his company's baggage and arms. Charlevoix makes the number of drowned 3,000, evidently mere guesswork, as fully six weeks elapsed before the disaster was known at Quebec. More or less accurate returns were made of the troops lost, but not of the shipwrecked crews. Only one of the New England transports went ashore, but without loss of life.

would have met the crisis differently. But Walker
and Hill flinched from it. In vain Vetch urged the
admiral to recall his decision. A way of retreat not
absolutely disgraceful
was quickly seized
upon, defeat confessed,

SCHUYLER AND THE INDIAN SCOUTS.

and the great fleet steered for Spanish River, now Syd-
ney, in Cape Breton, and thence for England, after
seeing the colonial vessels safe on their own coast.

Word was immediately sent to Nicholson, who, with the prospect of having all Canada upon his hands, had no choice but to break camp and disband his forces, in the deepest mortification at seeing his really great efforts twice brought to naught before he could even strike a single blow. *Fleet turns back.*

Upon New England news of the disaster fell with stunning effect. Success, full and ample, had been looked for, not defeat. Looked at in any way it was realized that all hope of the conquest of Canada was now at an end for years to come, if not forever. From the attitude of the commanders all along there were well-grounded fears that New England, and particularly Boston, would be made the scapegoat of the affair in order to shield themselves. *Effects of failure.* As usual, intense discouragement gave rise to a season of rigid self-examination by those pious souls who saw only in this signal overthrow the manifest anger of God for the sins of the worldly minded among them. In especial, Cotton Mather loudly bewails the decay of true piety as inviting the divine wrath. " Have not burdens been carried through the streets on the Sabbath Day ? " he pointedly asks his congregation of merchants, shipwrights, and petty tradesmen. " Have not bakers, carpenters, and other tradesmen been employed in servile works on the Sabbath Day ? "

With better reason, since they themselves had no hand in bringing it about, the Canadians also attributed their escape to " a Providence who in a singular manner watched over them, and who, not content with delivering them from the *Joy in Canada.* greatest danger which the colony had ever run, had actually enriched it with the spoils of an enemy it had not even had the trouble to vanquish."[1] Solemn masses were said, and votive offerings made at the shrine of Notre Dame de Victoires.

Strangely enough the earliest intelligence of the disaster reached Quebec by way of Albany, after Nicholson's retreat to that place. It was not until the middle of October that two French ships arrived there from sea, bringing news that no enemy had been seen in coming up the river. These tidings were presently confirmed direct from the scene of the wreck, which was reported strewn with corpses, lying in heaps among the wreckage of all sorts cast up by the waves. Wedged firmly in the rocks of the Egg Islands lay the stranded hulks that had borne them to their death, slowly dropping to pieces. Superstition had already fixed itself upon the scene of desolation. Mysterious lights, dancing over the water, were said to have heralded the disaster, and are, it is averred, still to be seen on the anniversary of its occurrence.

Vestiges of the wreck.

A great deal of plunder was secured from the wrecks. Among other things found there was a parcel of proclamations, which Hill had got printed at Boston, in bad French, for distribution among the Canadians. They could now afford to laugh at his threats.

The ill-starred fleet of Sir Hovenden Walker had not yet reached the end of its misfortunes. On the voyage home the frigate Feversham and three transports were lost in the Gulf of St. Lawrence. One week after the admiral's arrival at Portsmouth, the flag-ship Edgar, with the admiral's papers and journals, and four hundred men on board, blew up at her moorings.[2]

---

[1] CHARLEVOIX.

[2] WALKER says he lost the original of Sir William Phips's journal of his Canada expedition by this accident.

In England the Court went into mourning. Strange
to say no official inquiry was made into the causes
of the return of the fleet. The real delinquents,
however, sought to shield themselves by throwing
the blame upon Dudley, upon the Bostonians, upon
the pilots—in short, upon everybody but   New England
themselves. Dudley was notified of the   blamed.
coming storm and made a dignified answer. The pilots
were sent to England, in order to give their evidence,
but it was never called for. The policy of the Minister
seemed to be to let the matter die out. Silence, indeed,
best served to hide the cruel mortification of such a
wretched *fiasco*, which it was hoped might be the sooner
forgotten. This was all very well for England. But in
the colonies, where public expectation had been raised
to such a height, only that the fall might be the greater,
the universal discouragement found vent in mutterings,
long, loud, and deep.[1]

[1] Of what may be called contemporaneous authority, the journals of Walker, Hill,
Vetch, and King are in existence. Walker's was not published until 1720, when the
events were not fresh in the writer's memory. It was an attempt to exonerate himself.
Vetch's may be found in Vol. IV., *Nova Scotia Historical Society Collections*, King's
in the *British Colonial Papers*. See also Charlevoix and Penhallow ; also Lieutenant-colonel George Lee's letter of September 12, 1711. An extract from a letter of
Samson Sheafe, commissary to the New England forces, in *Hutchinson*, Vol. II., may
be considered contemporaneous. Hutchinson gives the best account of what occurred
while the fleet lay at Boston. There is also a reference to the expedition in the *London Magazine* for 1756, p. 231.

XXVIII

CONCLUSION

COMMISSARY SHEAFE, writing home from Annapolis, under date of October 6, 1711, truly says of the futile ending of Walker's expedition: "This will be a bitter pill for New England." His words regarding the outlook were no less prophetic: "The French will now employ their Indians with redoubled rage and malice, to distress and destroy our exposed frontiers."

To forestall these incursions, Colonel Walton marched in the autumn at the head of one hundred and eighty men as far as Penobscot, where he found two vessels being fitted out as privateers, and burned them. He also took a few prisoners here.

A single piece of good fortune may be placed to the credit of Walker's inglorious expedition. It was not much, but it counted for much just at this time, when the public mind was so depressed by defeat. It was now learned that Annapolis had been on the point of falling into the enemy's hands again. Indeed, very few people knew how narrow had been the escape, until the danger was over, or how determined the French were to repossess themselves of a place of such vital importance to the control of the fisheries.

Outside of the three-mile limit expressed in the articles of capitulation, the inhabitants were openly hostile, and inside of it covertly so. In the first place they were as strongly loyal to their old master as ever, and in the next, Nicholson's drastic treatment was not likely to reconcile them to their new one. To all intents, therefore, they were still enemies to be reckoned with. Vaudreuil, always alive to the importance of recovering Acadia, never ceased to exhort these people through his agents, the missionaries, to hold fast to their old allegiance, promising them his active assistance to maintain themselves where they were, rather than see them abandon the colony, as they had proposed doing. That would never do. Events were shaping themselves exactly to Vaudreuil's wishes. Annapolis had fallen in October. By June 1st, following, the garrison had lost two-thirds of its numbers by sickness,[1] if French reports are true, and in this weak   Situation at condition no doubt would have fallen an   Annapolis. easy prey to the exasperated Acadians, who were only waiting for reinforcements to arrive from Quebec to break out in open revolt, when certain news of the English fleet being seen on the coast caused the whole enterprise to fall to the ground. After the fleet's return, Annapolis was made secure against any sudden stroke.

Here began those anomalous conditions which finally resulted in the expulsion of the Acadians from their native country forty-five years later. From this time onward they were as undeniably the victims of French policy as soldiers ordered to hold a post, with the full knowledge that they are to be sacrificed to the last man.

[1] AN exaggeration, though some had been withdrawn, and their places taken by New England troops.

The Bostonians were in the first glow of mingled anger and mortification over the ill-success of the great expedition when a new calamity pushed the old rudely aside. On October 2d, early in the evening, a fire broke out "through the carelessness of an old woman," picking oakum by a lighted candle, by which most of the business part of the town, including its oldest church and its town-house—two buildings around which clustered its earliest and latest history—was laid in ashes. **Boston on fire.** All night the flames raged unchecked. When they had spent their fury the very heart of Boston was a mass of smouldering ruins. It had come like a thief in the night, when the inhabitants were wholly unprepared. Besides a number of lives lost, more than one hundred families were rendered homeless; and so far did this conflagration surpass any that had previously happened in the history of the town, that for fifty years it was always spoken of as the great fire.

A quiet winter was followed by the usual irruptions in the spring. The frontier fairly swarmed with small scalping parties, whose fury chiefly fell upon the towns lying to the east of the Merrimac. It was a sudden dash, a deed of blood, and the perpetrators had vanished as quickly as if the earth had swallowed them up. At Exeter, April 16, 1712, one Cunningham was killed while travelling from Mr. Hilton's to town. Soon after, Samuel Webber was shot between York and Cape Neddock. Three more were slain, and three wounded, while engaged in teaming at Wells. Lieutenant Josiah Littlefield,[1] one of the slain, had but just returned home

---

[1] LITTLEFIELD'S adventures are given in considerable detail in Bourne's *History of Wells*.

from a long captivity. Getting bolder, the marauders presently showed themselves in the middle of the town, where they secured two captives. They then went to Spruce Creek, in Kittery, killed one lad, took another, and though closely pursued, made their escape into the woods. Another party struck the upper branch of Oyster River, where they shot Jeremiah Cromett and burned a saw-mill. At Dover, Ensign Tuttle was killed and a son of Lieutenant Heard wounded while standing guard. On May 14th a larger party of the enemy, who had ambushed the road between Wells and Cape Neddock, fell upon a scouting party of English, killed the sergeant,[1] and took seven prisoners besides. The rest fought in retreat, until they came to a high rock where they held their pursuers at bay till relieved by Captain Willard. The only loss sustained by the Indians up to this time was eight slain during a scout up the Merrimac.

New Hampshire and Maine raided.

Notwithstanding the fact that scouting parties were kept out, John Pickernell was shot at Spruce Creek, as he was in the act of locking his door, his wife wounded, and a child knocked on the head and scalped. Stephen Gilman and Ebenezer Stevens were taken at Kingston, and Gilman was put to death. Two children of John Waldron were seized outside of Heard's garrison at Dover and brutally decapitated because the savages did not have the time to scalp them, and would not lose the scalps. The garrison itself was not molested, although there was no one in it at the time except a few women, one of whom, Esther Jones, kept up such a shouting that the assailants, deceived as to the fact, did no fur-

---

[1] PENHALLOW, whose account is here followed, calls him Nalton (Knowlton ?).

ther mischief there.[1]   Berwick and Wells again suffered
the loss of a man each, and at Wells, Sambo, a negro
slave belonging to Captain John Wheelwright, was carried off while out looking for his master's cows, but
quickly made his escape again by trusting to fleetness
of foot.[2] On September 1st John Spencer was killed
and Dependance Storer wounded.

In September a noteworthy event took place at Wheelwright's garrison. In the midst of all these alarms, or
rather in spite of them, his daughter, Hannah, and
Elisha Plaistead, of Portsmouth, were to have an old-
fashioned wedding, to which the neighbors far and near
had been invited, and had come in goodly numbers
to witness, as Wheelwright was a man
of some consequence in that section. But
there were other guests not far off who had come there
unbidden. After the nuptial knot had been tied, and
the company was separating to their homes, two horses
were missing. Some of the party started off to look for
the animals, which were supposed to have strayed away.
A few minutes after their departure several gunshots
were fired in quick succession. The trap laid for the
unwary whites was then exposed. Indian cunning had
been used to decoy them to their death. On the spur
of the moment, a dozen or more men hastily mounted
their horses and rode off to the rescue of their friends,
the bridegroom with the rest.

This party also fell into an ambuscade, from which
the savages fired as it was passing at a gallop, killing
one man, Captain Robinson, outright, and unhorsing
the others. All who were unhurt got safely off except

*End of a wed-
ding.*

---

[1] PENHALLOW: Belknap's *New Hampshire*.

[2] RELATED at length by Bourne, *History of Wells and Kennebunk*.

the unlucky bridegroom, who was quickly seized and dragged away by his tawny captors. Of the first party Joshua Downing and Isaac Cole were killed, and Sergeant Tucker was wounded and made a prisoner.

After this rebuff the white men acted with more prudence. A stronger party set out in pursuit of the marauders, who were presently found in strong force, brought to bay, and sharply attacked, though without making much impression. After the loss of a man or two on each side, the Indians slowly moved off with their captives. Soon after a letter came from Plaistead to his father, saying that his captors demanded £50 ransom for him and £30 for his fellow-prisoner, Tucker, besides certain articles of which they stood in want. He put the number of Indians at two hundred, and said they were from Canada. His letter closes with this moving entreaty :

" Pray, sir, don't fail, for they have given me one day, but the days were but four at first. Give my kind love to my dear wife. This from your dutiful son till death,
" ELISHA PLAISTEAD."

Had it been attended with no loss of life, the act of kidnapping a bridegroom, and at such an interesting moment, too, might be fairly classed among the humors of the war, instead of being only one more reminder of its stern realities.

With this affair hostilities definitely closed.[1]   In fact a treaty of peace had been signed on April   **Treaty of** 11, 1713, by the belligerent powers, which   **Utrecht.** Matthew Prior, who, with his patron, St. John, had

[1] A TRUCE was signed at Paris, August 7. 1712. old style. and ratified by Queen Anne on the 18th of the same month. News of this reached New England in October.

taken some part in the secret negotiations, tersely char-
acterizes as "the d——d peace of Utrecht." Strong
language that; yet it is doubtful if a more scandalous
story ever disgraced the annals of a nation; and there
were few who could speak with more authority than the
pliant tool of an unscrupulous minister. To the colonies,
however, who could have no hand in the settlement, the
result was everything. Only those who have witnessed
the ravages, the demoralizing influences of war, under
the weight of which the colonies were being slowly
pressed to death, can begin to realize what the sudden
lifting of the weight meant to an impoverished people.
To them, at least, peace came untainted with dishonor.
The loss of life, and that too of the very flower of the
country, had been such as to give a check to all thoughts
of triumph. From the beginning of Philip's War, in
Losses by 1675, to the close of Queen Anne's, in 1713,
war. it was reckoned that from five thousand to
six thousand had perished in the service—a most grievous blow to the growth of the country. To the miseries
incident to the total extinction of some families and the
dismemberment of others, were added the burdens of
private and public debts, incurred on account of the
war, and likely to last out a lifetime. Yet all disasters
had been patiently borne, all sacrifices freely made, in
the hope of putting an end, once for all, to a state of
things in which these complicated evils had their common source.

Under the treaty France gave up Acadia as lost,
though not without a struggle which should have been
Acadia a revelation to the commissioners charged
gained. with the duty of framing the various articles. One thing after another was offered to procure

its return and refused. During the negotiations preliminary to the signing, the following proposal was
made: "His Majesty offers to leave the fortifications of
Placentia as they are, when he yields that place to England—to agree to the demands made of the guns of
Hudson's Bay; moreover, to yield the islands of St.
Martin and St. Bartholomew—to give up even the right
of fishing and drying cod upon the coast of Newfoundland, if the English will give him back Acadia in consideration of these new cessions which are proposed as
an equivalent. In this case his Majesty would consent
that the river of St. George should be the limit of
Acadia, as England desired."

But after having obstinately refused to gratify Louis
by giving back Acadia to France, the English commis-

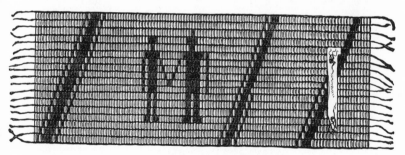

A WAMPUM PEACE BELT.

sioners immediately proceeded to make an exhibition
of imbecility, almost, if not quite, neutralizing the ad-
vantages of this hard-earned conquest. Louis was allowed to retain Cape Breton and to fortify Louis keeps
there, thus putting it in his power to cre- Cape Breton.
ate a much more formidable post than Annapolis had
ever been, and one far better situated for commanding

the entrance to the St. Lawrence. To the dullest com-
prehension this piece of folly, or worse, meant that in
the event of another war the work just finished would
have to be done all over again. To the bewildered colonists nothing, in short, could be plainer; but in England American objects were of secondary importance.

France also gave up all claim to sovereignty over
Newfoundland, although the privilege of drying fish on
the west coast was granted her—another stupid con-
cession which has periodically threatened to disturb
the peace of the two nations until a very late day. In
short, as a specimen of modern diplomacy, the Treaty
of Utrecht stands without a peer for what it left unsettled and undone.

The French view of the value of Indian alliances was
set forth by the pithy remark of De Costabelle to the
minister when going to take charge at Cape Breton,
" Point d'argent, point de Suisse."

One incident of the treaty is not without interest, if
only for its damning testimony to the bigotry of the
time. Under date of June, 1713, Lord Dartmouth
writes by the queen's orders to Nicholson, at Annapolis, that inasmuch as the Most Christian King had, at
her request, " released from imprisonment on board his
galleys sueh of his subjects as were detained there on account of their professing
the Protestant religion," it was her Majesty's good
pleasure that such of these unfortunates as might have
lands or tenements either in Acadia or Newfoundland, and
were willing to become British subjects, might retain
their property, sell it, or remove, as they should see
fit.

Galley-
slaves.

The hostile tribes were quickly apprised of the turn

of affairs through their allies, the French. Left to shift for themselves, no time was lost in sueing for peace. To this end certain of them came with a **Treaty with** flag to the fort at Casco, declaring their **Indians.** wish to enter into a treaty with the English. Captain Moody forwarded their request to Governor Dudley, who agreed to hold a conference with them at Portsmouth, which accordingly took place on July 13, 1713, when a treaty, couched in the usual terms, was duly signed and sealed by the contracting parties. It was an agreement in which all the demands were on one side and all the concessions on the other. The Indians, on their part, freely confessed to their past misdeeds, again acknowledged themselves lawful subjects of the Crown of England, promised for the future to forbear all acts of hostility toward the English or in any way obstructing the free entrance of the refugee settlers upon their old plantations. As a measure of security the Indians were prohibited from coming near any English settlement on the west of Saco. Other stipulations were similar to those embodied in the treaty of 1693, made between the Indians and Sir William Phips.

Kirebenuit.

Warraeensitt.

Bomazeen.

Wadacanaquin.

Æneas.

Iteansis.

Jackoid.

Joseph.

TREATY SYMBOLS.

Here ended twenty years of almost continuous warfare, broken only by a short respite of four years from its alarms, and during which the valor, patience, and endurance of the inhabitants of New England had been put to the severest test.   As the truest index to the character of a people, struggling with an adversary against whom it was impossible to cope on equal terms, it is a great story.

INDEX